HISTORY OF COÖPERATIVE NEWS-GATHERING IN THE UNITED STATES

GERARD HALLOCK, *President.*

GEORGE H. ANDREWS, } *Executive Committee.*
FREDERIC HUDSON, }

Hallock, Hale & Hallock.

[illegible]

James G. Bennett

Charles A. Dana, for the Tribune

M S Beach

J. & E. Brooks

Henry J. Raymond "Times"

SIGNATURES TO THE AGREEMENT FOR THE FORMATION OF THE GENERAL NEWS ASSOCIATION OF THE CITY OF NEW YORK

Adopted Oct. 21, 1856, "between Hallock, Hale & Hallock, of the *Journal of Commerce,* J. & E. Brooks, of the *Express,* J. G. Bennett, of the *Herald,* Moses S. Beach, of the *Sun,* Greeley & McElrath, of the *Tribune,* J. W. Webb, of the *Courier and Enquirer,* and Raymond, Wesley & Co., of the *Times,* to associate for the purpose of collecting and receiving Telegraphic and other Intelligence," under the regulations quoted in full in Appendix I.

HISTORY OF COÖPERATIVE NEWS-GATHERING IN THE UNITED STATES

BY

VICTOR ROSEWATER

FORMERLY EDITOR OF THE "OMAHA BEE"

ILLUSTRATED

D. APPLETON AND COMPANY
NEW YORK LONDON
1930

PRINTED IN THE UNITED STATES OF AMERICA

TO

THE MEMORY OF MY FATHER

EDWARD ROSEWATER

OLD-TIME TELEGRAPHER AND PIONEER JOURNALIST

FOREWORD

This volume is the result of a careful study of the history of news-gathering organizations in the United States which has extended over many years. At the foundation of the study is a life-work in newspaperdom and an unflagging interest in the subject, along with a close touch with the field of education for journalism. Membership for more than a quarter of a century in the old Associated Press of Illinois and its successor, the Associated Press of New York, gave direct contact with the main developments and the chief personages concerned in the later movements. I have had also the incalculable advantage of inside information and original papers, relating to preceding press associations, accumulated and preserved by my father during his long career as an old-time telegrapher and then as an editor of force and prominence, beginning with the pre-Civil-War era.

The documentary source materials are, I believe, amply indicated in the textual references and footnotes. While particular incidents and limited phases of the subject have been dealt with in the standard histories of American journalism and in the biographies of those carrying the leading rôles, nowhere have they been given perspective and sequence, or interpretative treatment. Collections of books and pamphlets under this heading are being built up now in many libraries of the country, and I have made use of the outstanding ones. Critical comparison of these collections would not be warranted, since in great part they supplement rather than duplicate each other. The New York Public Library is a treasure house of exclusive pamphlets and early newspaper files. The Library of Congress at Washington and the Library of the American Antiquarian Society at Worcester are both rich in their similar possessions. The shelves of the Library Company and of the Historical Society of Pennsylvania, in Philadelphia, contain some material not to be found elsewhere. A separate library of books and cuttings on journalism at Vassar College, begun by the late Professor Lucy Salmon, has proved valuable. Several schools of journalism have developed useful working libraries which have been drawn upon. I wish to pay this tribute to those administering each and all of these libraries, who without my asking any special privilege or favor, often without even making known my identity or divulging the object I was pursuing, granted me unfailing courtesy and considerate attention even further than I had a right to expect. The special libraries and morgues of certain great newspapers have also been freely opened for consultation, notably those of the New York *Times,* the Philadelphia *Public Ledger,* the Philadelphia *Bulletin,* and the Chicago *Tribune.* I am indebted largely to Adolph S. Ochs, of the New York *Times,* for otherwise unobtainable data concerning the Southern Associated Press; to the late Melville E. Stone for various suggestions; to Frank B. Noyes, of the Washington *Star* and president of the Associated Press, for going over the manuscript and giving pertinent advice; to Robert P. Scripps for permission to use material relating to the Scripps-McRae Press Association; to M. F. Moran, of the Associated Press office staff, for needed access to old reports and for sharing with me his fund of first-hand information; to the responsible officers of all the active press associations for helpful answers to my inquiries as to their organizations. It is quite impossible to mention each individual entitled to my thanks for encouraging and contributing to the continued prosecution of the study.

Aware of numerous shortcomings, I still venture to hope

that what is here recounted may illumine somewhat a phase of journalistic development which heretofore has had no comprehensive presentation and that it may be serviceable toward a clearer understanding of our institutional history and of the problems of our great news-gathering enterprises.

V. R.

CONTENTS

ILLUSTRATIONS

HISTORY OF COÖPERATIVE NEWS-GATHERING IN THE UNITED STATES

CHAPTER I

INTRODUCTION

News—the basic factor in journalism

It is a graphic picture of current life that is spread before us by the modern newspaper. As we glance over the sheet daily placed in front of us, we glimpse a view not only panoramic in scope but almost simultaneous with the occurrences depicted. The varicolored canvas, by means of its printed characters, puts us abreast of what is happening throughout the world, it illumines life in all its different phases, it reflects its ever-changing lights and shadows, it delineates the discordant blotches as well as the soft-blended tintings, it exposes the hideous scars along with the exquisite beauties, it holds up examples to be emulated and to be avoided. But it is more than a picture; it is the essential footing for the next day's step unless that step is to be taken in semiblindness.

How do we come to have this intricate chart of diurnal doings? What agency performs the needful service for us with such dependable accuracy, despite frequent and sometimes inexcusable blunders; and how does it do it with such exceptional initiative and driving force? How does this machinery work and how came it to be so delicately adjusted to the task of tracking and recording the succession of events on the rapidly revolving film of the newspaper cinema?

The history of news-gathering in the United States runs apace with the development of improved means of communication. American newspapers have been foremost in the field of news; here, more than anywhere else, emphasis is placed on the prompt collection and dissemination of news; here, sooner than elsewhere, each promising method of transmission has been tried out and utilized to the fullest extent.

It is hard to visualize the earlier conditions. The purview of the press has steadily broadened since the colonial beginnings. News brought in solely by the editor and his helpers, and only from territory accessible to them, could not long suffice. Journalistic enterprise pushed constantly forward. The assembling of the day's news has led, therefore, through cumulating stages to an intensively arranged reporting of events and also to an extensive scheme of coördinating the reports. In following the development of this organized news-gathering, we have a subject of study intimately interwoven with the industrial and cultural growth of the country, interesting and instructive, and certainly not devoid of its occasional lighter vein and picturesque aspects.

Generally speaking, before there can be coördination, there must be independent effort aiming in the same direction, even though unrelated. News-gathering has proceeded along the course, from couriers bearing messages embodying simple announcement and description, to an extremely involved interlocking set of globe-girdling forces utilizing for the purpose every available instrumentality of observation, collection, and transmission. As already noted, the progress of journalism on the news side corresponds closely to the invention, and introduction, and expansion of the means of rapid communication.

Pioneering is necessarily groping and plodding, and the pioneer newspapermen had to adventure into untrodden byways. When we examine early-day newspapers, preserved for us as curiosities of the past, we realize at once the narrow lines within which the first journalistic activities were hemmed; we see the obstacles which the ground-breakers had to contend with, the scant resources at their disposal, the slowness of their fastest transit. We can more readily understand, in the light of the meager equipment and facilities, how very vague or local was their news, how even their advertisements were confined to matters of importance to the particular community. Most of the space was given, in many instances, to essays and contributed editorials of interest mainly to those of culture or to those who had ideas and theories of government. For the academic and literary, there was poetry and sometimes ponderous literary work.[1]

---

[1] Payne, *History of Journalism in the United States*, p. 138.

CHAPTER II

THE BEGINNINGS OF SYSTEMATIC NEWS-GATHERING

First random efforts—The Merchants' Exchange: Topliff—Harbor News by rowboat: Blake; Bennett

SYSTEMATIC news-gathering naturally had to have its commencement in the most favorable field. For voyages to and from the mother country, the nearest and most active port in colonial America was Boston. At this point the most important information from abroad would be, ordinarily, soonest obtainable and, as Boston was first in printing and first in newspapers on this side of the Atlantic, it naturally should be first in instituting methodical collection of the news. Yet it can scarcely be said that the main credit for organizing the work belongs to the newspapers. The reasons are quite clearly disclosed by existing conditions of the times.

In all primitive communities, information is passed by word of mouth, and the news mart is found where the inhabitants are wont to congregate. In our colonial settlements, it was at the tavern or coffeehouse that reports of latest happenings were first bruited, that discussion of moot questions waxed warm, that the fads and foibles of the day were debated. To the coffeehouses, in particular, the merchants and traders of the town repaired to interchange the news that most intimately concerned them—the arrival and departure of ships, the sort of cargo carried, incidents of the trip, what passengers were aboard, what they had to relate of doings elsewhere.

In Boston, it was the Exchange Coffee House that long had the call. The news at such a place was, at least, fresh and prompt and continuous, and the early newspapers, appearing not oftener than once a week, could but follow in the wake. Indeed, the coffeehouse was the most fruitful fount of news for the paper and became the news stream of the rising press which obviously got together at haphazard the little additional material, and filled more of its space with controversial contributions, encyclopedic dissertations, official announcements, and doggerel poetry, than with information about events happening near or far.

The explanation as to why the first enterprise in newsgathering in colonial times lay in the field of shipping is, therefore, simple. The information obtained in the harbor was the vital news. Long after achieving national independence, as well as previously, the settlers were closely attached to the ancestral lands by their interests there; they were especially concerned in the changing relationships with the mother country, to which they were linked in many ways, and likewise in occurrences in the sister colonies. As the first comers inevitably chose the coast or river banks for their settlements, the first papers were printed in seaport towns where, aside from occasional land couriers, the ships constituted the chief carriers of persons, goods, and intelligence. Here, necessarily, the first organization for newsgathering was to be forthcoming.

Though the innovation hardly flashed with lightning suddenness, the year 1811 marked the advent into a novel venture of one whose individual impress proved long enduring. In its issue of November 20, the Massachusetts *Centinel* printed this item:

> *Exchange Coffee House Books.* These news books &c, commenced and so satisfactorily conducted by Mr. Gilbert, are now

transferred to the care of Mr. Samuel Topliff, Junr., a young gentleman of respectability, industry and information; and who will, we doubt not, continue the *Marine and General News Book* with great satisfaction to the patrons and friends of the Reading Room.

Born in Boston, April 24, 1789, young Topliff was then just past twenty-two years of age. The fourth son of a sea captain, he had shipped before the mast with no more than a grammar school education; but now, his father having been murdered by mutineers, he abandoned the life of a sailor to become clerk to Samuel Gilbert, proprietor and originator of the first commercial newsroom in the country.[1] In this employment, he proceeded at once to introduce his own method of news collection and to perfect a plan for keeping the information accessible. Instead of waiting for the reports to be brought in, he engaged a small boat and met arriving ships in the harbor, procuring the packets for which he had arranged, and all the quickly obtainable tidings, and forthwith carried back his material to post it where it could be read by any one who came to consult his volumes.

Within a few months the *Centinel* found occasion to commend the enterprise as follows:

Exchange Coffee House Books. Notwithstanding the recent dearth of shipping and commercial news, the industrious keeper of the books is alert in seeking out and recording intelligence. The establishment has become as respectable in point of utility as any in the United States and deserves every encouragement.

An advertisement inserted by Topliff shortly afterward had the evident purpose of persuading his readers to renew their subscriptions and to procure new subscribers. In 1814, Topliff succeeded Gilbert as proprietor, and the place hitherto known as "Gilbert's Coffee House and Marine Diary" became the "Merchants' Reading Room" and there is

---

[1] Bolton, "Memoir of Samuel Topliff," in *Topliff's Travels*, p. 3.

mention a year later of "Topliff's Private Marine Journal." After the burning of the Exchange Coffee House in 1818, the Reading Room was set up in the Merchants' Hall building and moved again about 1830, this time to the City Hall. A circumstantial description found in a contemporary guide-book is both interesting and instructive:

> Topliff's Reading Room, which is kept in the east side of the City Hall, is supported by subscribers consisting chiefly of the first merchants of the place. The annual subscription is $10.00 with the right of introducing a friend from any place not within six miles of the city. The room is furnished with all the principal papers in the United States as well as foreign papers, prices current, etc. Also seven books: the first is for the general record of news, on which is recorded daily all information of a general nature and such as is particularly interesting to the merchants of the place, as may be received from correspondents by land and water, and by arrivals at the port; the second is for the record of all arrivals from foreign ports or places, with the cargoes particularly specified to each consignee; the third for the record of all arrivals from other ports in the United States similarly noted as the second; the fourth for the record of all vessels cleared for foreign ports, time of sailing, etc.; the fifth for the record of all vessels cleared for other ports in the United States; the sixth for the record of all arrivals and clearances, from or for foreign ports, in all ports of the United States except Boston; and the seventh for the record of the names of all gentlemen introduced by the subscribers, the places whence they came and the name of the subscriber introducing them. In the room are also several of the most important maps, necessary or useful to the ship-owner or merchants, and a good clock. Attached to this establishment is a boat with two men ready at all times for the superintendent, who generally boards all vessels arriving in port, and all such information as he may obtain from them is recorded in the several books above mentioned as soon as possible for the benefit of the subscribers and all who have the privilege of frequenting the room.[2]

From 1818 on, newspaper after newspaper contains items of foreign intelligence "from Mr. Topliff's correspondent" at

---

[2] Bowen, *Picture of Boston,* p. 68.

Gibraltar, or Smyrna, or some distant port. Subsequently a visual telegraph was established on Long Island to signal messages, under arrangement with the keeper of the lighthouse, by dropping, from a 92-foot mast, balls six feet in diameter painted black. In 1828, leaving his brother in charge at home, Topliff spent the year in an extensive trip to Europe, during which time he wrote a series of travel letters, later published.[3]

Returning from Europe, he kept at his work until he had rounded out thirty years with a degree of success that has elicited for his enterprise recognition as the direct forerunner of the great press associations of to-day.[4] He disposed of his business in 1842 to Samuel Ellis and William B. Gray, who merged it with the exchange. A card of thanks to patrons appeared in the press over the name of "Topliff Brothers." For some years Samuel Topliff served as member of the Boston City Council, then lived in retirement until his death in 1864 in his seventy-fifth year. Long before this, the merchants' reading room idea had reached out to other ports and at least as far as Charleston. South Carolina.[5]

Suggestions of news-gathering exploits concurrent with, or antedating, Topliff's, crop out here and there, but such efforts were either narrowly local or by no means systematic and persisting. It is of record, for example, that Major Russell, identified with the *Massachusetts Centinel and Republican Journal*, which was started in 1784 and which he managed for forty-two years, was in the habit of visiting ships, on arrival in the harbor, for news.[6]

---

[3] *Topliff's Travels,* 1906.

[4] *M. E. S.,* p. 291.

[5] King, *The Newspaper Press of Charleston,* p. 77.

[6] Buckingham, *Specimens of Newspaper Literature,* II, 104.

Again, the *Palladium*, which was the name added to the *Mercury* in 1804, featured shipping news in a department uniquely developed by Henry Ingraham Blake, more usually referred to as "Harry Blake." Writing of Blake in 1850, Buckingham declared that "he may almost be said to have invented the present universal mode of reporting clearances, arrivals, disasters and the various incidents connected with the shipping interests of the country." [7] It was stated, too, that Blake "preferred running around the wharves and visiting merchants' offices picking up items of shipping news to standing all day in an office at ease." Moreover, "he knew all about the mercantile marine of Boston. Not a ship, not a vessel, indeed, belonging to that port that he did not know the history from the launch till she ceased to float. He knew her owner's name, her captain's name, when she was due at any port, could almost point out on the map where she ought to be on any given day." Upon Blake, "wonderful genius," numerous weird tales were hung testifying to his ship-infallibility.[8]

But when, after a long service on the *Palladium*, Blake was induced to go to New York to handle shipping news for the *Journal of Commerce* and afterward for the *Express*, he failed on both papers because, as Hudson believed, "New York, with her extensive range of short piers, her immense commerce, her mode of collecting news of this sort so entirely different from that which he had been accustomed to, bewildered an already worn-out and overtasked man." He returned to Boston, discomfited, disheartened, emphatically disgusted with the metropolis, his usefulness gone, and soon died. This encomium of Blake, for us anticipating a bit, must betoken Hudson's personal liking for the man, growing

---

[7] *Ibid.*, p. 169.

[8] Hudson, *Journalism in the United States from 1690 to 1872*, p. 190.

out of close association, and the further fact that Hudson won his own journalistic spurs in Boston and first scored a reputation as a ship news reporter.

Almost on the heels of Topliff's venture, a similar enterprise materialized in Charleston, and one more closely connected with newspaper publication. The proprietor of the *Courier* in this southern center of commerce, Aaron Smith Willington, possibly copying Topliff, since he was a transplanted Massachusetts man, had constituted himself, shortly after acquiring sole ownership of the paper in 1813, "a boarding officer" to meet arriving ships. This duty he performed "in an open boat 18 feet in length with width in proportion, sharp bow, square stern, and rowed by two stalwart slaves." [9] From a vessel up which he had clambered outside the bar, he obtained the first positive news of the treaty of peace between Great Britain and the United States, received through Savannah by express from Fernandina, Florida, which he announced to his readers February 14, 1815, the treaty having been consummated at Ghent nearly two months before.

As if directed by the stars, one James Gordon Bennett, a raw-boned Scotch-born youth, who had tarried awhile in Boston after landing as an immigrant in Halifax in 1819, had taken employment four years later with Willington's *Courier* in Charleston. At the time that Bennett came on the scene, it was the practice of Willington, or his substitute for the occasion, to meet particularly the boats coming from Cuba and to take off the latest Havana papers. On delivery at the office, they would be passed over to young Bennett, who would translate items from them. Thus, through the Cadiz packets which ran regularly to Havana, news from Europe would reach this country, at times prior to receipt in

---

[9] King, *op. cit.*, p. 105.

New York by the old London, Havre and Liverpool ships and, in this way, the *Courier* at Charleston often scored important beats. Can any one doubt that this early experience of Bennett's had a decisive bearing on his later performances in news-gathering?

It was inevitable that the gathering of news, the worth of which so plainly hinges on promptness and accuracy and which possesses an immediate commercial value only when undertaken with regularity and reliability, should become a function of the newspaper. Because of the relative costliness of news-gathering and the extravagance of duplication, it was equally inevitable that this should lead to the initial steps for a union of effort. What was needed was the development of the daily newspaper as distinguished from the preceding weekly or semiweekly papers. During the revolutionary era, there had been issues as often as three times a week, and "extras" were sometimes put out for unusual occasions, but it was not until 1784 that the first daily in the United States, the *Pennsylvania Packet and General Advertiser*, appeared in Philadelphia. Other daily newspapers followed in the larger cities, becoming eventually the big six-cent sheets. The earliest penny paper experiment, the *Cent*, made its bow likewise in Philadelphia, but not until 1830. A succession of one-cent dailies quickly followed. Many of them succumbed soon after, but several overcame their infantile ailments and served as the forebears of the cheap and popular journals that survive to this day.

Great and far-reaching changes had been taking place meanwhile in the condition and habits of the people, changes which almost imperceptibly created and speeded the newspaper efflorescence of the late 1820's and the beginning of the 1830's. The spread of democracy, along with the marked increase of population, the settlement of the western lands, the growth of the public school system, all came to a focus. The steamboat and the steam locomotive revolutionized transportation; a host of amazing inventions transformed the industries of the country; interest in foreign affairs became more general; domestic and foreign commerce expanded tremendously; politics grew more acrid; the foundations upon which popular intelligence rested were broadened. "No similar period in American history," we are authoritatively assured, "is so extraordinary for material development. At its commencement, the country was an overgrown type of colonial life; at its end, American life had been shifted to entirely new lines. Modern American history had burst in with the explosiveness of an Arctic summer." [10] Only the electric telegraph, already faintly ticking in the experiment laboratory, was lacking to furnish the means and the incentive, yes, the necessity, for news-gathering on a large scale.

It is in order to inquire first just how far the collection and publication of news had proceeded in America in advance of the innovating telegraph. Weeklies of fair pretension were being printed in all cities and towns of any size, dailies in the more populous communities. In Boston, Providence, New York, Philadelphia, Baltimore, Charleston, and New Orleans important news from abroad was brought by ships entering the harbors. Horse and stage expresses carried letters and other communications over the more traveled roads on something like regular time schedules and at tolerably good speed. Railways had begun to operate, but mainly for short distances and on lines not yet connected with one another. Journalism at these points was active, personal, and virulent, engaging a limited though steadily increasing number of readers but still seriously impeded by

---

[10] Johnston, *The United States*, p. 172.

small resources and inadequate facilities for providing the news of the day. The prevailing condition has been aptly described by William Durant, one of the early editors of the Boston *Transcript,* revealing graphically his personal experience:

> When I came to the office (in 1834), Mr. Walter was the sole editor; no staff aided him, no reporters assisted him. The ship-news man might occasionally bring him an item but otherwise the editor alone had to find material for his daily use. He made a daily call at Topliff's reading room, the insurance offices and public places, all conveniently located on or around State street; spending most of the day in the chair editorial, poring over the exchanges that came in the mail with more or less regularity, as the stages that brought them were oftentimes delayed by the bad state of the roads. Occasionally some sailing vessel would arrive, and by the courtesy of the captain a file of foreign papers with the latest European news, perhaps four or six weeks old, would gladden the heart of the editor, and some one to two columns of clippings could be had and food for criticism or comment for a few days more.[11]

This must not, however, be taken to mean that the papers of that era were generally lacking in energy and originality, or indisposed to make use of the available news-gathering facilities and to improve on them from time to time. Indeed, there were frequent examples of initiative and enterprise, but they were not sustained for long.

---

[11] Durant, *Fifty Years of Service,* p. 14.

CHAPTER III

EARLIEST NEWS COMBINATIONS

Webb and the *Courier and Enquirer*—Hale and the *Journal of Commerce*—Marine news coöperatives

In the interval, the rowboat method of procuring ship news in advance of docking had been introduced into New York. As competition at the oars offered no great advantage, the same boat sometimes served private merchants and news agents as well as the daily prints, and by the middle of the 1820's the latter were loosely united for the purpose of maintaining the service. The entire expense then never exceeded $2,500 a year.[1]

Lossing declares that it was James Watson Webb who inaugurated the regular collection of harbor news by boat for his paper, the *Courier*, and who not only had his men row out to the incoming ships but also forced the other journals to purchase their news from him.[2] If so, the start could not have been made until the spring of 1827, when the *Courier* was founded, which obviously puts it too late. What was called "The Association" was indisputably operating on a rowboat scale at that time. To whom belongs the credit of instigating the use of clipper and schooner is controversial and not easily determined from the boastful claims and counterclaims that have been made. But, in fairness, the credit warrants a division between Webb, of the *Courier*, and David Hale, of the *Journal of Commerce*. One version

---

[1] *Courier*, Sept. 24, 1831.

[2] Lossing, *History of New York City*, p. 220.

has it that the *Journal of Commerce* was excluded and compelled to go it alone; another, that the *Courier* set up its own boat and the *Journal* followed in an effort to match the speedier service. Webb's first fast craft was a Baltimore clipper, *The Eclipse,* "replaced later by the first clipper-schooner employed for such purpose which was built on his order with the stipulation that it need not be accepted unless it proved equal in speed to any New York pilot boat." This separate establishment was kept up for a year at an outlay of $4,300, when the *Courier* rejoined its former associates, sharing an expenditure of $10,000 a year, but pulled away again at the end of another two years.[3]

The quickening effects of Hale's activities are not to be ignored. Having taken charge of the *Journal of Commerce* in 1828, he proceeded to substitute a schooner for the row-boat, a move that left his competitors no choice but to adopt like devices. Hale's inspiration unquestionably traced its origin to Boston, where he had had his journalistic training. A native of Connecticut, nearly all of his life until then having been spent in mercantile occupations with varying fortune, he had nevertheless had a taste of newspaper work in his early youth, assisting his uncle, Nathan Hale, in the office of the *Daily Advertiser* there. The knack, then acquired, of writing articles for the press he steadfastly cultivated as a side line to successive excursions into business. Through this avocation, he came into contact with Gerard Hallock, who was making a profession of journalism and to whom, in 1825, he loaned a few hundred dollars to start a weekly paper. Two years later, Hallock, who had relocated in New York, reciprocated the favor by commending Hale to the Tappan brothers and urging his engagement

[3] *Courier,* Sept. 21, 1831; Bleyer, *Main Currents in the History of American Journalism,* p. 145.

to assist in their new project, the *Journal of Commerce*, which they were about to issue as a reform newspaper devoted to "high moral principles."

The earlier close contact of the two men makes it easy to understand how, upon the withdrawal of the Tappans after the reforming ardor had been cooled by mounting losses, they came together, Hale as business manager and Hallock as editor, and accepted the remnants of the *Journal* as a gift, with a $20,000 guaranty fund to keep going. Hale's biographer, writing his memoirs in 1850, is authority for the statement that at the time of the launching of the *Journal of Commerce* there existed "a combination of the leading morning newspaper establishments" of the city for obtaining foreign intelligence, which appeared to have been "rather a combination of laziness than of enterprise—the object being not so much to obtain news promptly as to insure that no one should obtain news to the disadvantage of the rest."[4] From this combination, he tells us too, the *Journal of Commerce* was jealously excluded, though, according to a different explanation, the exclusion was self-imposed, a tentative agreement to join the other papers being conscientiously rescinded when it was learned that their boat worked on Sundays.[5] So, whether by constraint of circumstances or by desire, the Tappans employed a separate news boat, well manned, to cruise in the harbor for the purpose of hailing vessels as they appeared and conveying their news to the city with the utmost dispatch. Presumably that boat was designated by the name of the paper it served; at any rate, the new schooner supplanting the rowboat was christened *Journal of Commerce* and its advent duly chronicled in the issue of October 9, 1828:

---

[4] Thompson, *Memoir of David Hale*, p. 54.

[5] *Journal of Commerce* (Centennial Edition), Sept. 29, 1927.

Yesterday our new boat, the "Journal of Commerce," went below for the first time, fully manned and equipped for service. We understand that her rival, the "Thomas H. Smith," is also in readiness for similar duty. An opportunity is now offered for an honorable competition. The public will be benefitted by such extra exertions to procure marine news, and we trust the only contention between the two boat establishments will be which can outdo the other in vigilance, perseverance and success. In one respect, and in one only, we expect to be outdone; and that is in collecting news on the Sabbath. This we shall not do, and if our Monday papers are, as we trust they will not often be, deficient in giving the latest marine intelligence, we must appeal to the candor and moral principle of our subscribers for a justification.

The schooner went out beyond the Hook, frequently as far as 100 miles, and, after sighting some packet and securing from it the latest foreign papers, raced to Fort Lafayette and handed the parcel to a waiting horseman, who spurred his steed for a quick run by way of the Fulton ferry to the home of the *Journal of Commerce.* Before long, a second schooner called the *Evening Edition* was added to the fleet, giving the *Journal of Commerce* two boats; but the prestige of the first was not dimmed. "Given an even start, the *Journal of Commerce* would outstrip both the *Courier and Enquirer* and the heavier *Evening Edition*."[6] By scrupulous adherence to the promise, "cruising was always suspended on the Sabbath," attests Hale's biographer, who adds that "by good luck as men of the world would say, but rather by the blessing of Providence on industry and enterprise controlled by right principle, the *Journal of Commerce* obtained important intelligence in advance of the entire commercial press of New York and thus established a character for energy and promptitude which proved invaluable. This was particularly true with regard to the French revolu-

[6] *Ibid.*

tion of 1830, the news of which was brought to the city by the *Journal's* news-boat and was read by Hale from the steps of the Exchange while extras were preparing in the Journal office."[7]

The year 1831 witnessed something like a newspaper boat war in New York waters. The secession of the *Courier* was ostentatiously announced and recriminations flew back and forth. The *Advertiser* accused the *Courier* of desecrating the Sabbath by giving information received on Sunday and also of trying to break down the other papers by increasing their costs of news-gathering. "The truth of the matter is simply this," retorted the *Courier*, "the association, for the purpose of saving a few dollars, refused, absolutely refused, to collect on Sunday; we, in consequence, left them and stated the fact to the public. They became alarmed—the *Mercantile* declared its willingness to work on Sunday; and to defeat us, all united on Sunday last and sent down two boats. They did not succeed—they are mortified at defeat—and the *Daily Advertiser*, without the least regard to truth, consistency or public opinion, throws itself upon the fanatic feeling of the community."[8] At the moment, there were six news schooners afloat, besides several small boats, and the total cost of running them was about $25,000 a year.

Whenever active competition broke forth, the rivalry grew extremely keen and not too courteous. A few days after

---

[7] The Tontine Coffee House had been the meeting place of the merchants since 1792, but a new one was opened in 1827, the Exchange, in whose principal room, oval in form and occupying the center of the structure, were posted the various notices which interested the merchants generally, such as the arrival and departure of vessels signalled from the station at the Narrows.—Wilson, *Memorial History of New York,* III, 334.

[8] *Courier,* Sept. 21, 1831.

the fall of Warsaw had been made known, for example, the *Courier and Enquirer*, bent on exposing those appropriating its news without credit, prepared a denial of the original account and printed a small number of copies solely for the other journals.[9] The second statement purported to have been gleaned from papers brought by the ship, *Ajax*. There was no such arrival. The article was reproduced by several sheets, and the *Journal of Commerce* sent it out in its country edition as news obtained originally by its own enterprise. In the city edition, however, credit was accorded to the *Courier*. Other papers disseminated the stolen news without giving credit to the source. The hoax created much excitement among journalists, and the public enjoyed the joke hugely.

The feats and failures in the harbor in due time brought a reorganization of the Association and a pooling of the operations of the *Courier and Enquirer*, the *Gazette*, and the *Mercantile Advertiser*. Three such associations to gather marine news were operating in New York in 1837-38, according to Hudson.[10] Captain Bancker was at the head of one for the *Courier and Enquirer* and the *Journal of Commerce*. Captain Hurley had charge of one for the *Express*, the *Mercantile Advertiser*, and the *Gazette*. Captain Cisco directed a third for the *Commercial Advertiser*, the *Evening Star*, and the *American*. By that time, the *Herald* also had its independent service, with a news boat commanded by Captain Hamill; and the *Sun* afterwards set up an enterprise of its own for important arrivals only, Captain Brogan, "the man with a glazed cap," being at the helm. The *Journal of Commerce* at this period was paying the *Courier*

---

[9] *Memoirs of James Gordon Bennett*, by a Journalist (said to be Isaac C. Pray), p. 135.

[10] Hudson, *Journalism*, p. 608.

and Enquirer $3,000 a year for its share of the joint service.[11]

In 1840, the *Herald* again smashed all records with a still speedier harbor boat named the *Fanny Elssler* after the then reigning popular dancer.

---

11 *Memoirs of Bennett*, p. 134.

CHAPTER IV

SPEEDING NEWS OVERLAND

Rival horse expresses: the "Black Ponies"—Temporary joint enterprises—First use of both horse and railroad—The railway express

THE collection and transmission of news over land routes was by no means wholly neglected. Probably the earliest newspaper express, of authentic record, to be run in this country was instituted by Samuel Hall in connection with the Salem *Gazette*, which he issued from 1781 to 1785.[1] Each day before publication, an express covered the distance of fifteen miles from Boston to Salem to supply the latest news to his readers. Special mounted messengers rode at various times, before 1830, between New York and Boston, Philadelphia, Baltimore, and Washington, but they never became permanent. Though these adventures were more or less sporadic outbursts of certain papers for themselves, there was, however, real rivalry.

"Some little idea of the opposition that exists among New York editors may be formed," observed the Boston *Transcript* in its issue of December 11, 1830, "when we mention that so great was the anxiety to get the start of each other, and have the credit of being out first, that three expresses were employed by the printers of that city. The *Courier and Enquirer* engaged one to bring in President Jackson's message to them only; the *Journal of Commerce* received it by special express; and other papers had a third in common to them all." Boasting the next day, the *Courier*

[1] Hudson, *Journalism*, p. 172.

and Enquirer gave these particulars: "It [the message] was delivered yesterday at 12 o'clock [in Washington] and conveyed from thence to Baltimore by express. From Baltimore to Philadelphia by boat; and from Philadelphia to this city by our own express in six hours and twelve minutes, notwithstanding the bad situation of the roads. We would have been able to lay it before our readers at an earlier hour had not our express between Baltimore and Washington lost all his copies. As it is, we have incurred an expense of nearly three hundred dollars." [2]

These expresses did not become permanently established at this time. Yet, significant was the selection in 1831 of James Gordon Bennett to go to Washington for the *Courier and Enquirer*, with which he was then associated, to arrange the preliminaries for securing the president's message of that year. On this occasion, Bennett counted on the express achieving the goal in 13 hours—in fact, 15 hours were consumed—and his paper had the document exclusive.[3]

In January, 1833, an express, begun by the *Journal of Commerce* to bring its own news from the seat of government, was at once followed by a joint horse express, in which eight relays of horses spanned the distance from Philadelphia to New York, to render the same service for several New York papers.[4] The combination continued only eight or ten days, and then the post office took it over. The *Journal of Commerce* thereupon extended its relays to Washington and was successful in beating the government express regularly by one day and sometimes, when heavy snows fell, by two and even three days. Once, it is related, the Norfolk, (Va.), *Beacon*, published 229 miles southeast of Washington, copied

[2] Stimson, *History of the Express Business*, p. 19.
[3] *Memoirs of Bennett*, p. 134.
[4] Hallock, *Life of Gerard Hallock*, p. 278.

the Washington news two days in succession from the *Journal of Commerce*, which it received from New York by steamer. The whole stretch of 227 miles between Washington and New York was often made within twenty hours.

In 1835, the *Journal of Commerce* took the *Courier and Enquirer* into the enterprise and again set in motion its "black ponies" to deliver a record of the proceedings of Congress throughout the session. In the winter of 1835-36, the *Courier and Enquirer* similarly maintained an express for its congressional news at a cost of $7,500 a month.[5]

The *Sun*, founded in 1833 by Benjamin H. Day, and the *Herald*, founded in 1835 by James Gordon Bennett, also maintained expresses in addition to their boats. The *Sun* went in for carrier pigeons and for some time had a dovecote on its roof, plainly shown in the pictorial prints of the day. In 1836, the *Sun* charged that "a diabolical plot" had been rigged up against it by a combination of the six-penny papers for the purpose of sharing the expense of running horse expresses from Philadelphia to New York to fetch the Washington news more quickly than the penny papers could get it by mail.[6] In retaliation, the *Sun* and the *Transcript* formed a union of their own and saved themselves from being beaten on Jackson's message to Congress. The accusation was made, and of course denied, that the *Sun* purloined the *Courier's* copy of Jackson's special message of January 18, 1836, by luring the messenger to the *Sun* office and surreptitiously opening the package, but the affair never came to an issue.

In the same year, no little sensation was produced by expresses speeding from Washington and New York with important news, one of which nearly cost a certain editor

[5] Lossing, *History of New York City*, p. 220.

[6] O'Brien, *The Story of The Sun*, p. 110.

his life through the overexcitement of riding a locomotive from Worcester to Boston, a distance of about forty miles, in as many minutes.[7] In a state of daze, he was hurried in a carriage to the office where, with greatest difficulty, the president's message was pried from his tightly clutched fingers. This express was run against the *Atlas* and one or two other papers by a concert of the *Courier and Enquirer* and the *Herald*, of New York, and the *Commercial Gazette*, of Boston.

Nor should it be overlooked that William M. Swain and Arunah S. Abell, two printers who had worked at the case in New York alongside of Day, and who, with A. H. Simmons, had founded the *Ledger* in Philadelphia and the *Sun* in Baltimore, also pampered their readers with news brought by special expresses. Washington tidings were procured for them by mounted messengers in 1837-38 and, in 1841, they outdid all others on the death of President Harrison.[8]

Certain coincidental happenings must be included to fill in our picture of American journalism of the 1830's. The inauguration of the *Courier and Enquirer's* Washington express necessitated the employment of a Washington agent, and this generated the species which has since come to be known as "the Washington correspondent." And, once more, the original of "that remarkable and peculiar class of reporters" was none other than James Gordon Bennett.[9] Furthermore, the expresses in the beginning looked largely to the gathering of election news. With a training as political editor on the *Journal of Commerce*, Richard

---

[7] *Memoirs of Bennett*, p. 372.

[8] Scharf and Westcott, *History of Philadelphia*, p. 2000.

[9] Shanks, "How We Get Our News," *Harper's Magazine*, May, 1867, p. 513.

Haughton subsequently established the Boston *Atlas* and introduced a system by which he was enabled, using horses and the few scattered lines of railroads then in existence in Massachusetts, to publish returns from every town in the state by nine o'clock of the following day. The work commenced on the *Journal of Commerce* by Haughton, was continued by Hale.[10] Systematic collection of election news within its own territory was similarly instituted by the Providence *Journal*, which many times also ran expresses from Boston where Haughton, "the most enterprising newspaper man of his day," always supplied it with the results of his own labor and expenditure.[11] An exploit of the Rhode Island paper in 1841 earned it great acclaim. Inasmuch as the only mail from New York arrived in the early morning, it had its news, including a letter from Washington, set up in New York, and the type sent in boxes to reach Providence in time for its morning edition, thus giving its readers the advantage of full twenty-four hours for everything which came from New York, and anticipating the New York papers themselves.

About the same time, private expresses, operating on the railroads, began to multiply and were promptly utilized by the newspapers. When Moses Y. Beach bought the *Sun* in 1838, there was still no express service to New York; in fact there had been none anywhere, except the one which Charles Davenport and N. S. Mason conducted over the Boston and Taunton Railway.[12] But in the spring of 1839, William F. Harnden initiated an express service, later the Adams Express, between New York and Boston, using the boats from New York to Providence and the rail from Providence on.

---

[10] *Journal of Commerce* (Centennial Edition), Sept. 29, 1927.
[11] Providence *Journal* (Semi-Centennial Edition), Jan. 3, 1870.
[12] O'Brien, *op. cit.*, p. 140.

This, we may readily conclude, was a wonderful help to the papers in both cities which were enabled thus to enjoy one-day intercommunication.

Up to the beginning of the 1840's, then, the joint news-gathering efforts were but temporary combinations and almost wholly local in their scope. Their performances were part and parcel of the sharp rivalry of the time, to match or outdo the feats of enterprise vaunted by competitors, rather than a persisting, steady endeavor to cover the day-by-day events. As on the editorial side of the newspapers, the news-gathering arm shone principally through the energy of the individuals who were doing the pioneering. In these activities, they were necessarily limited to an extremely narrow range of operations by the inadequate facilities at their disposal. Signs were pointing to the breaking of these bounds.

CHAPTER V

NEWS BY TRANSATLANTIC STEAMER

The private news agency—Emergence of D. H. Craig—Halifax as port of call—Exciting oceanic episodes

WHAT factor so out of the ordinary was taking place to cause these noticeable departures from a seemingly settled order? It was the prospect of transatlantic steam navigation, too long delayed, but at last assured for the near future by the successful voyages of the *Sirius* and the *Great Western.* Both of these vessels arrived in New York harbor on the same day, April 23, 1838, and the returning *Sirius* carried as a passenger the ever-alert James Gordon Bennett. Although his vision of immediate steamship lines plying regularly between New York and European ports proved premature, he proceeded to establish competent correspondents for the *Herald* in the great cities of the old world, the results of whose tact and industry were soon seen in its columns.[1] Before long, the six regular correspondents in Europe were reënforced in like manner in the more important cities of the United States, in Texas, in Mexico, and in Canada.

Competitors were naturally aroused. By 1843, the *Sun* had a correspondent in London, who ran a special horse express to take his dispatches to Bristol in order to make the boat there with the very latest intelligence.[2] It turned out that regular voyages were not to come for another two years,

[1] *Memoirs of Bennett,* p. 249.

[2] O'Brien, *The Story of The Sun,* p. 157.

and then, with the inauguration of the Cunard line, the fast boats connected Liverpool with Boston, instead of with New York. News-gathering had to be adjusted to the shifting conditions; news from abroad was accelerated, but also, for the time, rerouted, with the consequence that Boston, as the port of destination, and, a little later, Halifax, as the first port of call touched by the west-bound boats, monopolized attention in the race for news primacy. In this arena, wits were sharpened, stratagems concocted, resourcefulness displayed in novel and extraordinary forms by the rival newspapers, and equally by the private agencies that sprang up as commercial news-vending undertakings.

Under the direction of Bennett, the *Herald* started, without delay, to run its expresses from Boston with advices conveyed by the Cunard steamers; and the *Sun*, not to be left behind in journalistic enterprise, quickly followed suit. The *Herald* rarely left unseized an opportunity to parade its successes, for example:

> It is not a little laughable to see the efforts made by our neighbor of the *Sun* to get the news of the steamships. That concern sends printers and a steamboat to New Haven and Stonington and engages from one to a dozen locomotives and yet they never start or, at any rate, they never reach this city. That concern, however, publishes the news and the way he does it is funny. He meekly and patiently waits till we issue our Extra, one of the first of which he obtains by giving to a newsboy a shilling. He then sends for his printers, and in about an hour after we have flooded the city with the news, he brings out a miserable reprint of what we have published.[3]

The unrelished supremacy of the *Herald,* together with the enormous financial drain of these operations, led to a combination of sixteen papers in several cities, formed during

---

[3] *Herald,* June 3, 1844.

the Oregon excitement which had the country in alarm in 1845-46. To obtain earliest information from England—information which might spell peace or war—a pilot boat was chartered to cross the Atlantic, connecting with two special expresses, one from Halifax and one from Boston. This enterprise cost the participants $5,000 for the boat, $4,000 for the Halifax express, and $1,000 for the Boston express, "very large sums to be spent for news in those days." [4] In this exploit, the New York papers were joined by the *Ledger* in Philadelphia and the *Sun* in Baltimore.[5] From Halifax to Portland, troops of ponies fairly flew with the news brought by the steamers from Europe. Relays of ponies, extending from Halifax to Annapolis on the Bay of Fundy, and across Nova Scotia, a distance of 150 miles, took the news to Portland and thence, by express, soon by locomotive, to Boston and to New York, Philadelphia, and Baltimore. The distance of 1,000 miles was covered in fifty hours. Again, in the combination by which the *Romer* was sent to Liverpool in February to get the Oregon treaty, the *Ledger* and the *Sun* united with the New York papers, and all of them once more scored on their opponents. The *Herald* dubbed its antagonists "The Holy Alliance."

Keyed up by the advance trumpeting, the public hung on the outcome with the tenseness displayed at the racetrack. An entry in Philip Hone's diary, dated February 20, 1846, strikes the note of sustained expectancy prevailing on such occasions:

> The arrival of the steamer *Cambria* has been looked for with great anxiety, from the importance of the news she brings upon the great question of peace or war. Expresses were sent on by the newspaper establishments to anticipate the news at Halifax and

[4] Hudson, *Journalism*, p. 608.

[5] Scharf and Westcott, *History of Philadelphia*, p. 2,002.

bring it on before her arrival in Boston. She arrived at Halifax on Tuesday morning. The express started immediately and would have accomplished its enterprising object had it not encountered the great snowstorm. As it was, we had the news here in New York yesterday at noon; a rival express of the *Herald* being an hour or two ahead of the Nova Scotia racers. The distance from Boston, 240 miles, was traveled by railroad and steamboat in the astonishingly short time of seven hours and five minutes. What a change from the times when the mail stage left New York for Boston once a fortnight, and consumed a week in going to Philadelphia.[6]

Out of this strenuous contest emerged a towering figure, cast for a leading rôle in the development of news service in the years rapidly coming on. It was none other than Daniel H. Craig, whose name was to be almost a household word in every important newspaper office for the next twenty years. Born in New Hampshire, just as Topliff was setting up his historic reading room, he had started in the printing trade as an apprentice on the Plymouth, (N. H.), *Gazette* in 1825. Seven years later, with an intervening engagement on the Lancaster, (Mass.), *Gazette*, he went to Boston and issued what he insisted was the first prospectus for a penny paper in this country. He was, however, unable to finance it. "I then," to use his own words, "embarked in the importation and training of carrier pigeons for the conveyance of commercial and other news and, at different periods during ten or twelve years, used them successfully between Halifax, Nova Scotia, and Washington, D. C., having news relations with Harnden, Jacob Little, Moses Y. Beach of the New York *Sun*, and several other journals between Boston and Baltimore. Years before the establishment of the telegraph, I had a regular news reporting business by means of carrier pigeons from Halifax to Boston." [7]

---

[6] *The Diary of Philip Hone*, p. 756.
[7] Craig, *Answer*, p. 2.

SAMUEL TOPLIFF, JR.

A. S. WILLINGTON

DANIEL H. CRAIG

JAMES GORDON BENNETT

Having made contacts with foreign correspondents to supply him regularly with up-to-the-hour-of-sailing tidings, Craig's problem was to obtain this information from the incoming steamers and to distribute his reports to his clients in advance of the others, which, as a rule, he succeeded in doing. He got his news off the boats as they neared Boston harbor and sent it on by his winged messengers. The New York papers undertook to prevent him from taking his birds on board the Cunarders at Halifax. "On one occasion," he declared, "Captain Ryrie seized and held them until the steamer arrived at Boston. Apprehending the outrage, I had put one of my birds in my overcoat pocket before going on board, and, after putting the news on his legs, I went on deck and flew the bird close to the captain's head. He darted into his stateroom and caught his rifle, but before he got a chance to shoot, the bird was a mile above him, flying straight to his home in Boston, a hundred miles away, and safely delivered his news several hours in advance of the steamer."

Subsequently, the press of New York and Boston combined to charter a steamer to carry their news budget from Halifax to Boston, whence it was to be sent by telegraph and anticipate the arrival of passengers in New York. To head off this menace to his business, Craig stowed a couple of his birds in a basket and traveled by the land route to Halifax in time to take passage on the express boat as it started for Boston. When the shore of Massachusetts was sighted, his pigeons, heavily freighted with dispatches, were loosed from his stateroom window. With such adroitness was this done that, long before he and his fellow travelers landed, the pigeons had delivered Craig's news reports to his confederates in the city, and the reports were published first in the opposition journals. Craig's triumph and the heavy outlay for the special boat, it was said, led to a quarrel among the parties concerned, the boat was given up, and Craig was allowed undisputed possession of the field.[8]

Soon after the telegraph reached Boston, plans were laid to extend the wire to Portland, Bangor, and Calais, Maine, and by 1848 the line was opened to St. Johns, New Brunswick. At this juncture, Craig had the discernment to observe that pigeons could be no match for electricity and, accordingly, started a horse express, running 150 miles between Halifax and Digby, Nova Scotia, and a steamer from there 50 miles across the Bay of Fundy to St. Johns. At the outset, he had trouble with the telegraph manager in control at Boston, who also represented Boston and New York papers; but Craig won out in short shrift, putting his news through to its destination, and forcing the papers to accept it through his agents and to pay his charges. Awake now to the vigor and indomitable zeal manifested by Craig, Hudson of the *Herald* and Raymond of the *Courier and Enquirer,* for the combined New York papers, invited him to an interview, which resulted in the commissioning of Craig to act for them in procuring European news.

Under Craig's direction, the interception of steamers off the capes came to be an exhilarating sport, as witness this contemporaneous description:

> The steamers crossing from England or Ireland make for Cape Race and, when they approach the cape, they run up a signal or fire a gun to attract attention. The newsmen are on the alert and start off with the yacht to the large steamer. A tin canister, or box made water-tight, and to which a flag is fixed which can be seen at a distance when in the water, is thrown overboard, and this contains the latest news made up at Liverpool or Galway. The yachtsmen make for the small flag, pick up the box, and make all speed to St. Johns, Newfoundland, from which place the news is

[8] Reid, *The Telegraph in America,* p. 363.

immediately telegraphed to all parts of Canada and to the United States, a distance of more than a thousand miles. The news is carried across a country, a great part of which is little more than a savage wilderness, over lofty hills, deep swamps and almost impenetrable woods. It passes by submarine telegraph from Newfoundland to the American continent, over a portion of the lines to Nova Scotia and New Brunswick and thence to Portland, state of Maine, where the American system of telegraphs commences. The news from Europe thus precedes the arrival of the steamer by several days.[9]

Although somewhat modified to accord with the growth of ocean liners, their increased speed, and their more direct travel routes, this general method of securing and expediting overseas information continued for two decades and was discarded only when Cyrus W. Field, by his successful laying of the Atlantic cable in 1866, again revolutionized all preceding arrangements. To be sure, the semaphore at Sandy Hook, in giving notice of the approach of vessels, had saved a little time, and better telegraph facilities had made faster delivery of the dispatches when brought off the boat, but, until ocean cable service became a reality, ten days to two weeks was the normal time for getting news from Europe.

---

[9] McDermott, *Reporting by Telegraph*, p. 260.

CHAPTER VI

INVENTION OF THE MAGNETIC TELEGRAPH

Its vindication by news transmission—Haphazard extension of lines—Shortcomings of the service.

Going back a few years in point of time, let us hail the advent of the magnetic telegraph and visualize the extraordinary consequences for news-gathering of its achievement of time-effacing communication. We are not here concerned with the controversy long waged by champions of rival claimants to the discovery. No serious dispute envelops the practical application of the telegraph to commercial uses. The action of Congress, in voting an appropriation to enable Samuel F. B. Morse and his associates to erect the experimental telegraph line in 1843, is of official record, and the scene attending the first formal exchange of messages, on May 24th of the following year, has become history. By sheer accident, the initial telegraph joined Washington and Baltimore, and this fact served in a peculiar way to link in the newspaper from the start.

It happened that the Democratic national convention was assembled in Baltimore at that time to nominate a candidate for president. This supplied the dramatic incident needed to prove the utility of the telegraph, to command public attention, and to confound scoffers and skeptics.[1] After James K. Polk had been selected to head the ticket, the choice of the convention for vice president fell upon Silas Wright, then serving in the senate as a representative

---

[1] Reid, *The Telegraph in America*, p. 106.

of the State of New York. The information was communicated at once over the wire and, within a few minutes, all were astounded by the receipt of a telegraphed message from Senator Wright positively declining the nomination. The bewildered delegates refused to admit its authenticity; they appointed a committee to go to Washington and interview the senator, and adjourned to await its report. The committee, conferring over the wire, confirmed the telegraphic answer, and another name was agreed upon. The news of these almost unbelievable proceedings spread the fame of the telegraph to every corner of the land and helped immensely to strengthen confidence in its reliability as a means of communication. To confound persisting doubters, the *Herald* printed a certified verbatim copy of the telegraphic conversation a week after the event.

The jubilant inventor instinctively recognized how helpful this occurrence was to be. "The conventions at Baltimore," wrote Morse in a letter dated May 31, 1844, "happened most opportunely for the display of the powers of the telegraph, especially as it was the means of correspondence, in one instance, between the democratic convention and the first candidate elect for the vice presidency. The enthusiasm of the crowd before the window of the telegraph room in the Capitol was excited to the highest pitch at the announcement of the nomination of the presidential candidate, and the whole of it afterward seemed turned upon the telegraph. They gave the telegraph three cheers and I was called upon to make my appearance at the window when three cheers were given to me by some hundreds present, composed mainly of members of Congress." [2]

A previous use of the wire for an important news dispatch, furnishing similar testimony as to its value, had made com-

---

[2] Morse, *Letters and Journal,* II, 224.

paratively little impression. When Clay and Frelinghuysen had been nominated on May 1, a month earlier, by the Whig convention also meeting in Baltimore, its action had been announced in Washington on the strength of a message carried by train to Alfred Vail at Annapolis Junction, then the end of the line still under construction, who signaled it by key to Morse in his experiment room in the Capitol; but scant mention of this feat was made in the current newspapers.[3] A few items of congressional proceedings, handed occasionally to the Baltimore press free of charge, had also been printed as curiosities of transmission rather than as news beats. It required an incident really startling, such as soon emanated from the Democratic convention, to provoke attention to the news possibilities.

As a result, when the line was operated the next winter as an arm of the post office, with expenses paid out of money voted by Congress, a thin stream of press dispatches began to trickle over it and in time to become noticeable. Because the receiving magnet refused to register more than twenty words a minute, Vail invented a "dictionary" to meet the demand of the Baltimore papers. "Each phrase was indicated by a word taken from an ordinary dictionary, and the words were arranged alphabetically and placed opposite the phrases, also alphabetically grouped together under appropriate headings. The names of the officers and members of the two Houses were numbered." By this scheme, a large amount of congressional business was covered in a short space of time. The operator at Baltimore deciphered the messages for the reporters, and they wrote them down and carried them to their respective journals.

[3] Kirk, "The First News Message by Telegraph," *Scribner's Magazine* (1892), p. 654.

Shortly after the return of Professor Morse from Europe with a new and faster receiving magnet, he was able to dispense with the use of the dictionary. It was utilized, however, in transmitting the report of the proceedings at the inauguration of President Polk.[4] And in May, 1846, the Baltimore *Sun* had the President's message by wire exclusively, the first ever so transmitted.

Still, the telegraph was not to obtain full-faith acceptance by the press, or by the public, for some time. Its extension, though unchecked, was relatively slow and disconnected. After construction of the first short stretch already mentioned, the wires were strung, not from Baltimore or Washington, but out of Philadelphia to the north, south, and west. One wire reached Fort Lee, above New York, in January, 1846; another reached Wilmington, a little later, followed in June by a line bridging the gap to Baltimore; still another connected with Harrisburg, about the same time, going thence to Pittsburgh and, by the close of 1847, to Cincinnati, Louisville, and St. Louis. Construction was completed from New York to Albany, Buffalo, and Boston in 1846, and to Detroit, Chicago, and Milwaukee by 1848. The Boston line was pushed on to Halifax in 1849. Telegraphic communication across the continent to San Francisco was not consummated until 1861, and even then was sparingly employed because of the cost. So much for the chronology.

Throughout and long after this introductory stage, the telegraphic service varied greatly in different sections of the country, facilities in many places lagging far behind those in the territory of greatest development. The crudeness and inadequacy of the more primitive lines persisted in the out-of-the-way and sparsely settled regions, and what-

---

[4] Scharf and Westcott, *History of Philadelphia,* III, 2129.

ever progress was recorded must be understood to have been unevenly distributed and not necessarily prevailing in all parts of the country at the same time. It must be constantly remembered, too, that during this era the older means of communication and the prior methods of news-collection were not at once abandoned, but, on the contrary, were kept in use so far as serviceable and were supplanted only as improved mechanisms became available and economically more advantageous. Not until 1858, nearly 15 years after the first electric telegraph, did the pony express, carrying the first overland mail, make its advent into Sacramento, and it employed as many as 300 riders before it was crowded out by telegraph and rail.[5] So foot messenger and horse express, stage and locomotive, rowboat and schooner and steamship, were being used simultaneously and were complementing one another in bearing the news of the day from source to distribution outlet, just as, even now, special messenger, letter-carrier, telegraph, telephone, radio, airplane, and motor car bring news to the copy desk, according as each seems most suited or less expensive for the same work.

But the earlier use of the telegraph fell far short of completely satisfying those who were induced to make a trial of it. The tribulations besetting the news-gatherers proved often decidedly discouraging, and many an obstacle that now looks trivial loomed insurmountable. In all verity, it must be confessed that the common incredulity and suspicion aroused by the new telegraph were shared, to a large extent, in the newspaper offices as well as outside of them. The public prints were filled with descriptions of the astonishing invention, but the mass of readers failed to under-

[5] Young, *Journalism in California,* p. 10; see also graphic description by Mark Twain in *Roughing It.*

stand how it worked. We can scarcely imagine how confusing it must have been. Joseph Medill, noted editor of the Chicago *Tribune,* just entering upon his distinguished career of journalism in the Muskingum valley in Ohio when the wires came strung along from Cleveland and Pittsburgh, gives us a suggestive description:

> I often heard people ask how it was possible for the lightning to get past the telegraph poles and not run into the ground; and when it thundered, how the operators could play the ticker without being killed by the lightning striking the wire. Others could not comprehend how the electric fluid could make marks at the other end of the line without shocking every one in the room. . . . How little the journalists of the years closing the first half of the century imagined or suspected the revolution in news-gathering Morse's invention would cause before the end of the second half of the century! [6]

Resort to the telegraph for news in rare emergencies was, perhaps, conceivable to the more far-seeing and enterprising journalists, but its employment generally for gathering the day's happenings was regarded in the beginning as wholly out of the question and entirely incommensurate to the cost. No one even dimly dreamed what was to be the future relation of the telegraph to the newspaper.

---

[6] Associated Press Report, 1897, p. 155.

CHAPTER VII

NEWSPAPER AND TELEGRAPH

Swain of the *Public Ledger*—Bennett of the *Herald*—The independent reporters—Covering the Mexican War—Relay by horse and wire—Special newspaper combinations

THE first profound and practical interest in the telegraph as an adjunct of the newspaper was manifested by William M. Swain, proprietor of the *Public Ledger* in Philadelphia. When the lines of the Magnetic Telegraph Company were in course of construction from that city to Baltimore, the people were in the midst of an intense excitement over the menace of the Mexican War. Swain, as related by the historian of the telegraph, went to very considerable expense in maintaining a pony express to obtain the latest news and bring it from Baltimore, which was in telegraphic communication with Washington. He was described as a man "of great personal force," possessing "all the instincts of a news-gatherer in full vigor." [1]

The moment the electrical machinery began to click between Philadelphia and Wilmington, Swain sent agents of quick wit to Baltimore and to Wilmington to collate the news at these strategic points and to hasten it on to Philadelphia by wire. Although the ponies were kept running as before, he himself spent much of his time hovering about the telegraph office, where he remained until the early hours of the morning to carry to his waiting presses the last word from the seat of war.

[1] Reid, *The Telegraph in America*, p. 793.

Swain had full faith in the telegraph. He invested heavily in it, taking the principal portion of the stock in the original Magnetic Telegraph Company. He became a director and then president of the company; in fact, he transferred his energies largely from the newspaper field to that of the telegraph, whose administration he put on a sound footing. He also recognized the need of organic union of the leading lines and aided in its attainment, and then, feeling that his own work in this connection was finished, he declined re-election and retired, July 1, 1858. "No company organized in America has had its affairs managed with more scrupulous honor, or minute care, or intelligent vigor, than the Magnetic Telegraph Company under Mr. Swain," is the tribute paid by the one most intimately associated with him in these activities.

Another who lost no time in grasping the changed conditions was James Gordon Bennett. He saw the war with Mexico coming on and quickly learned his lesson from a painful experience in connection with the inaugural message of Governor Young to the legislature convening at Albany in January, 1847. The 5,000-word document went by wire to other New York papers in two and a half hours and was rushed into print while the *Herald* was depending on its special Albany Express. As the *Herald's* horseman, carrying its copy at full speed, rode into White Plains, he heard the newsboys in the street crying extras with the message, and he gave up the profitless race. This was a warning not to be ignored—a warning that, when the electric current could be employed, the horse was to be out of the running.[2] It made no difference that the governor's message was so mangled by the incompetent operators that correction by a

[2] *Ibid.*, p. 307.

second publication was found necessary, doubling the expense of the supplement issued to provide space for it. Bennett of the *Herald* at once became the heaviest patron of the telegraph.

The terrible plight attending the gubernatorial message on that occasion prompted a particularly appropriate suggestion from James Brooks, editor of the *Express,* with respect to the message that was to go to Congress the following December. Addressing President Polk, November 30, 1847, he wrote:

> Although a Whig editor, nevertheless, I do not wish to see the President's message butchered, and this is the cause of my writing you.
>
> The press here, ours among them, will receive your message by telegraph, for which we have made a contract. It will come mutilated, disjointed and full of errors. It will be the only copy in the New York papers and their extras the day on which it is delivered; and on our Packet ships on that day will go to all Europe as the real President's message. I should be sorry to see the President thus misrepresented there, or disgraced by the inevitable blunders of the Telegraph in hurrying on to New York so long a document the morning of its delivery.
>
> To prevent this, you have only one recourse—and that is to trust by your private secretary, or some other trustworthy person, six or ten official copies to the postmaster or collector here, under seal to be opened when the Telegraph announces a delivery in Washington. Under your own seal, nobody can betray your confidence, or break it but by Telegraphic order.
>
> Last year, we thus telegraphed Gov. Young's message, which he never ceased to regret, as thereby he was misrepresented all over the union. We shall do the same by yours, if you permit, but as an American, I have felt it my duty to inform you of facts of which you may be ignorant, or about which there may be inattention among the officials.[3]

Here we see a distinct proposal of what has become an established practice—that of furnishing advance copy to the

---

[3] In Library of Congress.

newspapers, to be held in confidence for future release—but nothing came of it at the time. The President, who was making alterations in his manuscript almost to the very moment of delivery, presumably had no notion that the corrections could be similarly effected by wire. So, having also had his troubles with "leaks," he retained the message in his personal possession until completely ready for the official printer.[4] His message of still another year was to strain the telegraphic service to the utmost. Incidentally, because of repeated breaches of confidence by unscrupulous reporters, to say nothing of crass bribery of clerks, efforts continued to keep these documents out of newspaper hands, until actual reading to Congress, through Lincoln's administration. Lincoln, too, found himself unable to prevent premature publication, despite every precaution.[5]

The advantage of the telegraph for news transmission was likewise perceived by certain scribes who vended their wares to the papers on their own account. The leader in this telegraphic press service out of New York was Alexander Jones, instrumental later in perfecting the machinery of collection and distribution, who, fortunately for us, wrote a history of the telegraph and included much first-hand information on this phase of the subject. Jones had handed in his initial press dispatch at the office opened at No. 10 Wall Street, the operating room being in Jersey City where it remained for another year or two. This was in the autumn of 1846. The message contained a brief report of the launching of the United States sloop of war, *Albany*, at the Brooklyn Navy Yard, and went to the Washington *Union*. Recalling once more that the wire to New York

[4] *Diary of James K. Polk*. See entries of respective dates.
[5] Gobright, *Recollection of Men and Things*, p. 339.

was opened in January of that year, this shows a lapse of eight or nine months before its requisition for purposes of news service on any scale worth mentioning. The reason, however, may be that the wire still stopped on the west side of the river because of difficulties encountered in attempting to carry it across. This purpose was accomplished, finally, by erecting a high mast for aërial suspension on each river-bank but it did not work dependably until 1850.

The Texas troubles inspired Bennett with premonition of a constantly growing public interest in what was to happen in that quarter. In January, 1845, the *Herald,* therefore, commenced publishing "certain later intelligence from New Orleans, Mobile and the South than can be found in any other journal this side of the Potomac," with the further information:

> This extraordinary piece of enterprise has been arranged by us in connection with another newspaper establishment in Mobile and in New Orleans, and will be continued through the winter months. It will furnish us and our readers in New York, and all the large towns from Washington north, with a day's later intelligence, and from one to two, three and four days' later, according to the state of the weather, than can be received from any other source. Not even the United States mail can compete with us, although we do not interfere at all with the transmission of mail matter or with mail arrangements.[6]

The scheme was discarded at the end of the month, however, for the reason that the post office, under pressure of the other New York papers, was inaugurating an express mail by running horses from Covington, Georgia, to Montgomery, Alabama. The *Herald's* venture could scarcely be called a shining success. "For some inexplicable cause, the express has succeeded only in several instances and the

---

[6] *Herald,* Jan. 6, 1845.

failure has, in all probability, been owing to some underhanded efforts on the part of the post office officials." [7]

With war with Mexico now formally proclaimed, the demand for war news waxed keen, and there was a question as to what extent the scattered telegraph lines could be utilized. As the fighting was pitched along the Rio Grande, the coveted intelligence had to come, for the most part, through the Gulf ports. The time then required for the regular mail from New Orleans to New York was seven days. The task, to beat the mail, devolved on the newspaper. Typical of ways and means improvised was the venture conducted jointly for the *Sun* in New York and the *Courier* in Charleston.[8] The managers of these journals, Moses Y. Beach and William S. King, respectively, projected a mutual enterprise to get ahead of the postal service and to distance competitors. The telegraph line to the South extended only as far as Richmond, Virginia. The gain of time had to be made between Mobile and Montgomery, where 150 miles of staging regularly consumed thirty-six hours, for which a pony express was now set up. By contract with private parties, this ground was to be traversed within twelve hours to overtake the previous day's mail, the riders fetching with them not less than three nor more than five pounds of mail matter. In this great undertaking, $750 was paid for each successful trip, and a failure rarely occurred. Several horses were sacrificed and, in one instance, a rider was killed for the glory of the venture, the detailed plan of which was carefully concealed.

For another combination in which the *Ledger*, in Philadelphia, and the *Sun*, in Baltimore, shared, an express comprising about sixty blooded horses was established from

---

[7] *Ibid.*, Jan. 30, 1845.

[8] King, *The Newspaper Press of Charleston*, p. 135.

New Orleans to Baltimore, which almost invariably anticipated the great southern mail by thirty hours.[9] The time consumed by these expresses was six days and the cost to each paper was quite large. The most significant beat was scored on the capitulation of Vera Cruz, announced in the issue of April 10, 1847.

In the autumn, this express was reorganized to connect with the telegraph, then working as far as Petersburg, Virginia. The first message thus relayed was captioned, "By Telegraph for the Ledger—By Special and Extraordinary Express for the Public Ledger—Twenty-four hours in advance of the mail," and the editorial promoter of the service exulted:

> This news is received by special daily express which the *Ledger* has just established for the purpose of communicating to the public, in advance of the mail and other newspapers, all the important intelligence which transpires at the seat of war and the commercial cities of the South. . . . All the journals which publish it this morning will, of course, be indebted to the *Ledger's* express for it, whether they credit it or not. Our benevolence is very large and we do not mind, however expensive it may be to us, furnishing the readers of the other papers in the city with news 24 hours after it has been published in the *Ledger*.[10]

Certain New York journals later participated in this plan, which became "a daily line of expresses between New Orleans and New York extending also, sometimes, to Mexico and Havana." The *Herald,* as one of the combination, proclaimed:

> These expresses will be continued through the approaching winter, probably up to the period required to complete the telegraphic communication between the two great cities of the union. This daily express will be organized for the purpose of giving the intelligence

---

[9] Scharf and Westcott, *History of Philadelphia,* p. 2002.

[10] *Ledger,* Nov. 19, 1847.

from the South and Mexico, the West Indies and the Western Territories, one day, or even two or three days, in advance of the government mails as they are now conducted by the present Postmaster General. It has been long seen by our contemporaries that there was a necessity of some voluntary association of the press of New York and the North, in union with the journals of New Orleans and the South, in order to obviate the blundering incapacity and ridiculous parsimony with which the Post Office Department is conducted under the present régime. A remedy is now at hand.[11]

Just at this time, too, came a spectacular feat widely blazoned as Bennett's culminating coup. Receiving advance notice that Henry Clay would deliver a keynote speech on Mexican war policy at Lexington, Kentucky, he issued orders to have it reported, for publication in the *Herald* the next day. Arrangements were thereupon perfected to run a night express over the 80 odd miles between Lexington and Cincinnati, with relays of horses every ten miles. Despite rain and bad roads, the distance was covered in eight hours. Transmission of the speech, which was put on the wire at Cincinnati, was interrupted for a while at Pittsburgh by the falling of a tree limb across the line. The operator in the Pittsburgh office rode out in the darkness and rain, found the place of trouble, and repaired the break. The dispatch was in the *Herald* office early the next morning, and its publication was the talk of the town. To get this one speech entailed an outlay of $500. The usual accounts of this great exploit, of which there are several, would produce the impression that the Clay speech was a clear beat for the *Herald* and leave unexplained the fact that it was printed also in the issues of other New York papers on the same day. In the *Herald's* own announcement we have the truth of the matter:

---

[11] *Herald,* Nov. 27, 1847.

Probably one of the most remarkable feats of newspaper enterprise is the result of that which appears in this morning's *Herald*—the speech and resolutions of Mr. Clay, delivered at Lexington the day before yesterday.

The distance is nearly one thousand miles. Knowing the importance of Mr. Clay's opinions and movements in the present contest now about to take place in this country, we made extraordinary arrangements last week to run an express exclusively for the *Herald*. We have, however, taken into the enterprise, since our arrangements were made, two of our contemporaries who will also publish the same this morning.

About eleven or twelve o'clock, on the day before yesterday, the meeting was held at Lexington. Our reporters were there, and when the resolutions were read, and Mr. Clay had delivered his speech, our express started on horseback, running 84 miles to Cincinnati. At Cincinnati, the notes of our reporters were written out, and the whole was sent on the electric telegraph to this city, a distance of nearly a thousand miles. The speech and resolutions were received early yesterday morning, and but for the intervention of Sunday, we should have been able to have published the whole Lexington proceedings in less than ten hours from their delivery in Kentucky.

This feat in newspaper enterprise has never yet been paralleled in the civilized world. In England where journalism is carried on with more enterprise than in any other country, nothing has taken place which can be compared with this extraordinary feat. But this is not all. In less than six months, when the telegraphic wires shall be completed to New Orleans, and to other points, we expect to publish intelligence fifteen hundred to two thousand miles distant, the day after it transpires at all the different extremities of the republic.[12]

An outline of Mr. Clay's speech, "expressed and telegraphed" to the Philadelphia *Inquirer,* was printed in that paper and copied, with credit, the next day in the *Public Ledger*. It is possible that the *Inquirer* was included in the *Herald's* arrangements.

---

[12] *Ibid.,* Nov. 15, 1847.

CHAPTER VIII

ALL-TELEGRAPH NEWS DISTRIBUTION

Initial experiments—Telegraphic codes—High cost of messages—Mistakes and break-downs—Conflict over priority

WHAT has been called the first deliberately planned effort to supply a piece of momentous news wholly by telegraph to the interior press came in December, 1848, when President Polk sent "a phenomenally long message" to Congress. The aim was to wire it by one manipulation to Pittsburgh, Cleveland, Detroit, Buffalo, Zanesville, Columbus, Cincinnati, Louisville, and St. Louis.[1] By reason of a severe storm which broke soon after the start, it took two nights and part of one day to send the message. The operators were thoroughly exhausted. At Pittsburgh the superintendent, without sleep for two nights, had to act as substitute operator. He took the key and pounded along several weary hours, concluding the message by unconsciously sending over the wire, in his joy of relief, the cry of the Spaniard with the name of the president, "God and Liberty! James K. Polk!" Some of the sleepy editors printed the copy as it stood. How they howled the next day! George D. Prentice asked in the Louisville *Journal,* with irreverent sharpness, "What had James K. Polk to do with either God or Liberty?" and suggested that the miscreant operator be publicly beaten with Santa Anna's wooden leg.

Publication of a presidential pronouncement two days late was nevertheless an immense improvement on what had

[1] Reid, *The Telegraph in America,* p. 794.

gone before. In December, 1844, the message, delivered on a Tuesday, had reached Cincinnati by special messenger the following Friday, was there put into type and copies dispatched to Louisville by steamboat, thence by coach express to St. Louis, the whole distance from Washington requiring something over six days. The message of 1847 had been received in St. Louis in four days, being telegraphed to Vincennes, thence forwarded by pony express, and was hailed as "the most magnificent enterprise of the age." In 1848, it was there in two nights and one day.[2]

The way the news of the Whig convention was handled the following June was no less characteristic of a transition stage. The presidential choice remained doubtful between four aspirants for the nomination, Henry Clay, General Taylor, General Scott, and Judge McLean. How to get the result to the New York papers most expeditiously was the problem. In the absence, as yet, of a wire across the Hudson, the tidings arriving in Jersey City would ordinarily have to be taken to their destination on a ferry boat. A set of flags, to serve as code of signals according to number and color, was improvised.[3] A young man from one of the papers was stationed on a pier, with instructions to wave a white cloth ir answer to a like display on the Jersey side of the river.

> It seems that there was, unknown to us [relates the chief actor in the play], a party employed by a company of brokers to telegraph the price of stocks from the top of the Merchants' Exchange to Jersey City. One man would be answered by another man who would wave a white flag as a token of his readiness to receive communications. The figures of prices of stocks would be indicated

---

[2] Hyde, "Newspapers and Newspaper People of Three Decades," in Missouri Historical Society *Proceedings*, p. 21; also Scharf, *History of St. Louis*, p. 909.

[3] Jones, *Historical Sketch of the Electric Telegraph*, p. 133.

by the motions from right to let, horizontally, etc., by the operator. The man who received the numbers in Jersey City would telegraph them to Philadelphia. After I had placed my young man at 11.30 A.M., the broker's man in Jersey City stepped out on the pier and waved his flag to the man on the Exchange as usual. Our young man, seeing this white flag waving on the pier, supposed it to be ours and immediately ran to the newspaper offices and informed them that General Taylor had been nominated. It produced great excitement and was telegraphed east. On reaching Portland, Maine, 100 guns were fired. The eastern line soon after gave out and the news could not be contradicted. It turned out that General Taylor was not nominated until the succeeding day.

To economize on telegraph expense, resort was had again to employment of a cipher code. The "dictionary," already mentioned, was followed by schemes suggested by the shorthand used in reporting.[4] Market quotations, in particular, were transmitted by an ingenious arrangement by which the receipts of produce and the sales and prices of all leading articles of breadstuffs, provisions, etc., could be sent from Buffalo and Albany daily in twenty words. This skeletonizing and coding of news dispatches, to be expanded after receiving, quickly produced expert "padders," and also stupid blunders of both transmission and translation, for which the blame was bandied back and forth. Delivery of a laboriously secured piece of news, twisted to unintelligibility in the wiring, was not conducive to uncomplaining acquiescence. Nor did the telegraph companies relish code messages that sought to curtail their revenues. When the abbreviated copy began to come in, the management of the line from Boston to New York promptly refused to accept the business at the regular rate of fifty cents for ten words. Notice was served that the letters in each cipher message would be divided by five to compute the number of words

[4] *Ibid.*, p. 123.

chargeable at that rate. When the reporters evaded the new requirements by substituting short words, the order was revised downward to three letters to a word with the result that the use of the wire was almost abandoned for a short while.

Owing to the expense, too, the papers would not agree to take more telegraphic news than would fill from one-half column to one column daily. They compelled the reporters to supply them under a weekly contract, defray their own telegraph tolls, and pay their own correspondents' fees. When a scrap of news came in by wire, it was rewritten to make the most the facts would justify, a small sheet of cipher copy often providing enough material to produce a full column. In spite of all such efforts, telegraph expense would not stay down. An exhibit by the *Herald* shows that in the first two weeks of 1848, its "telegraphic work" amounted to 79,000 words at a cost of $2,381, with reference to which it added: "In order to understand this statement, it is proper for us to remark that about one third of the work done by the telegraph in the above table is executed for us conjointly with several other of the morning papers; but two thirds very nearly, is performed for us exclusively, comprehending the debates in the Senate on the Mexican question and other important political movements of all kinds, at distant points of the country." [5]

Certain other unsettled questions helped to arouse a feeling of irritation not entirely on one side. Who, for example, should gather the news for telegraphic dissemination? Did the work properly devolve on the newspapers, on the independent news purveyors, or on the telegraph companies themselves? So far, there were no sharply drawn lines of separation. Except at critical moments, no rush of news

[5] *Herald,* Jan. 15, 1848.

dispatches threatened to swamp the wires. Many telegraph companies were having hard sledding financially and thought it necessary to demand rates that were practically prohibitive for press service. On the other hand, the wires and operators were frequently idle for hours, and it was a problem whether the slack should be taken up by lowering rates for press dispatches, or whether the company's employees should make up news messages for transmission when no other business engaged them. The company spokesmen also voiced complaint. "The telegraph companies were left to use the news for showy bulletins, which made splendid advertisements, or to present without charge to the newspaper which promised to give the best public acknowledgement of its receipt and the name, of course, of the polite manager presenting it." [6]

More serious to the papers was the fact that facilities for transmission from east to west were very limited. "For a year or two, only a single wire extended from Philadelphia to Pittsburgh and Cincinnati, over which to send the whole business of the company and the newspapers even then knew how to howl when a report had to be placed on the hook for a while until commercial business could be forwarded. And when some show of a daily report began to appear in semi-occasional strips, the few dollars assessed to help keep the telegraphic pot boiling were hard to gather." What the limited facilities meant to the newspapers need not be mere guess-work. After a severe snowstorm, we read: "We are thus by the vigilance of our messenger and by the interruption of the telegraphic communication to Boston, enabled to place the news before our readers considerably in advance." [7] Again, a little later: "The southern telegraphic

[6] Reid, *op. cit.*, p. 794.
[7] *Herald,* Feb. 2, 1848.

line was so much engaged with the transmission of the foreign news, brought by the steamer 'Washington,' to the south yesterday that affairs at the seat of government were entirely overlooked and we are without our usual congressional dispatches." [8]

Such exigencies of the news service sometimes took unexpected turns. It was the custom in Pittsburgh, for example, for each paper to have a reporter call at the telegraph office and copy what he wanted from the news messages received. Sometimes the chief editor, himself, would come in recognition of the responsibility of the task. Anson Stager was the operator, learning the telegraph from the ground up for the larger place he was to occupy in the military telegraph service during the Civil War and in the direction of a great country-wide telegraph system afterwards. One night, when the reporter arrived to make his copy, he found everything quiet and the operator sitting beside his instrument reading a book. Information was vouchsafed that there would be no news that night; the register which printed the characters on the strip of paper had broken; it could not be fixed. A steamer had landed in New York. No markets. Editorial despair. "Wait while I try another plan," said Stager. "I explained matters to the operator at the other end, asked him to go slow, and between my knowledge of the cipher and the good-natured repetition of each link of it by my down-east friend, I managed to get the whole of the market report." Listening mechanically to the clicking of the instrument, he had caught the idea that he could understand what it was saying by the sound, just as the office calls were recognizable to the ear. He had written it out as it sounded to him. The papers

---

[8] *Ibid.*, April 8, 1848.

were welcome to use it if they would take the risk as to accuracy. On comparison with eastern journals which arrived three days later, it was found that the copy had contained very few mistakes. In due time, press reports came to be invariably received by sound.[9]

The rules promulgated by the companies to govern service to the press were sowing seeds of seemingly endless contention. The award of priority privileges on any score was bound to create ill feeling, and the practice of "first come, first served," on its face the acme of fairness, only led to flagrant abuses. To capture the wire and then to hold it to the finish, to hold it even beyond the needed time in order to prevent its use by a competitor until the beat was cinched, to accomplish this at any cost and by any shrewd trick, threatened to become the regular procedure. The opportunity for personal favoritism, as well as for dubious inducements to get messages on the wire ahead of a counter-offering, was always present, and the temptation strong to make it excuse a fall-down. But the device, tried out as a remedy, of a time limit on service in the form of a fifteen or twenty minute rule, applying particularly to the line between New York and Washington, proved no more satisfactory. Under the new rule, it was the custom for a banker to hire the wire for fifteen minutes, and then for a newspaper to have it for the next fifteen minutes, to be followed by another paper or another banker, and so on.[10] With wire troubles, slow sending, interruptions, poor copy, and bad judgment of news values, "the newspaperman always noticed that his story left off at the most interesting point." The worst feature of this time-limit rotation was that it abso-

---

[9] Kennedy, "Anson Stager," *Magazine of Western History,* IV, 287; Reid, *op. cit.,* p. 570.

[10] Associated Press Report 1901, p. 348.

lutely destroyed all the advantage of enterprise among rival newspapers. The alternate use of the wire by two or more reporters placed them on a dead level, because rarely could either get more than a portion of a dispatch of any length through at one sending, and the last installment of the tardiest would be delivered very soon after the completion of the first.

CHAPTER IX

ORIGIN OF THE ASSOCIATED PRESS

Union of independent reporters—Union of newspaper proprietors—Credit for origin uncertain—Contradictory accounts—Question of precise time—Contradictory dates reconciled—What contemporary documents disclose

It was becoming more and more obvious that the system of telegraphic news service was wasteful, costly, and, too frequently, ineffective. The telegraph companies could not help seeing the evils which were growing out of disconnected lines, of cut-throat competition, of nonintercourse policies among themselves, and of "passing the buck" to the next line; and the process of tying them together and unifying their management was nearly ready to commence. The newspaper publishers also were bound to realize sooner or later that they were paying out huge sums of money for wiring messages without commensurate returns, and that a change to something more satisfactory was imperative and inevitable.

As a preliminary move, three or four of the independent reporters operating in New York united to engage others in various important localities to act with them in receiving and forwarding telegraphic news for the press.[1] Their services were paid for at stated weekly salaries, or in steamer news or other news in exchange, to be sold, presumably, to any who would buy. Each of the clients thus served was charged an agreed sum per week, while the reporters paid

[1] Jones, *Historical Sketch*, p. 136.

all incidental expenses. The date of launching this association is fixed only as "within a year or two" after the first telegraph reporting from New York, and its duration as "about twelve months." But we may definitely allocate it to the year 1847, since it did not endure long and, upon dissolution, was merged with another organization in which the newspaper proprietors and publishers constituted the controlling factors, and the reporters were relegated to the background in the capacity of employees.

It not infrequently happens that a move is made which, appearing inconsequential at the time, turns out to be of most far-reaching importance, and then is found enveloped in an uncertainty, arising from varying accounts, as to how it came about. The actual formation of the first associated press, the propagating root of all the different news-gathering associations performing a similar service, is conspicuously one of those epochal events difficult to assign to an exact date or to credit to a particular individual. It would be assumed, naturally, that an enterprise touching so closely upon the work of the newspapers would be reported in full in the contemporaneous prints, or at least accurately chronicled in Hudson's monumental history, since the author was actively identified with the principal participating papers and unquestionably cognizant of every step as it was taken. Yet, nearly every successive reference made by Hudson is at variance, if not conflicting. Thomas B. Connery, who was long and intimately associated with Hudson, once asked, "To whom belongs the honor of this idea?" and answered, "I am unable to state and I doubt if there be a man living to-day [1897] who can decide the point authoritatively."

Hudson, who above all might have furnished the most dependable testimony, seems to have been bent mainly on presenting a good human interest story. His first version reads:

One forenoon after the *Herald* had published some exclusive news, a knock was heard on the door of the editorial rooms of that paper.

"Come in," answered the editor. The tall gaunt figure of David Hale entered. One of the magnates of Wall street journalism was actually in the office of a despised penny paper! But Hale was a practical man. He saw the handwriting plainly enough. There was very little circumlocution about him.

"I have called," he said, "to talk about news with you. Have you any objection?"

"None," replied the penny editor. "Am always pleased to talk on that subject."

"We propose to join the *Herald* in getting news," continued Mr. Hale. "Have you any objection to that?"

This led to a brief conversation on newspaper enterprise, pony expresses and news boats. This conversation, on the establishment of the telegraph, led to the organization of the New York Associated Press. This interview was the origin of that institution. Out of this conversation grew up an *entente cordiale* in news between the old *Journal of Commerce* and the young *Herald* which was of great service to the former during the war with Mexico and in its competition with the *Courier and Enquirer*. When the Associated Press was organized, Gerard Hallock became its president and remained as such till he retired from the press, respected by every member of that body.

In another chapter, Hudson mentions, as a sequel to the momentous interview, "a great congress of the Republic of News" in which "representatives from the *Journal of Commerce, Courier and Enquirer, Tribune, Herald, Sun* and *Express* met at the office of the *Sun* and formed, first, the Harbor News Association and, second, the New York Associated Press." But careful perusal discloses nothing to show that the visit of David Hale to the *Herald* office was followed immediately, or even soon, by an inclusive news-gathering combination. On the contrary, the avowed purpose was a mutual alliance between the *Journal of Commerce* and the *Herald,* having to do with messages transmitted by horse expresses and news boats prior to the era of the telegraph, resulting at most in some united effort by these two papers and a more amicable understanding in place of antagonism. What the conference unquestionably did was to pave the way for a measure of coöperation and to make possible, or rather less difficult, the subsequent organization. The further declaration by Hudson that this interview between Hale and Bennett sought to avoid a ruinous competition, already in progress, in the use of the telegraph, savors of anachronism, though it does account satisfactorily for the selection of Hallock as first president of the Associated Press and as the representative of the only "blanket sheet" commanding the confidence of Bennett, the latter personifying the "cheap press."

Hudson's monumental history would confer the founder's medal on David Hale, with perhaps honorable mention for James Gordon Bennett. In an obituary of Hudson, *Harper's Weekly,* however, said that Hudson, himself, "organized the *Herald's* business of news-getting to a system and laid the early foundation of the Associated Press." [2] So it has been hinted that the credit may in reality belong to Hudson. Connery, however, definitely asserts, "I never heard Mr. Hudson himself make any claim of the kind. It seems only to be based on the fact that Mr. Hudson happened to be the first person whom Mr. David Hale saw in the *Herald* office when he went there to propose an alliance for news-gathering between the *Journal of Commerce,* then one of the 'blanket sheets' and the spritely *Herald* which was waking up the old fogy journals by its dash and enterprise." [3]

---

[2] *Harper's Weekly,* Nov. 13, 1875, p. 924.

[3] Connery, "The Collection of News," *Cosmopolitan Magazine,* May, 1897, p. 22.

Bennett, who was at no time timid about demanding recognition for his achievements, never, so far as is discoverable, paraded himself as the originator of the Associated Press. General Charles H. Taylor, long prominent with the press of New England as publisher of the Boston *Globe*, nevertheless is authority for the statement that Bennett, much aggravated by the futile, and almost fatal, fifteen-minute rule, and seeing eventual paralysis of profits in a competitive orgy of telegraphic news extravagances, called the other newspaper proprietors together and persuaded them to take the wire to Washington for a continuous report for two hours and divide the expense, and that "that was the origin of the Associated Press."[4] But Charles A. Dana represented Bennett as reluctantly joining the others in the combination and, after expatiating on the energy displayed in getting news for the *Sun* by special expresses and telegraph, manifested an inclination to give the credit to Moses Y. Beach, by declaring, "The final result was the organization of the New York Associated Press."[5] The one circumstance favoring Dana's preference for Beach is Hudson's notation that the all-important meeting took place in the office of the *Sun*.

Can the date of this conference be fixed? It does not seem precisely determinable either by formal agreement or by documentary evidence. It has been, as a rule, placed all the way from 1847 to 1851, and there is no concurrence of those who ought to speak with authority. Hudson's account of the "Congress of the Republic of News" states, "This was in 1848-1849." Writing in 1897, Connery gave the date of the meeting as 1847, and asserted, "There is extant one of the seven copies of the original agreement, with the auto-

---

[4] Taylor, "Reminiscences," Associated Press Report, 1901, p. 348.
[5] Wilson, *Life of Charles A. Dana*, p. 487.

graphs of the elder James Gordon Bennett, Gerard Hallock, Henry J. Raymond, C. A. Dana for Horace Greeley, Moses Beach, James and Erastus Brooks, and General James Watson Webb." Here, he was clearly mistaken if he meant to imply that this particular copy was one of the first compact, since, as we shall show, his was an inaccurate reproduction of a later agreement.

On the other hand, William Henry Smith, who functioned as general manager for many years and made a close study of press association history, distinguished 1849 as the beginning of the Harbor News Association, and made the New York Associated Press date from 1851, setting forth the wording of the signed paper as follows:[6]

> It is mutually agreed between G. Hallock of the *Journal of Commerce,* J. and E. Brooks of the *Express,* J. G. Bennett of the *Herald,* Beach Brothers of the *Sun,* Greeley and McElrath of the *Tribune,* and J. W. Webb of the *Courier,* to associate for the purpose of collecting and receiving telegraphic and other intelligence.

Let it be noted that the text, as quoted, is undated, though the fact that no signature is attached for any one representing the *Times* sets the agreement ahead of the appearance of that paper.

Bearing on the initial date, we have affirmative statements from two reliable sources that the great telegraphic triumph, in connection with Clay's Lexington speech, anticipated the press association compact. This address was delivered November 13, 1847. The narrative of it, incorporated into Dr. Jones's book, issued in 1852, declared distinctly that it was "before any regular association of the press was formed in New York."[7] Again, in his biography of Bennett, pub-

[6] Smith, "The Press as a News-Gatherer," *Century Magazine,* 1891, p. 524.

[7] Jones, *op. cit.,* p. 137.

lished in 1855, Isaac C. Pray, already a veteran of New York journalism, said, with regard to the same event, that "this was prior to the combination of the Associated Press."[8]

Study of the newspaper files of the period provides ample confirmation of this. The rival horse expresses to the south, it will be recalled, were established during this very month, with loud bugle blasts. The *Courier and Enquirer,* about the same time, announced special arrangements for covering the impending sessions of Congress and a plan to issue a supplement three times a week to take care of its full reports.[9] The *Herald* never ceased boasting of its exclusive reports from Washington: "They will not probably be found in full in any other New York paper this morning as we procured them by special express from Washington."[10] It was constantly asserting that its news "is more extensive and more complete than that of any other journal ever published in this country"; the treaty with Mexico "was originally published in this journal exclusively."[11]

In Philadelphia, the *Ledger* was playing up the intelligence received by its special daily express. "All the journals which publish it this morning will, of course, be indebted to the *Ledger's* express for it, whether they credit it or not."[12] We know now that not all of these enterprises were executed single-handed, inasmuch as temporary combinations had been formed for various projects, and the independent reporters were also serving identical news to quite a few papers. While making great ado over its liberal patronage of the telegraph, the *Herald* let slip a hint of this fact.[13] As

[8] Pray, *James Gordon Bennett,* p. 377.
[9] *Courier and Enquirer,* Dec. 14, 1847.
[10] *Herald,* Dec. 10, 1847.
[11] *Ibid.,* March 25, 1848.
[12] *Ledger,* Nov. 17, 1847.
[13] *Herald,* Jan. 15, 1848.

late as in April of 1848, the *Herald* was maintaining, on its own account, two special express steamers, the "Telegraph" and the "Jacob Bell," to board incoming ships outside of New York harbor.[14] It was a case of every paper for itself, and the devil take the hindmost.

The first sign of more cohesive union was visible in the chartering of a steamer, the *Buena Vista,* in the spring of 1848, to intercept the transatlantic boats at Halifax and put the foreign news on the wire at Boston. To facilitate the telegraphic transmission of the messages brought to Boston by the *Buena Vista,* and at the same time to reduce the expense to the participating papers, which was the object of the combination, a committee was appointed to negotiate with the telegraph company, and the correspondence arranging the terms throws real light on the details. Under the authority conferred, an inquiry was addressed to F. O. J. Smith, in charge of the Boston and New York line, as follows:

New York, May 13, 1848

F. O. J. Smith, Esq.

Dear Sir: The *Journal of Commerce, Express, Courier and Enquirer, Herald, Sun,* and *Tribune,* of this city have agreed to procure foreign news by telegraph from Boston in common and have appointed a committee to make arrangements with you for its transmission.

Acting on behalf of that committee of the Association, I beg to propose that you give us, from the moment our dispatch shall be received at the telegraph office in Boston, the use of all the wires that may be in working order for the uninterrupted transmission of all the news we may wish to receive.

Upon its receipt here, we will make copies for each paper entitled to it and shall desire authority to prevent any part of the news leaving the office until we choose to send it out.

---

[14] *Ibid.*, April 8, 1848.

The arrangement is also intended to apply to steamer's news that may reach Boston for us by express from Halifax.

Upon what terms will you secure for us, for one year from the present date, the use of the telegraph as specified above? An immediate reply will greatly oblige

Your obedient servant,

H. J. RAYMOND

Smith's answer, dated at Boston, May 15, 1848, was not only responsive to the suggestion, but submitted, in addition to the rates of compensation asked for, these further stipulations which he was willing to incorporate in the agreement:

I will contract the service of the Telegraph in respect to foreign news on this line to the proprietors of the papers you name for one year from this date on the following terms:

To give their despatch, on arrival of a foreign steamer, priority on any one wire which may be in order for work through to New York, and on all other wires that shall be worked through to New York, from the time the despatch shall be delivered to the Boston office, until its transmission shall have been completed.

You shall have the exclusive right to admit and to dismiss other parties to and from the benefits of the arrangement, on giving the president of the association, for the time being, written notice of admission and discontinuance of each, as it shall occur.

If you give other parties, private individuals, reporters or presses, the use of news before put into public circulation in good faith, payment shall be made as for a copy of the excess over 3,000 words, be the same more or less, by each party so furnished at the usual newspaper rates of transmission.

I will accord you the desired authority to prevent any part of the news from leaving the office at New York until you choose to send it out.[15]

The final acceptance, making the contract binding on behalf of all concerned, reads:

---

[15] Craig, *Review*, p. 18.

New York, May 18, 1848

Dear Sir:

I have received your letter of the 15th and have submitted it to Mr. Hudson, of the *Herald,* who with myself form the committee to act in behalf of the Associated Press. The object in making the arrangement proposed is to prevent the competition and the frequent changes of which you complain. We intend to forward the news so received, at once, to Philadelphia and Baltimore, so that the press of those cities will also be interested in the arrangement.

We understand your offer to be this: that our news shall come through without interruption; that for the first 3,000 words we pay a gross sum, $100, without reference to the parties using it; and that for the excess, we pay the regular rates, one full price and as many half prices as there are copies used, less one.

We therefore accept the offer and assent to the conditions you have named.

For Mr. Hudson and myself,

I am very truly yours,

H. J. Raymond [16]

Here we have the earliest record of the association, and the first official use of the name Associated Press. In view of the interrelated circumstances, moreover, the date, May 18, 1848, would indicate that the committee had lost no time in taking up its work—in a word, that the meeting which marked the birth of the Associated Press took place in the month of May, 1848, and that the expedition of foreign news was the prime object.

In point of fact, performance could not at first have been all that was hoped if we note information on this score given by the *Ledger:*

The steamboat chartered by some of the journals to run to Halifax and anticipate, by means of the telegraph at the east, the news by the steamships, has not been very successful so far. The "Buena Vista," the name of the boat, was announced at Boston and arrived at her wharf at precisely the same moment that the "Hibernia"

[16] Smith, *An Exposition,* p. 27.

arrived at New York. Her outward trip to Halifax was made in 60 hours, which included a stay of 12 hours at Shelburne. When one day out on her return, the boiler sprang a leak in the furnace room, and as it could not be stopped nor any head of steam maintained, the vessel was compelled to rely almost entirely on her sails for the rest of her trip. A new boiler is now being constructed to replace the one which gave out. Perhaps she will have better luck next time.[17]

Yet, before a month had elapsed, the big news of the day in the same publication was headed: "By Magnetic Telegraph for the Public Ledger—By Special and Extraordinary Express for the Public Ledger—Arrival of the Steamship Britannia at Halifax—By the Ledger's Special Express Steamer Buena Vista, we have just received the news by the steamer Britannia, etc."[18] The inevitable conclusion must be that the *Ledger,* in the interval, had become affiliated with the New York Associated Press.

That the new project was gaining headway in spite of initial difficulties was emphasized by two announcements of its extension, in June, to include a joint harbor news service:

The news steamer, "Naushon," recently purchased by the *Herald* and four of our contemporaries, arrived here yesterday afternoon from New Bedford. The name of the steamer is to be changed to "Newsboy." She is to be immediately put in complete order and will probably be ready for service on Monday. It is expected that her speed will fully meet the expectation of those who have entered into this piece of newspaper enterprise.[19]

The new ship news arrangements of the *Herald* and four of our contemporaries are now complete. The auxiliary fleet consisting of a swift boat at the Narrows, manned by Captain Robert Silvay, and two men; another boat at Quarantine, manned by Captain William Brogan; and another for the East river and harbor service, manned by Captain John Hall, commenced operations on Monday morning

[17] *Ledger,* May 30, 1848.
[18] *Ibid.,* June 26, 1848.
[19] *Herald,* June 2, 1848.

last. The news steamer, "Newsboy," commanded by Captain William Bancker, and manned by engineers, firemen, sailors, &c, &c, for outside or sea service, entered upon her duty yesterday morning. It will thus be seen that the leading journals of New York have now a most efficient Ship News establishment in operation.[20]

Whether the same combination took upon itself the collection and distribution of domestic telegraphic news at once, or deferred that until later, is less certain. There is reason to believe that the association organized by the independent telegraph reporters was continuing to function through the national conventions that named candidates for the 1848 presidential contest. The *Herald's* comment may be easily so construed:

During each day's sitting of the convention [at Baltimore], we received telegraphic reports from two sources—one through certain telegraphic reporters, who make it a business to transmit news, backwards and forwards, hitherwards and thitherwards, upwards and downwards, around, about and every way, for all newspapers and all journals that are willing to buy and pay for the news. This class of reporters are very competent men; but from their system, they are exceedingly careless and negligent in preparing and transmitting their intelligence. We know this to be a fact; for during last week, when our own special reporters transmitted intelligence to us, we receive it from the operators at both ends with perfect accuracy almost to the marking of a comma. The blunders arise from the news reporters who have attempted to invent a new mode of condensing language, by using particular words in order to reduce the expense of reporting.[21]

While not necessarily conclusive, since the *Herald* was prone to criticize the press reports and depreciate their reliability from time to time,[22] this description would indicate that the absorption of the general telegraphic news service

---

[20] *Ibid.*, June 10, 1848.
[21] *Ibid.*, May 22, 1848.
[22] *Herald*, Jan. 9, 1849; also Feb. 9, 1849.

by the association was not completed until a little later, which fact, furthermore, is supported by Hudson's remark that the arrangement for harbor news came first.[23]

The original Associated Press, then, was simply a mutual arrangement, or, more accurately, series of arrangements, for joint news-gathering at common expense by six of the New York morning dailies. Through an existence continuing forty-four years, it was never incorporated. It was reorganized at least twice, and its membership varied. These reorganizations produced much of the misunderstanding as to its earlier history. Presumably doing business by unanimous consent, the one condition imposed on the members, at the start, required prompt payment of an equal share of the cost, and the various rules were subsequently adopted only as other papers were taken along as clients. The avowed policy was to share the service with any paper "paying or securing payment of its proper proportion of the expenses involved" and "agreeing to abide by such regulations as the Association may find necessary for the protection of the parties to the arrangement." [24]

---

[23] *Ibid.*, Jan. 9, 1849; also Feb. 9, 1849.
[24] Smith, *op. cit.*, p. 23.

CHAPTER X

FIRST ORGANIZATION AND METHODS

The administration of Dr. Alexander Jones—Working under difficulties—Financial arrangements—Character of the news service

To accomplish its purpose, it became necessary for the new association to provide suitable machinery. Two broad divisions of the work were marked off, one relating to foreign news, and the other having to do with the collection and dissemination of domestic news. For the foreign news, interests were pooled for a harbor patrol and also to expedite the receipt and forwarding of dispatches and packets at Boston and at Halifax, this last through a representative there, appointed by a special committee in charge and working under its supervision. The domestic news service was given over to a general agent, with headquarters in New York, upon whom devolved the management of the office and the direction of the staff. In so doing, of course, the associated publications were working along lines already tried out in similar enterprises.

The first general agent was Dr. Alexander Jones, of Welsh descent, a graduate in medicine, and an experienced journalist, who had done reporting on both sides of the Atlantic.[1] Then forty-five years of age, he was described as a man of considerable force of character, but a little erratic. He had been a pioneer in independent reporting, and an early convert to the use of the telegraph for news-gathering, for which he had invented the first cipher code.

---

[1] O'Brien, *The Story of the Sun,* p. 166.

His intense interest in the infant telegraph was most fortunate, since it led him to write a book entitled, *Historical Sketch of the Electric Telegraph,* and to insert in it a chapter on the relations of the press, which supplies us with authentic information on many points that otherwise might remain obscure.

The office established by Dr. Jones had its location at Broadway and Liberty streets. The agent was allowed only one or two helpers and he complained about being compelled to take inexperienced and youthful parties and "by long drilling to create, as it were, our assistance." His was the task to hunt up and engage the best reporters in all parts of the country. He received and distributed the news sent by these correspondents from the principal cities of the United States and Canada, paid the tolls and other expenses necessary to conduct the business, and saw to the collections. Of each dispatch, eight or nine copies would be made, six for the New York members and the remaining copies for papers in other cities and towns. Compensation for the service depended chiefly on what Jones succeeded in extracting from publishers elsewhere, such as at Boston, etc., for news of all kinds thus reforwarded, including the local intelligence of New York. For the member papers of the association, extra news would be obtained on condition that any one of them might exercise an option to take what had been specially ordered, those using it sharing the expense.

As the first general agent, Dr. Jones put into operation, if he did not devise, the financial plan of the organization, which undoubtedly contributed a great deal to its long life. All the telegraph offices in the city were required to render their accounts weekly. These were examined and, after verification, set down in a general bill, to which was added the outlays for office and incidentals. The aggregate sum was then divided into six equal parts and submitted to the treasurer of the association, on whose approval the respective amounts were assessed to the member papers. In this way, "on each Saturday, we paid off all the telegraph bills and office expenses and commenced the following week *de novo*." In case any paper had failed to pay, its news, we are assured, would have been stopped. Papers supplied with news service as clients, as in Boston and various other places, were expected to remit monthly. Upon neglect of any country paper to settle at the expiration of each month, when the account was regularly forwarded, news was discontinued. The bills of out-of-town correspondents were also paid monthly by the general agent. "The system thus organized," we are naïvely advised, "worked quite smoothly and gave very little trouble." [2]

Of the money disbursed for news service, the telegraphs were the largest beneficiaries. The annual expenditures for telegraph reports of all kinds of the six associated New York papers ran as high as $30,000. The average for five years was between $25,000 and $30,000. During the Jones régime, the weekly expenses in the office did not exceed $50, exclusive of the rent, which was less than $500 a year, and the salary of the general agent, which was $20 a week, then considered good pay.[3] By 1855, the year's outlay of the association had risen to between $40,000 and $50,000.[4]

Among other possibly contributing causes, the onerous character of the duties shortened Dr. Jones's term of employment. He himself has indicated that he was by no means happy in his position. "Our services were severe,"

---

[2] Jones, *Historical Sketch*, p. 138.

[3] Connery, "The Collection of News," *Cosmopolitan Magazine*, May, 1897, p. 27.

[4] Pray, *James Gordon Bennett*, p. 377.

he confided, "and help with the proper tact and necessary prior instruction could not be had." The business demanded personal attention day and night, Sundays and week days. The outpouring of his trials and tribulations sounded pathetic. "Often on stormy nights in winter, when our errand boys were either ill or absent in Jersey City, have we gone round at twelve and one o'clock and delivered messages with a snow or sleet storm beating in our face; and having, at many of the offices, to climb three or four pairs of stairs to find the composing room. For months at a time, we seldom retired before twelve to one o'clock and then had to be on duty through the next day. During the state elections, we were frequently up all night; and, at the presidential election in 1848, we remained up for three nights consecutively." Dr. Jones submitted his resignation, which was accepted May 19, 1851, terminating a connection covering about three years. He went to the *Herald* in the capacity of commercial editor but continued to look after the market news for the association. Incidentally, he was holding forth as a practicing physician all this time. He was active as a journalist till his death, in 1863, at the age of sixty-one.

CHAPTER XI

THE ASCENDANCY OF CRAIG

His contest with "Fog" Smith—Reorganization of 1851—Reorganization of 1856—Minor competing agencies—The contest with Russell

THE successor of Dr. Jones in the position of general agent was David H. Craig, transferred or promoted from service as foreign news agent at Boston and at Halifax. By this shift, the management of the Associated Press fell under an aggressive and pugnacious hand, unscrupulous, maybe, as his foes charged, certainly stirring and tireless. Most conspicuous of all, in the mad scramble for transatlantic news during the fiercely competitive era, he had been annexed to the forces of the combined New York papers only in consequence of his demonstrated superior ability to control the situation against them. For fifteen years now, Craig was to hold the place and wield a power in the realm of news service akin to that of absolute monarch. The tenacious traits and thrilling performances that pushed Craig to the fore as an independent news-gatherer had already commanded wide attention. His engagement by the New York papers to be their representative for foreign news brought with him an acrimonious controversy over the telegraph facilities accorded his dispatches from arriving steamers. It was a fight without quarter between Craig, upheld by his papers, and the manager of the wires into Boston from the north, the same F. O. J. Smith who had made the special contract for uninterrupted use of the Boston to New York lines the previous year.

A native of New Hampshire, Smith, familiarly dubbed "Fog" Smith,[1] was a member of Congress from Maine when the appropriation for the Morse experiment still hung fire. After helping Morse wind the congressional mazes, he became one of the financial sponsors of his patents and now was principal owner, president, and in charge as manager, of the only telegraph line into Boston. For personal reasons, Smith resented the employment of Craig by the New York papers. At any rate, Craig accused Smith of sundry duplicities to obtain the appointment as press representative for John T. Smith, of Boston, member of another Smith family, and with him to create and control a foreign-news monopoly. Smith retaliated by reversing the indictment and also accusing Craig of manipulating the wires, and actually cutting them, to benefit private speculation in the stock market. Resultant libel suits and perjury prosecutions echoed in the courts for many years.[2]

In clash after clash between Craig and the Smiths, each side displayed singular ingenuity to best the other. Although the connecting line to St. Johns and Halifax had been constructed on the guaranties of patronage by the New York press, no sooner was it completed than John T. Smith, whom Craig had supplanted there in February, 1849, reappeared and declared himself empowered to superintend the news intercommunication of Europe and America over the telegraph.[3] When the next arriving steamer approached the port, both Craig and Smith were at the wharf, a mile from

---

[1] The name is variously given as Francis Orville Jonathan Smith, Francis Orman Jefferson Smith, Francis Osmond Jonathan Smith, and Francis Ormond Jonathan Smith.

[2] Craig, *Review of Differences,* 1850; Smith, *An Exposition,* 1850; Reply of American Telegraph Company, 1860; Arguments of Hayes and Smith, 1866.

[3] Reid, *The Telegraph,* p. 365.

the telegraph office, with the fastest horses in the province, ready for a race. Half the population lined the streets, eager to witness the trial of speed between the two "Yankees." As the boat came nearer, the excitement on shore grew intense. When within thirty or forty feet of the dock, the purser of the steamer mounted the paddle-box and tossed a parcel of London and Liverpool papers and a prepared summary of the fortnight's news to Smith, who, in a few seconds, was rushing on his way to the telegraph office. Long before Craig succeeded in boarding the vessel and obtaining his news packages, Smith had possession of the single wire leading to New York.

Realizing how badly he had been beaten, Craig instantaneously applied his wits to retrieve his damaged reputation. He telegraphed his superiors at New York to instruct their Liverpool agent to carry out scrupulously the directions to be sent by him. At the same time, by the outgoing steamer, he transmitted orders to the correspondent at Liverpool to depute a special messenger to succeeding steamers with duplicate copies of latest European journals and news summaries, one parcel to be thrown over to his news boat five miles below the city, and the other to another news boat stationed opposite the telegraph office, a mile from the wharf. In the meantime, Smith had also perfected his arrangements: he had the pursers liberally payed: he went around with an air of confidence contrasting noticeably with Craig's worried look. A week before the ship was due, Craig carefully manned his two news boats, engaged a fast horse express to run from a point five miles below the city and let the secret leak out to Smith that his parcels were to be hurled to his men as the steamer neared the city. On the eve of the test, Craig made up a dummy package of old European papers, including the best known, Willmer &

Smith's *European Times,* issued in Liverpool, taking care to expose a part of the name outside the wrapper, but to conceal the date. A trusted agent, standing on the bank, threw this bundle into the water as the steamer passed him, forthwith recovered it, sped to the telegraph office, placed it dripping on the table, and, almost breathless, announced, "Here is Craig's parcel of European news." Fifteen minutes later, Smith was driving a fast trotter from the wharf to the telegraph office. Before the horse had come to a full stop, Smith had leaped from the carriage and bounded to the top of the stairs leading to the operating room. The clerk pointed to the wet package on the table, indicating that it had right of way. With a single glance, and a "fearful malediction" upon his competitor, Smith turned on his heel, drove to his hotel, and in a half hour was riding out of the harbor on the steamer headed for Boston. Craig thereupon proceeded at his leisure, after receiving the packets from his messenger, to prepare his news for the wire.

But Craig was not to be left indefinitely in undisturbed supremacy. On his abandonment of the unequal fight, Smith turned over to E. S. Dyer the representation of the papers he served, chiefly Boston and New York evening publications. The conflict flared into the open again when the Boston Associated Press, by which name nine of the twelve papers there had joined forces with the New York combination, gave formal notice of dissolution effected at a meeting held November 17, 1849, and at once proceeded to reorganize under the name of the Morning Press without certain dissenting members. The papers retaining membership were the *Daily Advertiser,* Boston *Courier, Morning Post,* The *Atlas,* The *Times,* and The *Bee.* The withdrawing journals, according to Smith, had a triple grievance: first, the time limit cut their report off at two o'clock each afternoon;

second, the paying of an assessment of $40 per steamer for three evening papers as against $60 for seven morning papers; and finally, a disinclination to have to deal with Craig.[4] Invoking the rule of "first come, first served," avowing an opposition on principle to any monopoly of news, and assuming the rôle of champion of the smaller and weaker papers against discrimination and oppression by the New York association, Smith refused to forward the Associated Press dispatch ahead of news messages filed for transmission at Halifax, but otherwise held in abeyance to give the Associated Press priority.

Craig threatened to return to the use of pigeons and, to be in readiness, had his birds sent to him. He was meditating a master stroke to beat the telegraph, which project he incautiously proclaimed "a personal and private enterprise, in the results of which the press and the public will fully and fairly participate if they choose to pay me a quid pro quo; if not, I shall assume it as a right to sell my news as I would a string of onions, i.e., to the highest bidder."[5] Smith seized with avidity upon this rash declaration, lodged complaint with the committee of the Associated Press, and demanded Craig's dismissal. Craig, in some way, met the attack to the satisfaction of his committee. He countered strongly by inducing the telegraph management at Portland to hold fast to all dispatches coming there and to refuse to turn them over to Smith's operators for forwarding, until the Associated Press message, carried from Portland by special locomotive which Craig had chartered, had reached Boston and been put on the wire at that point, insuring delivery in New York in advance of all others. In the sharp interchange of letters over this performance, we may see

[4] Smith, *An Exposition,* p. 26.
[5] *Ibid.,* p. 36.

clearly the moves in progress. Under date of December 20, 1849, Mr. Darrow, in charge of the telegraphs at St. Johns, wrote to Smith:

During the frequent absences of Mr. Craig, Mr. Till, editor of the *New Brunswicker*, who took the news to his own office to make up the despatch, was frequently three-fourths of an hour before he gave us copy. In the meantime, one or two favored individuals would by some means possess themselves of the news, if of any importance, and bring in their private communications to be forwarded. Two or three times, they were successful in getting their news through; but, after a short time, not satisfied with their being before the news, they desired to have a longer time to operate and therefore broke our wires after their communication had passed. Once the line was down from three to four hours; and once over twelve hours; and they have now become so perfect that they have kept us down three days and we do not find the break . . . whereupon they (our directors) passed a resolution to cut off all private communications after the arrival of the steamer at the wharf—not because they want to prevent communications from passing, but because they wish to prevent the line being cut. This being made public, had the desired effect; and we had no trouble with our line until it was finished through Halifax.

But now comes the tug of war. The Halifax papers stated to the world that the government had adopted the principle, "first come, first served," in all cases. Advantage of this is taken by parties. Great opposition is raised. If one party gets in first, the other is sure to cut the wires and vice versa; and this is continually being done. The organization of these parties must be perfect, or we should not continue to lose the foreign despatch week after week.

Now, my friend, what are we going to do to protect ourselves against this continual breakage and loss of business? Are we to go on in this manner, giving preference to the first that comes, that no disappointed one may break the wires? or are we to adopt the strict rule that the whole public press, that will pay their portion of the expense, shall first be served at all hazards? This principle had its good effects with us at this point and I doubt not you will, after a time if not now, be forced to agree with me that it is the only line of action which will preserve us from a continual breakage—which four-folds our expense and destroys our business—as without the sum paid by the press, it would be impossible for us to support ourselves under the best of circumstances.[6]

Smith had proclaimed his determination to observe only one rule among the newspaper press, that is, "to enforce absolute priority to the despatch that first reaches this line, or the lines with which it coöperates, or treat all despatches as private and subject to the fifteen minute rule." He appealed to the government commissioners of Nova Scotia to uphold him in his position.

The argument was by no means one-sided in the camp of Smith's own telegraph people. Protests poured from allied companies which felt the effects, especially after Craig began to divert his Boston-to-New York business to the new Bain line, "the pirate line," and elsewhere to other competitors of the Morse system. This was the remonstrance that went to Smith from the president of the Magnetic Telegraph Company:

What is your position? A message comes to your line after having passed over three legitimate Morse lines and you assume a right to stop it—to send it no further. For what reason? Not that it is connected with any crime committed, or in contemplation; not that it would be encouraging piracy upon Morse's patent rights; not that it came upon the Halifax line through any fraud or deception; not even because it reached Halifax by a carrier pigeon; but simply because the agent of the Associated Press at Halifax is, in your opinion, a bad man, not to be trusted by the public; that he has avowed his purpose to employ carrier pigeons; and that he has threatened, under certain circumstances, to cut down the lines. No overt act has been traced to him; it is not shown that he has employed carrier pigeons, or cut the wires; he is sustained by the public authorities of Nova Scotia and his employers in the United States.

Under these circumstances, it seems to me you assume a high prerogative when you undertake to stop messages for no other

---

[6] *Ibid.*, p. 21.

reason than suspicion or dislike of the person who sends them. You virtually condemn the public authorities of Nova Scotia, and attempt to dictate to the customers of the telegraph whom they shall not employ as their agents, and in what manner their business shall be done, not only on your lines but on lines beyond, and even beyond the limits of the United States.

Whether the managers of the Nova Scotia line ought to receive and send messages which may have been brought to Halifax by carrier pigeons, is one question; and whether the manager of a line in the United States ought to stop them on that account, is another. Certainly, the manager of a line in Wisconsin would hardly venture to give, as a reason for refusing to forward an item of news, that it had been brought to Halifax by a carrier pigeon, or that he had not a good opinion of the man who sent it. In what does your position differ from his? [7]

The insistence of Smith that he was defending the public against control of the news sources by a self-seeking agent of an arrogant press, and against misuse of the wires for any special interest, to his disappointment failed to rally popular sentiment; on the contrary, it seemed to stimulate the financing of rival lines, promoted by poachers to whom reference was again made in the complaint voiced by Amos Kendall, speaking for the Morse group:

In behalf of my principals, I protest against the further use of their property in the Boston and Portland line in this warfare and request you to forward all despatches coming from the Maine line no matter by whom sent. I wish you and the country to understand that you alone are responsible for the course now pursued on that line. Would that I could as easily avert its injurious, if not fatal, consequences!

I have not thought it necessary to consider the question of your abstract power, as the owner of a large majority of the stock, on the Boston and Portland line. Power ceases to be rightful when perverted from its legitimate object and oppressed communities do not fail to find means to rid themselves of its dominion.

God forbid that, by any act of mine, the people of the United

---

[7] Reid, *op. cit.*, p. 366.

States should ever justly come to consider the pirates upon Morse's patents their friends and deliverers.

If, through the smoke of personal fusillade, doubt clouded the merits of the bitter feud, Smith's treatment of Morse would tend to incline one to favor Craig. Though Smith, while in Congress, had seen the value of Morse's device and had assisted him to obtain government aid (after an agreement to let him purchase a substantial interest in it and after avoiding legal entanglements by postponing the deal until his resignation of his seat), he proved to be a perpetual thorn in the flesh. Smith's investment of $7,000 in time yielded him more than $300,000, but did not satisfy his greed. In letter after letter, Morse lamented his association with him. "There are more F. O. J.'s than one, yet not one quite so bad," he wrote as early as January, 1847.[8] Two years later, he declared that Mr. Smith "is so utterly unprincipled and selfish that we can expect nothing but renewed impositions as long as we have any connection with him;"[9] and still later, "I wish nothing short of entire separation from that unprincipled man if it can possibly be accomplished. . . . I can suffer his frauds upon myself with comparative forbearance but my indignation boils when I am made, *nolens volens, a particeps criminis* in his fraud on others. I will not endure it if I must sacrifice all the property I have in the world."[10] What Morse's biographer calls "the meanest case of extortion," was Smith's claim of a share of the honorary gratuity of 400,000 francs voted to Morse by the congress of ten European powers at Paris in recognition of his service to mankind. This demand for $25,000 was submitted to referees, who rendered a decision

---

[8] Morse, *Letters,* II, 271.
[9] *Ibid.,* p. 308.
[10] *Ibid.,* p. 312.

against Morse in the sum of $14,000, which the latter, in sheer disgust, refused to contest further. The climax came in the public letter, addressed by Smith to the Morse Monument Association, in 1871, objecting to making the aging Morse the central figure on a monument at Washington to symbolize the electro-magnetic telegraph. Morse's final jibe at Smith excoriated him as "one of the most revengeful of men."[11]

The fuss and fustian between Smith and Craig gradually subsided, and the issues at stake eventually settled themselves. While the commotion was at its height, the New York Associated Press had made its offer, on January 3, 1850, to let any paper share the foreign news on equitable terms. In this statement, it was specifically set forth that Boston might have the service at $100 per steamer, "same as heretofore," and take as many papers in Boston as they pleased into the association; it was also made known that two additional New York city journals had come in with them within the preceding two weeks and that arrangements with the press of Philadelphia provided that the news be offered to all alike.[12] It was at this moment, too, that Craig magniloquently advertised himself as representing, through the Associated Press, "all, with a very few insignificant exceptions, the commercial journals between Boston and New Orleans and between New York and Quebec." This boast was, we may be sure, as vaingloriously overdrawn as his subsequent assertion that, through all this period, "fully four-fifths of the papers sustained an opposition news association."[13]

Rival news services there were, chief among them Abbott

---

[11] *Ibid.*, p. 502.
[12] Craig, *Review*, p. 20.
[13] Craig, *Annual Report*, 1862.

and Winans with offices at No. 3 Hanover Street, right across the roadway from the Associated Press quarters. We can readily believe that such annoying competition had something to do with the supplanting of Jones as general agent, and the promotion of Craig, but the decisive factor was the latter's success in downing Smith, a victory nailed tight now by the completion of a second telegraph from Boston to Portland, abating the necessity of using the Smith lines for the press dispatch from Halifax, and providing independent transmission all the way to New York.[14] The division of the business forced a consolidation after a year or two, a consolidation unprofitable to both companies; but, by that time, Craig was established in the New York office, and the fires of belligerency merely smoldered.

With Craig transferred to the seat of authority, a new momentum in the activities of the association was manifest; indeed, it had already commenced. The Harbor News Association, the same group engaged in an integral part of the work, had been reorganized early in 1849, and its methods recast. The boat, owned in common, which had been acquired at a cost of $30,000 and ostentatiously christened *Newsboy* the previous year, was thrown out of commission and ordered sold on joint account. The carefully composed description, incorporated into the invitation for proposals to purchase, furnishes certain information found nowhere else:

> For Sale—The Steamer "Newsboy" which, for several months past, has been employed by the News Association of this city for the collection of ship news, &c. She was built in New York of the best materials, by Joseph C. Coffey, in August, 1845; is coppered and copper fastened, and of the following dimensions: Length, 134 feet 4 inches; breadth, 22 feet 2 inches; depth, 8 feet 3 inches; ton-

[14] Reid, *op. cit.*, p. 369.

nage, 240 18/95 tons. The engine is a powerful one, having a 34 inch cylinder and 8 feet stroke and is in excellent order. Her boiler is entirely new and cost, including fixtures and the expense of putting on board, about $3,000. She has two large tanks for fresh water; and for strength, speed and other good qualities is believed not to be surpassed by any steamer of her class in our waters. For further particulars, apply at this office.[15]

In passing, it may be noted that the current demand for fast boats could not have been very brisk, since the advertisement ran in the *Courier and Enquirer* for nearly three months before it was withdrawn. Coincidentally, or soon after, the underwriters were prevailed upon to unite with the papers for securing the construction of an electric telegraph from New York to Sandy Hook, whence steamer news was expedited as delivered by pigeon express from the boarding fleet operating outside the bay. Before Craig left the north, he had resumed the practice of having a sailing vessel lie in wait at sea on the track of the incoming ships off the coast of Nova Scotia, taking off the packets and transferring the most important news to pigeon carriers, to be dispatched on the wire from Halifax well in advance of the boats' landing. So the receipt and expedition of foreign news, on which the greatest store was placed, was better organized than ever before.

In this new capacity, Craig was confronted with the persistent purloining of his reports by outside publications and opposing news venders. The foreign language papers, whose readers expected to be kept advised constantly of events in the home countries overseas, were chronic offenders, bribing workers in the press rooms to furnish an early copy struck off the press, or resorting to some of the expedients always open to those employing illegitimate means to obtain news.

---

[15] *Courier and Enquirer,* Jan. 13, 1849.

Craig, himself, confessed that "there never was a time between 1850 and 1855 that the opposition agents could not get hold of important news within five to thirty minutes after delivery to newspaper offices of the association."[16] The perennial problem was already up, not only to obtain and transmit the news ahead of all others, but to safeguard it from unauthorized publication.

The task of maintaining and perfecting the alliance with the telegraph companies demanded watchful attention. Various preferential agreements had been entered into, by which assurance of the press patronage obtained priority rights and favorable rates. The Nova Scotia line, for example, had been built to do away with the need of an express to St. Johns on a guaranty of a stipulated payment for every arriving steamer over a period of ten years, dating from 1849.[17] Similar contracts were negotiated with other lines, the exclusive business of the press being skillfully played for better terms wherever there was more than one line to bid for it. In 1853, the New York-to-Boston wires of the Commercial Telegraph Company were offered to the Associated Press for $40,000 and, while the papers declined to go into the telegraph business at that time, they agreed to have all their reports sent over this line to pledge it a certain revenue as an inducement for other parties to take it over.[18]

Dependence on a precarious single thread of metal was being lessened, too, by the expanding facilities of the Morse lines: by 1852, the Morse system had three wires running from New York to Boston, three to Buffalo, five to Philadelphia, four to Washington, and two to New Orleans. Sending capacity improved as operators became adept with ex-

---

[16] Craig, *Annual Report*, 1862.

[17] Reid, *op. cit.*, p. 348.

[18] *Ibid.*, p. 410.

perience; a record was made by one office with two wires, one 500 miles and the other 200 miles in length, which, after spending three hours in the transmission of news, telegraphed in a single day 450 private messages averaging twenty-five words besides address.[19] It was becoming more nearly possible to obtain regular and unbroken service to and from the principal news centers. But it still devolved on the papers to encourage additional construction, and repeated changes in telegraph ownership and policies admonished vigilance on the part of the association for the protection of its contract rights and privileges.

The autumn of 1851 had marked the admission of the just-launched *Times* to a full share, with the six New York morning papers, in the news-gathering organization. The agreement, quoted by William Henry Smith as the original compact, set forth heretofore, must have been drawn before this stage of development to define the aims of the group with which the *Times* was now to unite—an organization previously without written articles of association and with few conditions of membership or patronage except that of paying promptly or being cut off. Seven papers, instead of six, were, from this time on, equal partners in the enterprise conducted, generally speaking, on the basis of unanimous consent, while others receiving news service occupied the position of customers or clients. Under these conditions, it was inevitable that established practices should crystallize into more or less rigid rules and regulations and be set down finally in formal articles designed to stabilize mutual obligations and to limit occasions for controversy. This is what led to the notable reorganization effected October 21, 1856, when representatives of these seven member papers affixed

---

[19] Turnbull, *Lectures on the Telegraph*, pp. 55, 122.

their hands and seals to an instrument of indisputably prime importance in the annals of news-gathering. The document in question, the Magna Charta of all the Associated Presses, was headed as follows:

> General News Association, of the City of New York. It is mutually agreed between Hallock, Hale and Hallock, of the Journal of Commerce, J. & E. Brooks, of the Express, J. G. Bennett, of the Herald, Moses S. Beach, of the Sun, Greeley & McElrath, of the Tribune, J. W. Webb, of the Courier and Enquirer, and Raymond, Wesley & Co., of the Times, to associate for the purpose of collecting and receiving Telegraphic and other Intelligence, under the following regulations:

In the autographed copy, the signatures were varied slightly and not exactly in the same order as in the printed text. The second name, for example, was that of "James Watson Webb, per G. H. A."; for the *Herald*, it was "James G. Bennett"; also "Charles A. Dana, for the *Tribune*"; and last, "Henry J. Raymond, *Times*." An examination of the subjoined "regulations" disclosed how the machinery was set up.

By way of prelude, it was stated that this was a consolidation of the Harbor News Association, formed January 11, 1849, with "the subsequent Telegraphic and General News Associations, entered into since that time, between the parties hereto or their predecessors." There being no change in membership or ownership, all properties in boats, furniture, or other articles belonging to either of the other associations were simply transferred, "all the rules and regulations of the former associations being annulled." The same continuation of existing arrangements was seen in reference to the officers; the incumbents, "to wit, Gerard Hallock, President; Moses S. Beach, Secretary; George H. Andrews and Frederick Hudson, Executive Committee;" remaining during

JAMES WATSON WEBB

DAVID HALE

MOSES YALE BEACH

HENRY J. RAYMOND

the pleasure of a majority of the members, with the usual duties attaching.

No addition to the membership listed in the agreement was to be permitted without unanimous consent. "But the news obtained may be sold to other parties for the general benefit of the Association, on the vote of six-sevenths of its members." Withdrawal from membership was provided for on six months' written notice, while expulsion was the penalty for deliberate violation of the rules and, particularly, failure, for thirty days, to pay a proportionate share of the expenses, one week's delinquency causing a stopping of news. In either event, cessation of membership called for the resale of all interest in the association to the other participating papers at two-thirds of the appraised valuation of the visible property, "but not any supposed value in the share itself, over and above the value of the visible property." In safeguard of rights, however, the provision for expulsion was not to apply to an honest difference of opinion as to the meaning of any rule or article, but "a majority of votes shall decide what the meaning is," and be binding.

Administrative responsibility was reassigned to the general agent, working under direction and supervision of the executive committee. The general agent was to receive all telegraphic communications for the Association and to transmit them immediately by manifold copies to each of the papers entitled to them. He was to collect weekly all bills of tolls and other expenses, first submitting them for audit, and, when collected, to pay all approved bills and accounts. Agents or correspondents were to be maintained at Washington and at Albany and correspondents at such other points as the executive committee designated. Though telegraphic news arriving at any hour of the day or night was to be sent to the offices "without unnecessary delay," its delivery or publication might be withheld until a specified time, the "hold-for-future-release" obligation. The ship and port news was to be attended to by a specially appointed "Marine News Collector," transmitting his reports direct to each party to the agreement and also delivering promptly all packages of newspapers or news addressed to any of them. To avoid possible favoritism, where full files of foreign papers could not be obtained for all, the Marine News Collector was to deliver those which he managed to get to the general news agent, who should proceed to extract the items of special interest and furnish a copy, "simultaneously as near as possible," to each paper already advised of the title and date of the papers so obtained. For this service, the beneficiaries were to bear the cost equally.

With certain specified exceptions, all telegraphic news received by any of the member papers was to be pooled and placed at the disposal of every one of them. It was distinctly set forth that all European and California news and all election news, received by special express or telegraph by any member of the association, should be common property and that all such news must be handed over immediately to the general agent. Designated items of news might be ordered through the general agent, but such reports must be offered to all and paid for by those using them, or any portion of them. No paper might receive news by telegraph from its own correspondents, or by special arrangement, "without first informing the other members of the association and tendering a participancy in them." Excepted were reports of conventions, political meetings, trials, executions, public dinners, sporting intelligence, and legislative proceedings of other states. Excepted, furthermore, were dispatches from a resident editor, or resident reporter, and news originating in Washington or Albany. Papers might decline "such news as they may think proper," and be released from sharing the cost but, if declining a class of news, could not have reports of any one day, or of any special point. Similarly, Sunday papers might have all telegraphic messages received too late for Saturday papers by paying for them; and the leading items of foreign news, not exceeding a quarter of a column, by paying one-fourth of the expense, unless issued in Sunday extras, in which case the entire cost was to be charged.

Protection of the service was not confined to prohibition of premature publication. No participating paper "shall enter into arrangement with rival Telegraphic news agents in this city or any other city"; nor receive from them any telegraphic news; nor shall such parties, nor any persons not connected with this association "be permitted to avail themselves of the facilities of this association." Improper use by an employee of the press reports, presumably for the advantage of rival news agents or for speculative purposes, should be followed by reprimand or discharge, and a second offense by immediate discharge and barring from employment in the office of any member, unless by unanimous consent. Anything overlooked, or any unusual situation, could be dealt with by the Executive Committee—a committee of two men who could get together and act on a moment's notice—fully empowered "to make all necessary regulations" and "whose contracts shall be binding on the Association."

Maverick tells us that Bennett once or twice threatened to take the *Herald* out, but was persuaded each time to reconsider his determination and to continue to receive the news through the regular channel with the others.[20] The seven original members, with the *World* substituted for the

[20] *Henry J. Raymond and the New York Press for Thirty Years,* p. 326.

Courier from 1859 on, remained till the end the only fully participating members of the New York Associated Press.

Realizing its strength, the press grew perceptibly aggressive, almost dictatorial, in its attitude towards the telegraph companies. Another tilt with the wires was plainly invited and could not be long deferred. It soon came and provided a bold episode in the history of both telegraph and newspapers. As already narrated, the line from Halifax to Sackville had been constructed by the Government of Nova Scotia on a pledge of patronage by the New York Associated Press, executed as a definite agreement, in 1851, for payment of double the commercial rate in consideration of preferred and uninterrupted transmission. When it passed to a private company the next year and, in November, 1853, this company demanded exorbitantly increased tolls, negotiations resulted in a compromise on a charge of $150 per steamer dispatch not exceeding 3,000 words.

In the summer of 1858, Craig found himself able, through the success of his improved arrangements for intercepting the ships off Cape Race, to get the gist of the foreign news expedited via Newfoundland and, in order to save expense, undertook to send only a brief supplemental message through Halifax, for which he proposed to pay the regular commercial rate. On repeated drafts by the Nova Scotia company for the full amount of the agreed $150, regardless of the curtailment of the dispatch, Craig took advantage of the clause permitting rescission on six months' notice and announced that further payments under the special contract would cease May 1, 1859. Accepting this as leaving it free to consult its own interests, the telegraph company thereupon perfected arrangements on identical terms with George W. L. Johnson and Michael A. Zabriskie, styling themselves representatives of the United States Associated

Press, for exclusive use of the wires for steamer news. Here was a prospect of rival news purveyors in a position of vantage; trouble was easily sighted for the moment when the New York Associated Press dispatch should be cast aside to give way to a competing concern. The protests voiced by Craig and by William Hunter, whom he had commissioned as his local agent, exceeded all bounds in violence; "insulting and vulgar" was the characterization of James C. Cogswell, president of the telegraph company. in the ensuing correspondence.[21]

As the next step, Craig and his associates seem to have induced Peter Cooper, at the moment heading the connecting American Telegraph Company, to remonstrate and to demand reversion to "first-come-first-served." The action of the Nova Scotia company, it was urged, conflicted with the antidiscrimination law of New York, which controlled the American company in its operations in that state, whose exceptions were for news messages only—of course, not for what Craig denominated "the speculators' report." Cooper's communication drew a firm refusal together with a reminder that the New York Associated Press itself had violated its preferential contract, then terminated it, and now was making threats to force the Nova Scotia company to submit. Reviving methods that had proved effective in previous bouts with the telegraphs, Craig procured an order from Cooper to his company to transmit no private messages coming from the Nova Scotia line, unless the charges were paid in advance in money (an order soon withdrawn) and also to stop forwarding news messages from the same source until the New York Associated Press dispatches had first come through. Renewed insistence on the "first-come" rule

[21] *Herald,* June 4, 1859.

was followed with this additional demand: "The Directors . . . . request that you will direct their agent to be received at the office at Halifax in order that these resolutions may be carried into effect." To which came the reply: "Your request is a singular one. Would you permit an agent of ours to sit in your office to superintend and report on your procedure? We think not, and we must decline your request as unreasonable."

As a possible solution, the Nova Scotia company suggested purchase of the contract rights of the upstart association, which seemed to be the obstacle, and return to the old terms with the New York Associated Press, now going through the form of offering its messages for transmission at the lower commercial rates. This idea was doubtless expected to meet no more responsive reception than it got. Craig blew another blast; and the Nova Scotia's spokesman wrote his American Telegraph correspondent, "We find it difficult to separate you and Mr. Craig." While the battle raged, Peter Cooper had retired from the presidency of the American company and Abram S. Hewitt had taken his place, and presto! the control was found to have shifted suddenly again with a consequent installation of another set of officers. The new president was Zenas Barnum and the new secretary Robert W. Russell, the latter largely represented in the stock ownership and, in reality, the dominating personage. From intimate alliance and coöperation with the New York Associated Press, the American Telegraph Company, one of the most powerful telegraph systems in the country, if not the most powerful, veered practically over night to an exactly opposite position, and the contending forces were drawn up under leadership of two astute and implacable foes.

In command on the one side stood Russell, "an Englishman, able, imperious, willful and persevering," and on the other, Craig, the New Englander, "his cool gray eye, his placid assertion of power, his merciless Saxon," making the blood of the Englishman hot.[22] Russell had been active in the consolidations out of which the big company had been evolved, and harbored visions of telegraph supremacy for it. He had hatched a scheme to reverse the existing order of relations with the press. He saw no reason why the telegraph company should not be the collector and distributor of all current intelligence rather than the mere mechanical agency of transmission, the retailer of foreign and domestic markets, and the press wholly dependent on the telegraph not only for the conveyance, but also for the contents, of its news.

That the basic object of the new policy was the mastership of the press by the telegraph, was something of which the papers took every advantage to evoke its popular disfavor. The first move consisted in abandonment by the company of the practice of "detaining" forwarded news messages, independently filed, until after arrival of the Associated Press dispatch, and a payment to Johnson and Zabriskie, who had instituted suit for damages, of the sum of $962.08 in settlement of their claim.[23] This was followed by a rate revision affecting news reports with a view to stimulating rivalry in news service, and at the same time to bring in more revenue. Where the press rates from St. Johns, or Cape Race, were formerly the same as for private messages, the charge was to vary according to the importance of the intelligence; for example, "whether the news was a certain number of days later."[24] In general, the rates on press

[22] Reid, *op. cit.*, p. 424.

[23] Russell, *Reply*, p. 3.

[24] At this period, foreign news appeared quite generally in the papers under headings emphasizing principally the timeliness of the information as compared with the last previous publication.

messages were materially increased all along the line, calling forth strenuous objections from Craig, threats to get up an opposition telegraph line, a demand "by the Boston and New York newspaper gentlemen" for five places on the corporate directory, a fruitless appeal by the preceding president, Abram S. Hewitt, and from Cyrus W. Field, and other newspaper spokesmen in the company, from this action of the executive committee to the whole body of stockholders.

It was a wordy warfare, extensively aired in letters and pamphlets, yet, to some advantage in yielding here and there information usually kept under cover. Boston papers formerly enjoyed a special arrangement for daily transmission of their reports without limit from New York for the sum of $650 per month. These messages averaged about 6,000 words a day. They were dropped at Providence, Worcester, Springfield, Hartford, Bridgeport, and New Haven, for the papers in those towns which, together, paid approximately $353 per month for their service. This press business occupied three wires and interfered with other patronage because of commanding priority. Russell insisted that Craig and his papers had no good ground for grievance as to rates; that the New York press was paying, for transmission of reports from Washington, less than the much nearer Philadelphia press; that the Boston papers had a rate of three cents for the first 500 words, two cents for the next 500 words, and one cent for all over 1,000 words; finally, that it made no difference to the Craig organization what rates might be exacted, because whatever was charged was taxed back to the customer publications. Russell, particularly, asserted and reiterated that there would be no controversy if the Associated Press would abrogate its rule for exclusive use of its European news by the papers which it was serving. "The immediate result of such abrogation would be," he declared, "that the newspaper press in various parts of the country would take additional telegraphic messages containing foreign news; other associations would be formed, in and out of New York, to take that and other news; and, in some cases, the great newspapers would have special despatches containing foreign news for their own columns alone. Our eastern lines would then pay handsomely." [25]

Having absorbed the pioneer Magnetic Telegraph Company into the American Telegraph Company, Russell appeared to be riding the crest of the wave, when, proceeding to intrench himself still further he dug the ditch into which he was to fall. To relieve the pressure of a discordant minority and, by the same stroke, to add weight to his methods of administration, he bought out the holdings of Cyrus W. Field and Abram S. Hewitt at considerably advanced prices and procured the election to the board of Col. E. S. Sanford, the well-known manager of the Adams Express, and Cambridge Livingston, prominent in financial circles. Russell should have realized that such men would not be content to be dummy directors; that they would prove too wise to ignore the peril of a telegraph company, whatever its inherent strength, waging perpetual warfare with almost the entire press of the country. After much excited discussion, a reorganization was effected in the executive committee. Russell and his friends were left out, and Sanford and Livingston installed. Amicable relations with the Associated Press of New York were resumed, the United States Associated Press soon faded from view, a new reign of prosperity for the telegraph company was in-

[25] Russell, *op. cit.*, p. 49.

augurated by the elevation of Colonel Sanford to the presidency at the close of 1860, while, with approaching war clouds, attention had to be centered elsewhere. One immediate outcome must be mentioned, however, the leasing and operation, and for a time the ownership, by the Associated Press of the Newfoundland lines and certain subsidiaries required to bring in the news summary of the European packets.[26] Otherwise, the American Telegraph Company, which concurrently bought up the interest of F. O. J. Smith in the Morse patents, as well as the Morse lines in New England, harmonized its policies, as far as possible, with those of its newspaper patrons and carried on without noticeable friction until it, in turn, vanished from the scene upon its absorption by the Western Union in 1866.[27]

[26] Hudson, *Journalism,* p. 613.
[27] Edward Sewall Sanford, *In Memoriam.*

CHAPTER XII

THE CIVIL WAR PERIOD

Growth and expansion—Reporting the war—Changes in the official roster—The sudden exit of Craig

MEANWHILE, the business of news-gathering, conducted by the association, had been going ahead, along the lines marked out, and inevitably expanding. Broader service went with the enlarged clientele which also brought increased income and expenditures. The average payments by each of the seven members ranged from year to year from $200 to $230 per week. The evening journals paid about half as much; the morning and evening papers outside the city paid fixed amounts to the local agents, aggregating from $10,000 to $12,000 a week, exclusive of additional charges for special reports.[1] The general agent's confidential report for 1862 showed that the total outlay that year was $123,408. Under a new arrangement of weekly assessments, the regular morning papers were paying $214 per week, and the three evening papers in New York, $119 per week each; one German publication, the *Staats-zeitung*, had been advanced, over its protest, from $40 to $101 weekly; another German paper, the *Demokrat*, was paying $30; and the French *Courier*, $25 a week. The recent order to procure $12,000 more revenue was adding $5 to the bill of each of these foreign language sheets and $13.33 to those of each of the local evening papers. By the end of this period, the total

[1] Craig, *Answer*, p. 5.

outlay rose to about $200,000 annually, of which the New York press was called on for about one-half, while the remainder was divided among those served in other sections of the country, the bulk coming from the larger cities as against the country papers, some of which were taxed only $30 to $40 per month each.[2]

Besides measurable relief from the cost burden of news transmission, members of the association reaped direct and indirect advantages, estimated by Craig in 1862 at "$20,000 virtually saved," very likely in telegraphic news from the local fields furnished without charge which otherwise would have had to be paid for. "Indeed," so the beneficiaries were reminded, "holding practically a monopoly of the telegraphic news of the country, you are saving the expenditure of many thousands of dollars which would be required in case you had determined opposition"; moreover, the association was not only receiving from outside sources one-half of its entire expenses but these were "immensely greater than the outside papers require" for their reports, "in the ordering of which they are not permitted to interpose."

Better success with the foreign news at Cape Race was recorded. In 1861, thirty-four reports had been received and distributed; in 1862, about sixty reports. Wages of the boatmen were $60 a week, and the expense for boatmen for the year, $2,000, while the whole cost of the sixty reports was about $18,000. The Buffalo line, and the telegraph lines of the Western Union west of Pittsburgh, had adopted the same sliding scale of rates for press dispatches prevailing on the American lines, which was what the Associated Press desired, namely, one-third off for reports from

---

[2] Prescott, *History, Theory and Practice of the Electric Telegraph*, p. 384.

100 to 500 words, one-half off on the second 500 words, and two-thirds off on all over 1,000 words; also the further worth-while concession that all messages from any one point were to be regarded as continuous during the entire day.

Besides the regular representatives at the usual news centers, special correspondents had been sent into the field to obtain war news for the association. Associated Press agents were at General McClellan's headquarters; also with General Banks; an Associated Press correspondent was with the Army of the Potomac; while official intelligence came mostly from Washington.

Under the pressure of individual initiative and rivalry among the constituent papers for supremacy in war news, the bars against exclusive telegraphic reports had to be let down. As a rule, the *Herald* led the others, although the *Times* and the *Tribune* were not far behind. Anticipating hostilities, the *Herald* had stationed correspondents in different strategic points in the South to watch and report developments. At the commencement of the war, it established a southern bureau which set about to accumulate and file all information obtainable about the Confederate states. Correspondents within the rebel lines were to obtain and forward southern newspapers at any price, and from these were compiled lists of the military forces of the Confederacy. Finally, the *Herald* came out with a review of the military strength of the South, so complete and comparatively accurate that it created a commotion in the War Office at Richmond. Several clerks there were arrested on suspicion of treason and, in the North, it was intimated that the *Herald* had too intimate relations with the Confederate authorities. Bennett is said to have spent more than $500,000 in covering the Civil War; everywhere at the front there was a *Herald* man; its correspondents were at every battle;

with each army corps, there was a *Herald* tent and a *Herald* wagon.[3]

Many stories were told illustrating the desperate devices utilized to get news through. On one occasion, a Union soldier was released from Libby Prison, where several northern correspondents languished. On reaching New York, this soldier called at the *Herald* office, cut from his coat one of the brass buttons and handed it to the editor in charge. The button was hollow; it contained a letter finely written on thin tissue paper, describing conditions in Richmond; rewritten, without undue padding, it made three-quarters of a column of prime news.

But it was not an altogether rosy picture of scoops and successes. The difficulties interposed by stupid or short-sighted authority were disheartening.[4] Occasionally, one of the quick-witted, plucky young men who had invaded Washington, by eulogizing a general in command, was enabled to go to the front as a gentleman but, more generally, they were one and all proscribed and hunted out of the camps like spies. Stanton bullied them, set up a censorship, from time to time imprisoned one, or stopped the publication of the paper for which he corresponded. Halleck denounced them as "unauthorized hangers-on," who should be compelled to work in the trenches if they did not leave the lines. Meade was unnecessarily severe in his treatment of correspondents whose letters were not agreeable to him. So the newspaper-men were, as a rule, forced to hover around the rear of the armies, gather up such crumbs as they could, and then ride in haste to the nearest available telegraph station to send off their dispatches. The Washington press, which should have

---

[3] Hapgood, "Great Newspapers," *The Bookman,* XV, 26; Bent, *Ballyhoo,* p. 161.

[4] Perley Poore, *Perley's Reminiscences,* p. 126.

been a reliable cache of news for the papers elsewhere, was despotically repressed by a censorship under the direction of men wholly unqualified. Entire printed editions of influential journals, republican and democratic alike, were more than once seized by order of Stanton because of presenting intelligence which, in his judgment, should be withheld. Bulletins were issued by the War Department, but were often incorrect. It was known that Washington papers containing military information were being forwarded through the lines daily, yet the censors would not permit paragraphs clipped from them to be telegraphed to Boston or Chicago, where they could not possibly appear sooner than they would be printed in the Richmond papers.

Interviewing had been originated just on the eve of the outbreak between the sections. At the time of the raid on Harpers Ferry, a reporter from the *Herald* had been sent to Peterborough to talk with Gerrit Smith, a man who had been implicated with John Brown. What Smith said was published in full, in conversational language, and created a sensation. Interviewing had the call; its scope broadened at once and it continued in high favor throughout the war. The interview became a choice channel for communicating important news impressed with the weight of some prominent person as its authority. Correspondents were ordered to the far corners to obtain comment or information of supposed value from some one of note. From now on, at least for a few years, the cost of procuring big news was no deterring factor. The *Herald* had the whole speech of the Prussian king, after the Battle of Sadowa, transmitted by cable at an outlay of $7,000 in gold. It commissioned Henry M. Stanley as its representative in the Anglo-Abyssinian expedition of 1868. In 1870, it fitted him out to find Livingstone in darkest Africa. For the Franco-Prussian

War, the palm was awarded to the *Tribune,* whose war-news service, organized by Whitelaw Reid, produced "the most remarkable cabled accounts of the great battles between the French and the Germans, the siege of Paris, and the conclusion of peace."

An incident of our conflict over slavery caused a change in the presidency of the New York Associated Press, filled from its inception by Gerard Hallock, editor of the *Journal of Commerce.* Because of its too outspoken presentation of the claims of the South, that newspaper was branded as disloyal and was excluded from the mails, and the government authorities indicated that resumption of publication would be permitted only if another were placed in editorial charge. Whereupon, Hallock, thoroughly disgusted and disheartened, decided to eschew journalism absolutely and negotiated the sale of his half interest to William Cowper Prime and David Marvin Stone. On his retirement, in 1861, his position as head of the news association passed to Prime. The fire was rekindled in 1864, when the *Journal of Commerce* was temporarily suppressed again as a result of a crude imposition to which it fell victim because cloaked in the guise of an Associated Press report. Quickly exposed, it transpired that a spurious proclamation, over the name of President Lincoln, countersigned by Secretary Seward, had been concocted, which appointed a day of fasting and prayer in view of military disasters and called for thousands of fresh volunteers. It proved to be part of a well-laid scheme of reckless stock market speculators, who engaged a former Associated Press employee to make copies and to send them, late at night, to all the newspaper offices as coming from the Associated Press. Every paper but one had the proclamation set in type, and the *Herald* printed 25,000 copies before the fraud was perceived and the edition killed. The bogus document reached the *Journal of Commerce* after all the editorial force had left, and the printers, still at work, accepting it without question, took the responsibility of inserting it in the paper. The office and equipment of the *Journal* were promptly seized by Federal troops, and the arrest of its editor ordered, from which release came on the uncovering of the author of the forgery and its purpose.[5] A few years later, Prime ceased his connection with the *Journal of Commerce* and also with the Associated Press, being succeeded, as its president, by his business partner, David M. Stone, who was to retain the office for two and a half decades. The presidency manifestly appertained to the paper rather than to the person of its representative, necessarily changing from time to time.

Through this period, Craig remained monarch of all he surveyed. Nothwithstanding sharpened competition between newspapers, the association had managed pretty well to maintain a solidarity of its own and to hold down occasional differences inside, to say nothing of smoothing over clashes, now and then, with Craig as the general agent. To stop the display of grievances to the public, members had agreed, by a resolution formally adopted in 1857, "to publish no more complaints against Mr. Craig or others of its agents without first submitting the same to the Association and also that Mr. Craig be instructed to make no public reflection upon the members of the Association, their associates or agents, in or out of the city, without first submitting the same to the Association."[6] That disciplinary action had to be taken at times may well be inferred from the obligation imposed in 1859, "not to furnish news to any newspaper outside of New York City which shall use the reports of a

[5] White, *Cyclopedia of American Biography,* I, 205.

[6] General News Association Rules, 1874.

rival organization." The purpose and policy of the association, to build up and maintain a news monopoly, was ill concealed. In this effort, declared Craig, "we succeeded and compelled the editors to abandon their arrangements and come into ours." The nature of the compulsion employed was illustrated by an example, furnished by him in another connection, wherein he told how the only morning paper in one of the largest up-state cities, unheedful of every admonition against using the lines of a recalcitrant telegraph company, was forced to capitulate by offering free service to the evening journal there, if it would start a morning issue.[7]

Yet, in all fairness, Craig must be credited with opposing both the cutting adrift of outside papers and the equally unwise policy of increasing the charges beyond their ability to respond. This, however, did not forestall the development of a community of interest among the papers of other cities, or sections, and particularly of the Middle West. It had so happened that the western telegraph lines raised their assessments for news service at the same time as did the Associated Press, and some of the editors, supposing, "very stupidly," that the Associated Press controlled the telegraph lines, wrote abusive articles against the association and finally stirred up a meeting at Indianapolis. Apprised of what was in the air, the shrewd Craig assigned one of his western agents to represent the Associated Press at the conference, "and reached satisfactory arrangements," as, at any rate, he believed. Perhaps he revised his verdict when the meetings were regularly repeated, and steadily augmented their demands for concessions until, before long, the pressure from these groups of outside papers, ranged in united forma-

---

[7] Craig, *op. cit.*, p. 24.

tion, was to become a factor of greater and greater magnitude.

From the inception of the New York Associated Press to this time, the six or seven big dailies of the metropolis were in absolute control of the news-gathering of the country. They held the steering-wheels of all the machinery employed, and arbitrarily set the course. The news was collected primarily for them. They determined all questions of policy without consulting any others. They had developed a relatively high degree of efficiency and did not stint in expense, most of which they recouped from the clients. They got what news they wanted, and the rest could take it or leave it. But the geographical balance of journalistic power in America was shifting along with the growth and redistribution of our population. Power and control cannot long be far apart, and some measure of readjustment here was inevitable. A more benevolent rule was in order, if not a complete overturn of the self-serving oligarchy. Only the occasion for an upheaval was awaited and such occasions, sometimes spontaneous, are also frequently deliberately produced. The end of the Craig régime was certain to mark noteworthy changes.

Craig's dominance in the affairs of the New York Associated Press terminated abruptly in 1866. Whether altogether unforeseen or not, it involved highly melodramatic features, bidding strong for front-page publicity. The story, wired to all papers receiving the Associated Press service, over the signatures of W. C. Prime, President, and Joseph P. Beach, Secretary, and dated November 5, 1866, broke the news that Mr. Craig "is discharged by unanimous vote of the members," and "Mr. James W. Simonton has been appointed General Agent." Craig lost no time in making a rejoinder:

NEW YORK, Nov. 5, 1866

To All Editors and Agents of the Associated Press:

I have read the notice sent over the wires this evening signed by Messrs. Prime and Beach and pronounce its assertions utterly and infamously false.

I have not been discharged unanimously nor at all. My responsibility is to the Executive Committee and to them only; and they have not and will not unite in the lying assertions of Prime and Beach.

It is true that I have for some weeks past headed a movement here to remodel and improve our association, as you will learn from my printed circular now on its way to you, and it is also true that all these arrangements are completed and will go into effect next Monday.

My resignation has been in the hands of the Executive Committee for several weeks, and whether accepted or not, I should have retired at the end of this week, at which time, as I have good reason to believe, every agent or reporter of the association will earnestly co-operate in the new movement, which I assure you is started with the most ample backers, and its results will largely promote the interests of all the papers outside of this city, and I shall confidently hope for your earnest approval.

D. H. CRAIG
General Agent New York Associated Press

Reviewing the event with less of a partisan spirit, we have this contemporaneous statement:

In common with other journals belonging to the Associated Press, we received a despatch announcing that Mr. D. H. Craig, who had been for so many years the General Agent of the association, had been unanimously discharged. Accompanying this, we received a message from Mr. Craig denying his alleged discharge and commenting upon the first despatch in rather offensive terms. We printed neither of them. . . . There can be no doubt that Mr. Craig has been discharged, or will shortly cease to be the General Agent of the New York Associated Press, and it appears from a circular that he has issued, that he has become president of another news association. . . . The machinery of the Associated

Press has not given general satisfaction to newspaper proprietors and editors for several years past. There had been inconveniences and delays and just cause for complaint of a great many kinds. There is opportunity now to remedy this.[8]

And a little later:

A dispute has been going on concerning the Associated Press and a concern that has been set up to rival the old association. . . . Controlled by the caprices of one man, and based upon the idea of giving the news in advance to a few favored subscribers before it goes to the general public, its operation must be very unequal. . . . On the other hand, the primary idea of the Associated Press is to give all the people the news that comes to it, at the same time.[9]

The attending circumstances surely invite denunciation of Craig's action as unconscionably treacherous and disloyal and this verdict is mitigated only slightly by his own subsequent version, being the best face he was able to put on it.[10] For justification, he explained that the Western Union, which had just taken over the American Telegraph Company and was being remolded as a giant system of telegraphs, had proposed that he form a general news company and give them one share more than one-half. "It was expected that I should organize a Commercial News Bureau in all the cities of the union to which all bankers, brokers, merchants and speculators would be forced to subscribe—yielding an almost unlimited revenue. My own estimate was one million dollars net, and half as much more from the press." Whether the proposal, in fact, emanated from the Western Union or from Craig, is immaterial, since it was prematurely disclosed. "The result was a quarrel between myself and four of the seven members of the Associated Press," and, for fear of

---

[8] *Philadelphia Ledger,* Nov. 7, 1866.
[9] *Ibid.,* Dec. 5, 1866.
[10] Craig, *op. cit.,* p. 6.

consequences, the Western Union withdrew its offer. "I accordingly abandoned the general news business to my successor in the management of the Associated Press who agreed, through the president of the association, not to compete with me in the commercial department of telegraph news reporting, and I proceeded to develop what is now known as the Commercial News Department of the Gold and Stock Telegraph Company." Here, he did not last long. Craig accuses the Western Union of wresting the business from his control in 1869, after he had it well developed, and of doing this in alliance with the Associated Press. The remainder of Craig's career was devoted to the perfection of an automatic telegraph system on which he was already working and continued to work while variously employed. During the summer of 1878, Western Union wires were placed at his disposal to test out his mechanism, but when he failed to enlist Western Union backing, he organized the Rapid Telegraph Company, in 1879, which afterward, despite its grand prospectus, went into receivership. Undaunted, Craig conceived the plan of enlisting government aid, just as Morse had done at the inception of the telegraphic era. He appeared as a witness before the United States Senate Committee on Education and Labor, at a session held in New York in 1883, to answer interrogatories.[11] He came once more to light in the summer of 1888, when Senator Blair, as chairman of that committee, reported a resolution "to provide a suitable place in the Capitol building," without other expense to the government, for D. H. Craig to test his improvements in the art of telegraphy with a view to insuring their benefits to the American people.[12] Craig lived into his eighty-first year.

[11] *Ibid.*

[12] Fifth Cong., 101st Sess., Sen., Misc. Doc. 2: 157.

CHAPTER XIII

RISE OF THE AUXILIARY ASSOCIATIONS

The Western Associated Press—The fight of 1866 and its outcome—The Northwestern Associated Press—The New York State Associated Press—The New England Associated Press

The plan of the New York association was to deal with the outside papers by localities and in groups, necessarily so because of the limited means of telegraphic communication. The privilege of sharing the foreign and other news reports and contributing pro rata to the expense of collection and transmission had been accorded to other publications associated together, where possible, instead of separately. The arrangements were with the Boston press, or the Philadelphia press, or the Baltimore press, the New Orleans press, the State press. We see here recognition of a community of interest among those papers engaging the service for a particular city where a single delivery of the dispatches was to be for joint benefit and use and the charges apportioned equally in each class, morning and evening, as among the New York papers themselves. This was apparently the simplest, the easiest, and the most effective mode of operation, its guiding principle being subsequently adopted by nearly all of our news associations and enduring to this day. But it should have been realized that this method of dealing with the clients must tend to accentuate and encourage claims and complaints in common, and to make for a class solidarity wherever the relations of the clients with the dominating New York press were involved.

To a certain extent, the disposition to coöperate in telegraphic news-gathering manifested itself among some of these clients prior to, and independently of, the organization of the big dailies in New York. One such movement, at any rate, had developed quite early among the up-state New York papers when, to mark the completion of the line from Albany to Buffalo, the president of the company, T. S. Faxton, invited the editors along the route to celebrate the Fourth of July, 1846, by attending a meeting, by telegraph, in the various offices open at that time, from which sprang the idea of a federation for the supply of telegraphic news. In fact, the first daily dispatches to the press of the state were started January 1, 1847.[1]

When competing lines were built, Faxton went to great lengths to hold the business; he advised the agent of the New York association that unless all the news that he was in the habit of sending out went west over his line, he would refuse to accept dispatches except prepaid at private message rates.[2] "As we persisted," says the naïve Dr. Jones, "in dividing our news as requested by the press which we served, we soon after received a notice from the chief operator at the office in New York, Mr. Johnson, that other arrangements had been made and our news would not be sent; that is, Faxton had engaged to serve a majority of the papers we had been supplying for less money and to include the expense of reporting." Sharper yet was Jones' outcry against the employment, to carry out this project, of a man "whom we had instructed and brought up to the business," and who also worked with another line's "Eastern arrangements in combination with a portion of the Boston papers." This situation, taken in hand by Craig, resolved itself into a regular Associated Press report wired to the New York

---

[1] Reid, *The Telegraph*, p. 307.

[2] Jones, *Historical Sketch*, p. 141.

State papers as far as Buffalo, but firmly fixed only after a trial of strength. The first agreement entered into by the up-state editors obligated the agent of the Associated Press to furnish them two daily reports, but, for some cause, his reports were so irregular and unsatisfactory that the papers, after suffering much inconvenience, were compelled in self-defense to return to the "only line that makes news a commodity." [3] Soon, another change in practice saw the news business "left exclusively to the newspapers to manage for themselves." It was thus demonstrated that reciprocal advantages could be obtained by exclusive contracts between the press and the telegraph companies enlisting their patronage.

It was in the wide-stretching West that progress toward territorial autonomy in news-gathering sped faster, reached out farther, became more restless of restraint. Though still struggling for existence, the papers in the interior cities behind the Alleghanies took all the news that the New York association was willing to send them and paid what was demanded, so far as they could pay at all, but they chafed at Craig's high and mighty demeanor in his intercourse with them. "If any of us grumbled at the lateness of his news, or its quality, or talked back to his autocracy, he cut us off, stopped our news, and, after we had begged his pardon and promised never to repeat our offense, he would let up but fine us to the amount of the news if we had received it." [4]

Was it any wonder that the western newspapers grew more dissatisfied each year with the telegraphic press service, the inadequate country news, its burdensome cost, and the arbitrary treatment to which they were subjected? Year by year, too, they were waxing in numbers, strength, resources,

---

[3] *American Telegraph Magazine,* October, 1852, p. 10.
[4] Medill, in Associated Press Report, 1897, p. 158.

and enterprise. The Westerners resented, more and more, being kept in leash to the self-vaunting New York papers. When civil strife came on, by sending out their own special war correspondents, they distinguished themselves in the field of war news quite as well, with two or three notable exceptions, as the big city dailies. The war made it plainer to them than ever that, as to the contents and treatment of the news served them, they were not in complete harmony with the New York papers, whose wishes alone governed. The unsatisfactory situation became the theme of correspondence and consultation and finally resulted, late in 1862, in calling a conference of the principal newspaper publishers of a half dozen western states at Indianapolis. Here, again, we have the beginning of a momentous movement attracting such scant attention at its inception that few details are preserved. According to the only available source of information, "there were certainly present, Mr. Haldeman, of the *Courier*, and Mr. Osborne, of the *Journal*, Louisville; Mr. George Knapp or Mr. John Knapp, of the *Republican*, St. Louis; Mr. Medill, of the *Tribune*, Chicago; Mr. Walker, of the *Free Press*, Detroit; Mr. Fairbanks, of the *Herald*, and Mr. Cowles, of the *Leader*, Cleveland; Mr. Brigham, (probably) of the *Commercial*, Pittsburgh; Mr. Bickham, of the *Journal*, Dayton; Mr. Richard Smith, of the *Gazette*, and Mr. Potter, of the *Commercial*, Cincinnati; Mr. Holloway and other representatives of the Indianapolis papers." [5]

No business of importance was transacted at this initial meeting beyond an agreement to act together and to reconvene the next year, and the appointment of an executive committee, with Medill as chairman, to represent the western publishers in any negotiations with the New York association. "We formed an organization under the name of the

[5] Smith, in Western Associated Press Report, 1876, p. 28.

Western Associated Press," said Medill, "and adopted some rules which would not disturb the Associated Press of New York or arouse the suspicion of its amiable agent." Possibly this had reference to the second meeting, held at Dayton, the following year. Of this session, Bickham, who acted as host, is quoted as remembering only that Richard Smith, Medill and Haldeman assembled in his office and talked over plans looking to an informal organization with a committee of directors. At all events, a committee soon visited New York under the leadership of Medill. "We succeeded in being allowed to put a news agent in the office of the New York Associated Press with authority to make up and send a 300-word extra dispatch to afternoon papers and a 1,000-word message to be put on the wires after 10 P. M. for the morning papers. It was called the midnight dispatch and was published in an extra edition. We secured it at low tolls. The extra day dispatch was comparatively expensive as the wires were occupied at that time on commercial business." [6]

The difficulty evidently was met at the start to suit, with a single service, journals possessing very different needs. At the next meeting at Cincinnati, a motion emanated from Halstead that arrangements be made "allowing newspaper establishments with large resources and enterprising dispositions to obtain more news by telegraph than the proprietors of papers with small revenues, or who were wanting in an enterprising spirit, could or would pay for." The contract for the extra service was revised, increasing the payment to the New York Associated Press from $10,000 to $15,000 and the number of words daily from 1,000 to 1,500 a night and also an extra 300 words for afternoon papers.

When, at the 1864 meeting in Detroit, it was decided to

---

[6] Medill, *supra*, p. 160.

take steps for a charter of incorporation, the execution was entrusted to Judge Walker, of the Detroit *Free Press*, and he speedily prevailed on the legislature of Michigan to pass a special act for that purpose.[7] Formal qualification under the law took place at the ensuing session at Louisville. A covertness of proceeding is distinctly indicated by the title of the act, "An act to provide for the incorporation of associations engaged in the publication of newspapers, periodicals, books and other matter," the first section of which says that "any three or more persons may associate themselves together for the purpose of procuring intelligence for the newspaper press from all parts of the world by telegraph or otherwise, upon such terms and conditions, and subject to the liabilities prescribed in this act." Capital stock was not to exceed $500,000 and property was to be used only for the legitimate business of the association, empowered to form by-laws, elect officers, and "to do any and all things, lawful."

The report submitted by the general agent disclosed that the first representative of the Western Associated Press was Thomas Wallace Knox, to be famed later as a writer of boys' travel tales. There was doubtless appropriateness in the selection. Going from New England, in the gold rush, to Colorado, he had been a reporter, and then city editor, for the Denver *News*. Wounded in the war, he served awhile, on recovery, as field correspondent of the New York *Herald* and then located in New York for a career in journalism. He could attend to the extra and midnight dispatch for the Western Associated Press with true western discernment. Indeed, he elicited an encomium for being faithful in the discharge of his duties and ready at all times to conform to the views of the members but want of fixed rules, and divergent

---

[7] *Laws of Michigan*, 1865, Chap. 299.

instructions as to what his reports should be, prevented him from giving entire satisfaction. To remedy the difficulty, although Colonel Knox's service was soon to be cut short by the vision of a telegraph line through Southern Asia enticing him afield, a set of rules was framed and adopted for his guidance which, so far as known, has not since been improved on:

1. Telegraphic reports are interesting in proportion as they are reliable; therefore nothing should be telegraphed that is manifestly sensational merely.

2. Reports should be prepared with a view to presenting facts as briefly as possible, consistently with their importance and nothing should be sent for quantity.

3. It is not desirable that importance should be attached to statements merely because they are telegraphed to New York papers. Nor is it our wish that the editorial comments of New York papers be telegraphed, except on rare occasions, when such views really be of the greatest public concern.

4. As a rule, our agent should compile in concise shape all the items of news, without giving credit to papers, except where the authority is an essential part of the statement transmitted.

The Western Associated Press felt itself now on solid ground and in a mood to assert its demands with the vigor of the West. The fateful year 1866 had arrived, which was to be called the "Year of Independence." Significant changes were in the air. The successful operation finally of the Atlantic cable was about to revolutionize once more the system of procuring foreign news. The telegraph lines were being consolidated under unified management. The zest for all the news, sharpened by the war, continued insistent; new papers were springing up, warning the older papers to protect themselves against competition. The western publishers put their complaints into a bill of particulars:

1. That the reports were made wholly in the interest of the proprietors of the news, to wit, the seven leading papers of the City of New York.

2. That, as the outside papers were taxed pro rata for the cost of all the reports, which included marine reports from the Atlantic and Pacific coasts, local legislative and political intelligence at great length, cable announcements of the arrival and departure of vessels at foreign ports, and of markets wanted only by the commercial classes of New York, they paid largely in excess of what was just and what would be required to procure the news adapted to the wants and tastes of their own customers.

3. That, by controlling the making of market reports, they made the commercial interests of the rest of the United States unjustly dependent on those of New York.

4. That, while all of these expenses were lumped in what was called "the original collection of news" and charged to the outside press pro rata, no member of the outside press was permitted access to the accounts.

5. That this monopoly of management enabled the New York Associated Press to prevent the establishment of new papers in New York and to encourage the establishment of new papers elsewhere.

Either the inroads of the outside publishers brought the New York Associated Press to the verge of collapse, or the internal disruption of that association nerved the dissatisfied clients to rebellion. Craig, for fifteen years the autocrat of the news service, let it be recalled, severed connection with his former sponsors the first week in November, 1866, and announced his readiness to give a better news report than ever to all who would go with him. Seizing the opportunity of the moment, though doubtless in full understanding with Craig, the directors of the Western Associated Press, meeting at Cincinnati, fulminated their ultimatum:

Resolved, That the Western Associated Press will furnish to the New York Associated Press, at a point to be agreed upon, all news and markets of sufficient general interest to be telegraphed to the press of the country from the West and Southwest, in exchange for the news collected from the East and Canada.

That the Western Associated Press will make their own report of the proceedings of Congress and provide for the transmission of the same.

That the New York Associated Press shall furnish the Western Associated Press the usual report of miscellaneous news from Washington.

That the news of the Atlantic cable, or from the Pacific coast, shall be subject to special arrangement.

That the Western Associated Press shall arrange with the telegraph company for transmitting the news of the New York Associated Press from New York.

That the New York Associated Press shall arrange for transmitting the news of the Western Associated Press from a point to be agreed upon to New York.

The fight was destined to be short, sharp, and decisive. Full powers were vested in the executive committee consisting of Halstead, Brigham, and Horace White. Craig was already running his "opposing" association. Under date of November 27, Halstead and White addressed a note to the New York Associated Press which could be considered only as a challenge. It read:

The Executive Committee of the Western Associated Press proposes to get news from all parties who have news to sell and to provide for its transmission to their respective journals. They propose to take the regular report of the New York Press at Buffalo and provide for its transmission to the various Western cities. For this news, they will pay their own equitable proportion of the cost of collection. They propose also to appoint their own agent in New York to collect and buy additional news from all sources accessible to him and to provide for the transmission of the same to the various cities.

The expected answer came: "The New York Associated Press will permit no newspaper accepting its news to enter into any arrangement with any rival organization." The

Philadelphia papers endorsed the action of New York. The generalissimos of the Western Press proceeded east in person and, on arrival, "unintimidated by threat of the New York association, threw down the gauntlet by making a contract with the United States and European Telegraphic News Association and appointed D. H. Craig general agent." On the same day, Craig instructed his agents to give notice to editors receiving the New York Associated Press reports that they could not have the Western Associated Press service. Was this step warranted? Oh, yes. "Hypercritical persons may see an inconsistency between this order of exclusiveness and the ground on which the break with the New York Associated Press was justified, but the enemy was unscrupulous and—there is high authority for fighting the devil with fire." [8]

The committee entering into these arrangements evidently believed a more frank explanation to be due to their constituency. Here are extracts from their circular letter to the members:

> By establishing competition, there will be a constant incentive to the rival organizations to excel in their legitimate functions of obtaining and forwarding news to the press accurately and promptly.
>
> It is agreed with Mr. Craig that the Western press shall receive news reports from all parts of the country and from Europe that shall compare favorably with those sent by the New York Associated Press upon terms as favorable as those heretofore prevailing and, if the press outside of New York unite with him, he engages to make a reduction of ten per cent on the present rates on news dispatches and 50 per cent on European dispatches. He consents to surrender, at any time, all facilities of the opposition news association, which he has organized, to the proprietors of the papers of the country associated in general news arrangements in competition with the New York Associated Press. It is provided that the new opposition

[8] Smith, *op. cit.*, p. 39.

association shall never exercise, or claim to exercise, any control over local associations or individual editors as to their right to receive news from other associations or parties in New York, or elsewhere, and the Western Associated Press is conceded the exclusive control of their news report within their own territory.

We have no connection whatever with Mr. Craig's projected commercial news system.

So many difficulties present themselves in negotiating for a special report of Congress to be sent direct to the West that we decided to abandon that for the present and trust to individual enterprise in that direction.

Nearly all the western and southwestern agents had adhered to Craig. According to one summary, the new line-up included "the leading journals of Cincinnati, St. Louis, Chicago, Louisville, Cleveland, Pittsburgh, Indianapolis, Memphis and Nashville in the West, the majority of the newspapers in Arkansas, Mississippi, and Texas in the Southwest, every newspaper in Louisiana with a single exception in New Orleans, all the newspapers of Virginia with but three or four exceptions, four-fifths of the press of Georgia, all the newspapers of Washington City, one-half the press of Baltimore, eight out of the thirteen Philadelphia newspapers which publish news by telegraph, two of the three of the prosperous city of Newark, the entire press of Brooklyn, and three of the nine newspapers of New York."[9] This list subsequently embraced also the Buffalo *Commercial Advertiser* and the Troy *Times*. At first, the *World*, one of the Associated Press's big seven, sought to ride in both wagons. A resolution to expel that paper was actually adopted, but rescinded a few minutes later and softened into a caution that left the latch string out. Despite efforts to avoid the threatened break in the ranks, despite the "gentlemen's agreement" with its requirement of six months'

[9] *World*, Dec. 11, 1866.

written notice of withdrawal, the secession of the *World* was proclaimed editorially in its issue of December 3:

> The *World,* which is a member of the Associated Press, has been informed by the Executive Committee of that organization that acceptance or use of news from other sources will be considered as a withdrawal from the Association and has also been informed by the Secretary that expulsion will be the penalty of with-holding an immediate assent to this rule.
>
> It is a question in which the public has a very slight interest whether the Associated Press has a right to make and enforce such a rule and penalty. In our opinion, it has no right not derived from its articles of association, and those articles justify no such rule and penalty.
>
> But the *World* is a newspaper. Its business is to obtain news from every quarter of the habitable globe and to publish the same at the earliest possible moment. It cannot consent to be hampered by the inferior enterprise of rival newspapers. It cannot consent to be bound by obligations imposed by rival newspapers in their own interest, and to which its own assent has never been given. Least of all, can it consent to lay before its readers only meagre, trivial, worthless despatches from half a dozen cities when news of importance teems forth every day and hour in all parts of the New and Old World, which by enterprise and money it can publish for the benefit of the American people.
>
> In the judgment of the *World,* not to publish all of the news when it is news, is to cease to be a live newspaper. The *World* must publish all the news, and will, whether its rivals do or not. They have concluded to commit their business to feeble, incompetent hands. They have also concluded to attempt to fetter the enterprise of the *World* and other journals throughout the country, and abridge it to the pattern of feebleness and incompetency. Their own business they can manage as they please. The *World* is a newspaper and will contain every day all the news.
>
> This morning, therefore, we lay before our readers special news which will be found in no other New York journal, and we shall continue to do so.

In subsequent self-justification, the *World* posed as a victim of discrimination, complaining that the rule for sharing all special dispatches had never been enforced against the *Herald*. Nevertheless, it was maintained that, in theory, the *World's* membership in the original association was never completely forfeited.

Following these developments, the New England and the New York State press exhibited distinct signs of restlessness. The elder Bennett had engaged in private conferences with the Western Press committee. "It looked as if the New York Association would be destroyed." But the adventure of the westerners into the wilds of New York failed to bring down its quarry. After several sessions with representatives of the New York papers, they could only report, "Our propositions 'could not be considered.' " And further:

> It appeared not only that there remained in the New York Association, after Mr. Craig's connection with it ceased, the old and well-known despotic exclusiveness and intolerance, but that there had been added a hitherto unknown and most offensive stupidity.
>
> If he [Craig] is the great rascal members of the New York Association say he is, it would do less discredit to their sagacity if they had found him out before he had been eighteen years their confidential and exclusive agent. We found him using much less harsh language than his opponents with, as we have every reason to believe, a most extensive and efficient machinery on hand for the collection and diffusion of the news of the world, while his quiet, vigilant, methodical ways of doing business gave us a measure of confidence in his competency much greater than we would entertain for his competitor whose excitement it was painful to witness. We found Mr. Craig seeking what we may suppose may be termed his revenge on the Associated Press and offering the only opportunity we ever had, and the only one likely to be presented to us, of establishing competition in news-gathering in New York.

The need of organized reënforcement greatly impressed the western committee which recommended immediate activity in this direction, with the declaration that influential gentlemen connected with the press in the Southwest and along the Atlantic seaboard, in the middle states and New England, were urging the formation of associations like that in the West, "or rather like that which we must make our Western association." And then, returning to the main issue:

> Mr. Craig is a man of large means acquired through the rise and expansion of telegraph stock and not by robbing New York papers of the money they never spent, and has no special ambition to continue in the news business. His quarrel is our opportunity. When he takes revenge by establishing a competitor with the old monopoly, we will have justice. Instead of being subordinate to the New York press, we will be masters of the situation.

The desire to be "masters of the situation" was not shared by all the Western Associated Press publishers. A counter circular issued by James E. Scripps, of the Detroit *Advertiser and Tribune,* charged openly that a ring made up of the Cincinnati *Gazette,* the Chicago *Tribune,* and the St. Louis *Republican* was conspiring "to prostitute the machinery and influence of the association to the promotion of their own individual interests." [10] Ignoring denials, he asserted:

> The plan undoubtedly was and is to break up the existing telegraph news arrangements and compel the smaller journals to look to the three Western cities for their news, instead of to New York as at present.
>
> It now remains for smaller publishers to decide whether it is better to submit to the old mild tyranny of a distant and hence impartial master, like the New York Association, or whether we shall place ourselves in the clutches of a Western Monopoly whose interest will ever lie in a tampering and crushing us for their own aggrandizement.

With conditions thus tense, the membership was called to a special meeting in Chicago, December 12, to ratify the

---

[10] Smith, *op. cit.,* p. 50.

committee's actions. It had been announced that Erastus Brooks, of the *Express,* would be in attendance to represent the New York organization, and he was there accompanied by Joseph P. Beach, of the *Sun.* As a welcome, the *Tribune* of that morning came out with an editorial roasting the New Yorkers and poking fun at Brooks and bragging that "the Western Press can buy and sell the ring which he represents and have spending money left." At the meeting, Halstead repeated in substance the contents of his circulars, and a fervid discussion followed. President Walker, in the chair, ruled out of order the attempt of Brooks to speak, though later he was accorded rather ungraciously the privilege of the floor.

As reported, Brooks reminded those before him of the turbulent proceedings he had just witnessed. "There had never been shown a greater spirit of dictation, of aggression, and of oppression in the New York Association than he had seen to-day." (Cries of "No" and "Yes.") "He proceeded to lecture the Chicago *Tribune* for its impertinence in stating that the New York *Express* was a paper of little influence."

Medill replied that the Western Associated Press had been formed for mutual defense, "in order that there might be two sides to the telegraph news business, if possible." He expatiated on the much-noised grievances involving points on which "their views and ours have not corresponded or harmonized," and went again into the grievances:

> This New York Association is a monopoly in the worst sense of the word. It contracts and collects the telegraph news to suit its own wants and tastes and then deals out scraps of it to others on such conditions and at such prices as it chooses. What voice have we had in that New York Association? We are told that we pay but a trifle towards the expense. I contend that we have paid more than our full quota on all the dispatches we have received. When

the cable dispatches were added as a portion to the news of the day, the New York Associated Press apportioned out to the various places their quota of the expense. Did they take five sevenths of the cost themselves? Not exactly. They charged one full third to the association represented on this floor; another third on the papers south of New York; an additional fraction on those west and north of New York; and the residue, if any, they pay themselves.

The outcome was a vote to sever all relations with the New York Associated Press and to inaugurate a proselyting correspondence with news associations outside of New York state, and with the newspapers in New York connected with the New York Association. to induce them to join the newly launched organization.

For a few weeks, the rivalry was brisk and the expenditures of both associations mounted far above the receipts. The New York papers were first to signal their readiness for a treaty of peace in a communication to the western publishers asking for terms. Acceding to the request, Messrs. Medill, Smith, and Walker were named as a committee empowered to negotiate, and General Anson Stager, western superintendent of the Western Union Telegraph Company, went along with them to New York to help. Things moved slowly. All the efforts of the New York committee to win over the western men proved unavailing, for the latter felt themselves well in the saddle. They were relying absolutely on the coöperation of the press of New England and also of the New York *Herald*. But they were deprived of that aid by the craft and strategy of the enemy. They awoke one fine morning to learn that Simonton had slipped over to Boston and concluded a fresh contract with the New England Association, and that Bennett had accepted concessions as to his special news service in consideration of remaining firm. Realizing that neither was now in a position of superior advantage, the two sides got down to business and soon evolved, by a process of compromise, a mutually acceptable basis for renewed relations. There is a hint from the outside that the telegraph company, having found its wire equipment unequal to a duplicated service of such magnitude, was the main factor in producing agreement.[11] The circumstance that the treaty of peace embraced new and exclusive contracts for telegraphic transmission at any rate lends some color to the statement. The irritating personalities were to be entirely eliminated; Craig was to retire from the news field; the New York Association promised to put some one else in Simonton's position; the Western Associated Press was to be represented by a new general agent, George B. Hicks, not a journalist but an experienced telegrapher, with headquarters at Cleveland. "This part of the agreement was not fulfilled in every particular," e.g., the retention of Simonton as the general agent of the New York Associated Press.

What was to be the program now for collecting and distributing current intelligence to American newspaper readers? The controlling features of the scheme were embodied in the tripartite compacts sealing the close of the great news war of 1866. These contracts were all executed as of date, January 11, 1867. The combat had lasted less than four weeks. The documents in question bore signature on behalf of the New York News Association, "known as the New York Associated Press," by W. C. Prime, President, and Jos. P. Beach, Secretary; on behalf of the Western Associated Press by H. N. Walker, President, and Murat Halstead, Chairman of the Board of Directors; on behalf of the Western Union Telegraph Company by Hiram Sibley, Acting President. Generally speaking, what was agreed on was a division of territory with exchange of news, certain

[11] Shanks, "How We Get Our News," *Harper's*, May, 1869, p. 514.

payments to the New York Associated Press for foreign and other specified service, mutual respect for each other's monopoly of the self-assigned field, most favored treatment in the matter of rates by the telegraph company. Stated more in detail, it was provided, in substance:

1. Those papers that left either association during the difficulties are re-admitted.

2. The New York Association is to furnish "all their news" of all kinds for the exclusive use of the Western Associated Press within its territory to its agent in the New York office.

3. The Western Associated Press is to collect and furnish all news of its territory to the agent of the New York Associated Press at Cleveland or Pittsburgh.

4. Delivery of news is to be made as rapidly as received.

5. Both agree not to compete for papers in the other's territory, "nor will either association sell, or permit to be sold, to any paper or papers within the distributing territory of the other association without the express assent of such association."

6. The territory of the Western Associated Press is defined, namely, that west of the Alleghanies and north of the Ohio.

7. The Western Associated Press is to make arrangements with the Southwestern press.

8. Previous arrangements are to continue with the Northwestern Associated Press.

9. All copy is to be manifolded for delivery to each association.

10. The New York Associated Press may order special reports from Western agents which may be taken also by the Western Press on payment of tolls.

11. Members may have special correspondents in both territories unless forbidden by the rules of their own association.

12. The Western Associated Press is not to use telegraph companies competing with the lines of the Old American Company (in violation of unexpired contracts).

13. The Western Association is to pay: For general news, $8,000 per annum; for cable news 22 per cent of the expense of obtaining the same, but not exceeding in gross expense $150,000 per annum; for California news, 20 per cent of the whole cost to the New York Associated Press at Chicago.

14. The Western Associated Press is to deliver at Chicago its

report for California customers of the New York Associated Press and for customers at other points west of the territory of the Western Associated Press.

And with the telegraph company:

15. The Western Press is to pay $60,000 a year for transmission of a 500-word morning news report from New York, 300 words noon, 3,200 words night, and 2,000 words local.

16. Payment at regular press rates for the excess over 6,000 words a day as a monthly average.

17. Employment of the Western Union wires exclusively.

18. Agreement on the part of the Telegraph Company not to sell news or serve other associations in said territory.

Communicating this information to the members of his association, Halstead commented on the outcome in a confidential circular. dated from his office in Cincinnati, as follows:

Our contract with the New York Associated Press is regarded as of considerable value to us. For some time after its ratification there were differences as to the interpretation of details that seemed likely to give serious trouble. All difficulties have, however, as it appears at present, been adjusted and there seems to be no reason why our relations with the New York Associated Press should not continue to be amicable.

The contract establishes the independence of the Western Associated Press, its complete control over its own affairs, the collection, compilation and transmission of news, and over the news agents within its own lines.

Arrangements with the papers outside the territory of our organization, but made tributary to it, in the Northwest have been perfected and negotiations are in progress with newspapers in Missouri and Kansas and also with the Southwestern Associated Press. In these negotiations, news is recognized as a commodity of value and we sell it to the outside papers for moderate sums, expecting in the aggregate to derive from them a considerable revenue but one that is by no means out of proportion to their ability to pay.[12]

[12] Western Associated Press, confidential circular, April 15, 1867.

The contract with the Western Union Telegraph Company, Halstead characterized as "hardly second in importance," stressing the obligation of the association not to encourage and support any competing telegraph line, and of the telegraph company not to sell news in the territory of the Western Associated Press. The difficult task involved in the adjustment of assessments was dwelt on at the same time. "We had to give some heed to precedents, some to ability of the papers to pay, some to dimensions of the cities in which they appeared, some to the value to journalism of the territory in which they circulated." So the best that could be done was to strike an average which, though in certain cases arbitrary, on the whole would be conceded substantially fair. Notice was served that the general agent was to cut off all newspapers refusing to pay for a single week, and that the division of the charges in any one town was left to the participating local papers unless they found themselves unable to agree. The initial schedule of assessments, as listed under the new dispensation, was:

Cleveland	$150	Toledo	$108
Detroit	175	Louisville	200
Chicago	375	Columbus	60
Cincinnati	375	Zanesville	25
St. Louis	375	Wheeling	40
Milwaukee	150	New Albany	40
Pittsburgh	200	Dayton	30
Indianapolis	150	Sandusky	25

The number of member papers in the particular city, of course, determined the portion of the assessment each was called upon to pay.

The return to tranquil conditions thus inaugurated a form of federation of news-gathering associations occupying separate, though not always sharply defined, areas in which rested responsibility for the supply of news from such territory. The New York Associated Press still held the primacy through its handling and virtual control of the transatlantic service, coupled with the important market reports and the news from the seat of national government.

The auxiliary associations, among which the Western Associated Press came first with a status but little short of junior partnership, made their arrangements with one or the other of these two for an exchange of news conditioned on payment of a proportional quota of the general and overhead expense. The policy of encouraging the organization of auxiliary associations and accepting the group as a client merely extended a practice that already existed, along with an apparently larger grant of local home rule. Membership in a news association became a "franchise," an exercise of privilege, to be guarded and defended against the encroachment of outsiders or newcomers. For the most part, the auxiliary associations were loosely united and sometimes temporary in character. Among those referred to at this period may be mentioned the New England press, the Philadelphia press, the Baltimore press, the Southern press, the Southwestern press, the Northwestern press, the New York State press, the Missouri and Kansas press, the Colorado press, the California press.

Of these, certain ones came to play larger parts that entitle them to closer attention. The example set by the Western Associated Press in its incorporation and plan of unified negotiations was quick to inspire imitation. The publishers of the smaller papers in adjoining western states, who would have to obtain their news from that association, took immediate steps for incorporation under a special act obtained from the legislature of Illinois,[13] creating "The Northwestern Associated Press." The stated object was "the procuring, dissemination and publication of general news and intelligence for and through the newspaper press of the Northwestern states, making use of the telegraph, or otherwise, and employing such means and agencies, on such terms of supply, service and compensation, as the by-laws, orders, and regulations shall prescribe." While six charter members were named in the law, and constituted the first board of directors, the significant provision was a requirement that a call be issued "to all the daily newspapers in the Northwestern states," for an organization meeting, at which books of subscription shall be opened, the down-payment not to exceed 10 per cent, and all the capital stock, $20,000 in shares of $25 each, divided equally "among all the daily newspapers of the Northwestern states who shall desire to become subscribers." Could any news-gathering association have projected a more democratic and all-inclusive ideal than that of the Northwestern Associated Press at its inception? Accepting the invitation and qualifying as members at Chicago, February 22, 1867, the publishers of the following journals enrolled:

ILLINOIS

Alton	*Democrat, Telegraph*
Bloomington	*Pantagraph*
Freeport	*Journal*
Galesburg	*Register*
Jacksonville	*Journal*
Peoria	*Democrat, Transcript*
Quincy	*Herald, Whig*
Rock Island	*Argus, Union*
Springfield	*State Journal, State Register*

[13] *Private Laws of Illinois,* 1867, p. 515.

Iowa

Burlington ....*Gazette, Hawkeye*
Council Bluffs ....*Nonpareil*
Davenport ....*Democrat, Gazette*
Des Moines ....*State Register, Statesman*
Dubuque ....*Herald, Times*
Keokuk ....*Constitution, Gate City*
Muscatine ....*Courier, Journal*

Nebraska

Omaha ....*Herald, Republican*
Nebraska City ....*Press*

While several of these papers dropped out, some of which purchased the reports as clients afterwards, only two more were admitted to full membership in its entire span of twenty-five years, namely, the *Bee*, at Omaha, and the *Journal*, at Sioux City. This rigidity of membership was due to the fact that, despite the liberality of the original plan, the by-law governing admissions made necessary an affirmative vote of two-thirds of all the members, and also the unanimous consent of the members in the city or town in which the applicant was to carry on his business. And the franchise monopoly received still further strengthening in the contracts concluded with the Western Associated Press, barring extension of the service except by its consent as well, in consideration of its agreement not to give the use of the news to places which, "from near location," conflicted with the interests of the members of the Northwestern Associated Press. By mutual understanding, and by practice, "conceded and approved," the latter's exclusive jurisdiction prevailed in the territory embracing all of the State of Illinois, outside of Chicago, all of Iowa, and the eastern portion of Nebraska. Could assurance be made doubly sure, it was done by the contract with the Western Union, whereby that company stipulated that it would not sell or be interested in selling for private use, within the territory expressly defined, any news except election returns and strictly commercial reports and market quotations, unless by consent, in which event no price would be fixed less than a proportionate rate to that charged members, and 15 per cent of the amount collected would be remitted to the association.[14]

In the same year, 1867, the up-state New York papers emerged as a legally chartered "body corporate and politic," entitled, "The Associated Press of the State of New York," whose objects were declared to be "the mutual protection of members of the press, procuring and supplying its members with telegraphic news, upholding and elevating the character and standing, and the promotion and maintenance of the general interest and welfare of the profession and its members."[15] Specifically authorized were "a uniform system of fees for admission to membership and also a uniform system of dues, payable periodically at such intervals as may be prescribed by the rules"; also the right to hold real estate not exceeding in value $200,000 "for the purposes of said association and no other."

Rules and by-laws, promulgated from time to time under this authority, showed how the association was to carry on. Membership was to be open only to the proprietor, or part proprietor, of a daily newspaper published in the State of New York, inseparable from the paper, under which description came all the incorporators, eleven in number. Any such newspaper proprietor might become a member but only with

[14] Clendenin, *Autobiography,* p. 146, refers to "members in Wisconsin," mistakenly, since they were merely clients.

[15] *Laws of New York,* 1867, p. 1860.

the assent of the other member papers, if any, in the same locality. The admission fee eventually reached a sum equal to five years' weekly dues, these dues being not less than $25 for afternoon papers and $30 for morning papers. The customary officers administered the affairs of the association —an executive committee, at first of five, later ten, geographically distributed. Nonpayment of dues or violation of the conditions of membership risked suspension and expulsion after hearing. Obligations included safeguarding the news report against premature publication, against unauthorized publication out of hours or in extras, prompt payment of assessments, a special levy in case of deficit apportioned in the same ratio as the regular weekly dues. The roster, allowing for variation at different times, comprised these journals:

Albany	*Argus, Express, Journal, Times*
Auburn	*Advertiser*
Binghamton	*Republican*
Buffalo	*Commercial, Courier, Express, Democrat*
Elmira	*Advertiser, Gazette*
Hudson	*Register*
Ithaca	*Journal*
Kingston	*Freeman*
Lockport	*Journal, Union*
Newburgh	*Journal*
Oswego	*Palladium, Times*
Poughkeepsie	*Eagle*
Rochester	*Democrat, Union*
Saratoga	*Union*
Schenectady	*Union*
Syracuse	*Courier, Journal, Standard*
Troy	*Telegram, Press, Times*
Utica	*Herald, Observer*
Watertown	*Times*

The report was to be made up by an agent stationed in the New York office of the Associated Press from the manifolded copy furnished to him there. The state was divided into news districts, each in charge of a member of the executive committee responsible for his allotted territory and "authorized and directed to command the service of any and all members of the Association within his district." All complaints relating to the news, however, were to be addressed to the president whose duty it was to submit, at the annual meeting, a detailed statement of them for the year and of the action upon them. Arrangements with the New York Associated Press and the telegraph companies provided for an exclusive news service for a definite sum annually in equal weekly payments and, in addition, the collection "with thoroughness," of all the news of the territory, described as "New York State, north and west of Newburgh," and its transmission for the use of the New York Associated Press and its affiliated organizations.

Before the decade ran out, the New England Associated Press was similarly organized under the lead of the Boston papers, whose local association was thereby supplanted. It undertook to gather the news of New England for its members and for the New York Associated Press, with which it established the customary exchange relations, and to further mutual service and protection. The papers published in Maine, and certain others in Connecticut, made their arrangements collectively. For fifteen years, Edward L. Beard was in charge. In 1887, the New England Associated Press absorbed the outside service, which the journals it had excluded had been forced to take, and, two years thereafter, came under the direction of Herbert H. Fletcher, who remained until the final merger in the Associated Press, of which we shall learn later.[16] At its height, the

16 Fletcher, Letter, July 15, 1927.

association was sending its reports to 103 members and clients, including morning, evening, and Sunday papers in all the New England states, New Brunswick, and Nova Scotia. Among the influential journals included at one time or another were: Boston—*Advertiser, Post, Herald, Globe, Transcript;* Springfield—*Republican, Union;* Worcester—*Gazette, Spy;* Hartford—*Courant, Times;* Lewiston —*Journal;* Bangor—*Whig;* Kennebec—*Journal;* Nashua—*Telegraph;* Manchester—*Union.* W. W. Clapp was president, then Joseph L. Shipley of the Springfield *Union,* finally John H. Holmes, of the Boston *Herald.*

CHAPTER XIV

POST-WAR RECONSTRUCTION

The régime of James W. Simonton—Scope of operations—Relation to members, clients, and patrons

In putting James W. Simonton in the place so long occupied by Craig, responsibility for the smooth running of the service was restored to a man of journalistic training. Coming from a rural section of New York, Simonton was, at twenty, a reporter on the *Courier and Enquirer* and, a few years later, went to Washington with Henry J. Raymond as one of its correspondents at the Capital. He must have earned the favorable opinion of Raymond and reached terms of intimacy with him, for, when the latter embarked on his venture with the *Times* in 1851, Simonton was associated with him.[1] As Washington representative of the *Times,* Simonton achieved the delicate distinction of being barred from the floor of the House for exposing certain members implicated in a land steal.[2] It made a ripping story. When his first letter, embodying the charges, came back to Washington in print, a wonderful amount of virtuous indignation burst forth in the House, particularly from the gentlemen overeager to rebut suspicion. Poor Simonton was being hotly berated by those making a show of injured innocence, "as a terrier treats a rat," when, at the moment of highest excitement, "a respectable member" rose in his seat and avowed that he had been approached with a

[1] O'Brien, *The Story of The Sun,* p. 174.

[2] *Congressional Globe,* Feb. 28, 1857, p. 952.

bribe-offer of $1,000 if he would advocate the passage of a pending land-grant measure. The announcement had the effect of a bombshell among the very people who had been decrying all newspaper charges with ineffable contempt. An investigation simply had to be ordered, though preordained to be a job of whitewashing. The guilty members caught in the net of exposure resigned to escape expulsion, but, of course, that in no way mitigated the heinousness of the offense of the too observant reporter. Simonton had been held in custody through the session for refusing to divulge the name of his informant and his floor privileges as a correspondent were annulled.[3] It goes without saying that neither with the public nor in newspaper circles was his reputation damaged or his usefulness impaired.

Soon after this episode, Simonton was sent across the plains with Albert Sidney Johnston's expeditionary force against the Mormons, and he went on to the coast and was lost to the *Times*.[4] He must have visited California prior to 1857, however, inasmuch as he had referred in his testimony before Congress to a friend "whom I knew in California when I was there several years ago." [5]

Locating in San Francisco, Simonton became interested in the *Bulletin* which, under his management, soon ranked as the leading paper of that city. What occasion found him back in New York in the fall of 1866 is unexplained, but his presence no doubt served to renew the old contact with Raymond, at the moment a potent factor in the critical affairs of the New York Associated Press. What could be more natural than for Raymond to turn to Simonton as

---

[3] Perley Poore, "Washington News," *Harper's Magazine*, 1874, p. 229.

[4] Davis, *History of the New York Times*, p. 41.

[5] Quoted in "One of the Reasons for Telegraphic Reform," pamphlet, 1873, p. 37.

a man of proved ability and dependability? This was the man propelled, as it appeared, in a flash, into the trying position of general agent so suddenly vacated by Craig's discharge on that late afternoon in early November. This was the man whose incumbency was to equal in duration the fifteen-year record of his immediate predecessor. Though devoting his time and talents to the business of the Associated Press, Simonton retained his financial holding in the *Bulletin* in San Francisco, which connection, as we shall see, was not always free from its embarrassments and, when his health broke down, returned to California where he died, not yet sixty, in 1882.

While Simonton's methods were more diplomatic, his manners less blustering, and his viewpoints more sympathetic to the side of the newspaper publisher than to the telegraph companies whose lines constituted the means of communication, his path still ran over not always even roads. The advent of the oceanic telegraph had brought a problem he had to work out at once. The no longer needed fleet of news boats off Cape Race was disbanded.[6] The conjoining telegraph lines, for whose control there had been so much contention, could be almost altogether dispensed with as news carriers. James Gordon Bennett, at least, had not failed to estimate the worth of cable service to his newspaper; within six months after completion, he had let Cyrus W. Field know of his willingness to sign a contract to pay $3,750 a month for assured use of the cable for political and foreign news.[7] Neither had the western editors failed to see the value of the cable, for, at their session in Detroit in August, 1866, the principal topic of discussion concerned arrangements with the Atlantic cable

[6] Philadelphia *Ledger,* Nov. 3, 1866.
[7] Judson, *Life of Cyrus W. Field,* p. 181.

SAMUEL F. B. MORSE

WILLIAM M. SWAIN

ANSON STAGER

CYRUS W. FIELD

for a more satisfactory foreign service.[8] During the split between the news associations later in that year the cable bills had risen as high as $2,100 a week for these enterprising metropolitan journals, reduced after the peace to about $800 a week.[9]

In the settlement with the Western Associated Press, cable news stands out for the first time as a separate item. Twenty-two per cent of the cost was to be borne by that organization out of a total expected to approximate $150,000 a year. In the beginning, it had been figured that the bill for 200 words a day at the initial rates would amount to $300,000, but that must have been quite exaggerated. Examination of the newspaper files of the period reveals the items printed as cabled news in dailies outside of New York averaging from 250 to 400 words, including market quotations, after expanding and padding. What the reader saw was not to exceed a quarter of a column of type, headed "Cable News," over a jumble of short items in casual disarrangement. And the same complaints as to precedence in transmission developed with the cable as originally with the land lines. Aired in printed correspondence, Simonton protested against discrimination, in that cable messages were not transmitted in the order of filing. Field got back at him by producing the request that Simonton himself had made the previous year to have press dispatches accorded priority.[10] Disputes over cable transmission of news could be acute, of course, only so long as the cable facilities were restricted and their capacity inadequate to maximum demands, a difficulty gradually self-remedying.

The character of the news served drew fire from several

---

[8] Schurz, *Intimate Letters,* p. 159.
[9] Shanks, "How We Get Our News," *Harper's,* May, 1869, p. 516.
[10] "Atlantic Cable Mismanagement," Correspondence.

directions. Congress more than once took notice of the alleged unreliability and mendacity of reports in which senators and congressmen were concerned. Even before this, Senator Grimes, of Iowa, had offered a resolution to inquire "what action may be necessary to secure more accurate reports of senate proceedings."[11] The grievances paraded in the debate had mostly to do, as would be surmised, with failure to print remarks for which the senators who made them wanted publicity. A year later, the subject again precipitated discussion which incidentally disclosed that the Associated Press reporter was on the Senate payroll as a clerk to a committee, and that it was a common practice for committee clerks to act as special correspondents for the newspapers.[12] The question recurred when the Senate was asked to admit the Associated Press reporter to the floor during the impeachment trial.[13] As one good reason for granting the request, Senator Conklin informed his colleagues that 840 dailies were being supplied with news of the case by the New York Associated Press. On the side of the reading public, one critic voiced a complaint that, whereas the use of the telegraph originally was to transmit intelligence of real moment, of late it seemed to be to give significance to unimportant news.[14]

By this time, the Associated Press was occupying six rooms in a building at Broadway and Liberty Street, adjacent to the telegraph offices, one, a committee room in which the representatives of the seven member papers met once a month.[15] The agency was the heaviest customer of

---

[11] *Globe,* Dec., 1865, p. 36.

[12] *Ibid.,* Jan. 24, 1866, p. 391.

[13] *Ibid.,* April 4, 1868, p. 2234.

[14] Browne, *The Great Metropolis,* p. 302.

[15] Aplin, "At the Associated Press Office," *Putnam's Magazine,* July, 1870, p. 23.

the wires. Dispatches were trundled across the street, from one side to the other, by three miniature elevated railways, "to the apparent bewilderment of humanity below" as they rattled to and fro, night and day, bearing news from all quarters of the globe. The usual day's grist was 150 sheets containing 35,000 words. The delivery messengers made thirty to forty "routes" with the manifold copies, of which there were twenty altogether, to the *Herald*, the *Times*, the *Tribune*, the *World*, the *Sun*, the *Journal*, the *Post*, the *Express*, the *Commercial Advertiser*, the *Staats-zeitung*, the Brooklyn *Union*, the Newark *Advertiser*, and to the reporters of the state press, the Boston press, the New England press, the western press, the southern press, and the far southern press, leaving one copy for the office record.

It was the manifolding process that rendered possible simultaneous copy. To write out twenty identical messages separately would have taken much longer and have called for many more clerks. So the receiving operator performed this amazing feat all by himself by using a "book" of manifold paper, alternating thin tissue with sheets of black paper "as thick as blotting paper," so that the pressure of an ivory stylus, or anything with a hard, smooth point, running over the upper sheet, transferred the lines to each—"every letter, dash and dot formed by the ivory point."[16] The sheets of the manifold, torn apart, would then go to the papers entitled to them "by means of that lively boy." "Manifold paper and miscellaneous" formed a distinct item in the early financial exhibits of the Western Associated Press to the tune of nearly $6,000 a year.

The regular members of the Associated Press in New York were paying annually at this time about $14,000 each

---

[16] Hill, *Secrets of the Sanctum*, p. 82.

for the news service, those having Sunday editions about $15,000, the three evening papers about $8,000 apiece.[17] Each of the auxiliary associations had agents, or reporters, in the manifolding room night and day, enjoying access to all the Associated Press news received, and sending out such parts of it as were likely to interest the people of their respective sections. As fast as they compiled their reports, they would forward them to the telegraph office by the overhead mechanical conveyor, directed, "State Press," or "Southern Press," etc., and at certain regular hours, convenient alike for telegraph and the editors to be served, the operator, "with one manipulation of his magic key," would transmit the words in the copy to all the papers on the circuit. Incoming western news was sifted through the hands of the agent at Cleveland. No southern news would arrive except that forwarded by the Washington agent.

When the revenue law was enacted, imposing a tax on telegrams, the Associated Press cleverly rose to the emergency to lighten its share of the burden. "By an innocent fiction," the local agent, who ordinarily dispatched a dozen messages a day, was enabled to send one telegram only by treating the first eleven as parts of a single dispatch, ending each one, "more," or "more coming," and subscribing his name in full to the twelfth at midnight. It became almost second nature for an Associated Press correspondent to conclude his message, "more," in place of his own signature, and the practice even yet continues. The word rate on messages of not less than ten words ranged from three cents from Boston to New York to five cents from Washington, fourteen cents from Chicago, twenty-three cents from New Orleans, fifty-seven cents from San Francisco.[18]

---

[17] Aplin, *op. cit.*, p. 27.

[18] Shanks, *op. cit.*, p. 517.

As for the papers receiving the reports, the main solicitude strove to keep off news poachers as much as to get the news for themselves. The commercial news department of the telegraph company gave cause for incessant dispute; this bureau, and the Gold and Stock Telegraph Company which it absorbed in 1871, supplied and sold commercial news and market quotations to private subscribers in all the larger cities of the country. The dividing line between general and commercial news was a hazy one. But the telegraph company, then and for a long time thereafter, assumed the right to appropriate to its own use whatever information, transmitted over the wires, it believed to be relevant to its commercial news service.[19] "The persistent invasion of the province of the press," by the commercial news department, brought in response to repeated representations "evasion, procrastination and promises, but no reform." [20]

It had been the boast of the western association at the close of the great news war that no means whatever remained of obtaining the telegraphic news within its territory or that tributary to it, "except through our agents," and that in the absence of any opposition news agency, "our contract gives us, for our territory, a monopoly of the news of the world on the wires from Liverpool to San Francisco." [21] If true, such a condition could not but be a standing invitation to attack. The idea of competition in news, so beautifully painted in alluring colors by the selfsame word artists, could not be extinguished by an agreement between warring claimants to parcel out the empire of news. The constantly increasing numbers of outside

---

[19] Reid, *The Telegraph,* p. 825.
[20] Western Associated Press Report, 1873, p. 11.
[21] Confidential Circular, 1867, p. 3.

papers, of papers in sections not served, of papers excluded by local competitors in possession of exclusive franchises, were bound in time to form the starting point for further efforts.

CHAPTER XV

THE SUCCESSION OF RIVAL AGENCIES

Henry George's efforts—The Hasson News Association—The American Press Association—The National Press Association—The United Press

Rather curiously, the next move in the news arena cut all the way across the continent from the Pacific coast. Curiously, too, the central figure in it was destined to achieve great fame wholly apart from his work as a journalist. In the beginning, three newspapers, the *Alta* and the *Bulletin* in San Francisco, and the *Union* in Sacramento, had made an arrangement with the overland telegraph company whereby only those in the combination could receive the press reports at first hand. Against this embargo, Senator Conness had sought vainly to force delivery of the news to all public journals in his state of California at two cents a word.[1] This tight shut policy—so tight that the slightest revealment of eastern news was prohibited until a day after its publication in the protected papers [2]—had been broken once by the San Francisco *Times*, and its hard won success in this exploit was stimulating rather than deterring the starting of other papers. Henry George, a newcomer from Philadelphia, who had served apprenticeship both as a seaman and as a typesetter, had been doing editorial work on the *Times*. Dissatisfied with his salary, George left the *Times* in the summer of 1868 and, con-

[1] Bancroft, *Chronicles of the Builders,* V, 321, 339.

[2] Mark Twain, *Roughing It,* I, 69.

cluding a short engagement with Charles De Young's project to convert his *Dramatic Chronicle* into a morning daily, he fell in with John Nugent's scheme to revive the old *Herald*. His special assignment was to go to New York and try to get the Associated Press reports for the *Herald*, or, if that should be refused, to set up a news service for the paper.[3]

Crossing the plains in a wagon, and then connecting with the luxury of a sleeping car in which he had to share his berth with a stranger, George went first to his old home where he engaged John Hasson, one of his boyhood friends, to join him. The two proceeded to New York and made formal application for the Associated Press news for the San Francisco *Herald*. Writing to Charles A. Sumner, the managing editor, in January, 1869, George said:

> Nobody received me with open arms, unless I except the Peter Funks. I have made no acquaintances beyond those necessary for my purpose and not yet delivered any letters except business ones. The newspaper offices here are like big manufactories and they don't seem to be in the habit of asking strangers to take seats and look over the exchanges. The bosses come down for a few hours occasionally; the managing editors get down about twelve and leave about four or five in the afternoon; and I don't think the smaller guns begin to work as hard as those on the Pacific Coast.

After provoking delays, the application was unceremoniously rejected by the Associated Press management, and independent machinery was the sole recourse. In the belief that Philadelphia would be a more suitable base of operations, George and Hasson returned there and opened their press bureau in the little coal office occupied at the time by Henry George's father, on Third Street almost opposite St. Paul's church. "Here they collected by wire

---

[3] Henry George, Jr., *Life of Henry George*, p. 180.

from various sources their news, and dressing it up to fit their California requirements, putting as much as possible into a prearranged cipher, to save expense, telegraphed it by the Western Union Company, which controlled the only route to San Francisco, at a rate fixed by a clear agreement and based upon a schedule adopted before any news war was in sight. In exchange for the full credit, access was given to the New York *Herald's* special dispatches, and in this and other ways a good news service was supplied; so much better, indeed, than that which the Associated Press papers in California received that they made a great commotion inside the association and that body urged the Western Union Telegraph Company to interfere."[4]

The company, hiding behind alleged rules, vetoed the use of the cipher code and refused to accept the service for forwarding from Philadelphia; when the agency was moved promptly to New York, a new and discriminating rate sheet was promulgated to be effective on short notice. Protests, interviews, appeals, all piled discouragement on discouragement. Desperate and indignant, George fulminated a printed broadside, addressed to the executive board of the company, but in fact directed to the general public. The New York *Herald* was the only publication of moment that found space for it. Could the author have hoped for anything different? Is it not more reasonable to believe that he was pleasantly astonished to see it in the *Herald* where it bristled through nearly two columns of fine type with alternating argument and defiance?[5] The unmistakable purpose of the new rates, of which he had just been apprised, was to crush out the paper he represented and give its competitors a veritable monopoly of eastern telegraphic

[4] *Ibid.*, p. 183.
[5] *Herald,* April 25, 1869.

news in California, "a proceeding repulsive to every idea of justice and fair-dealing." Under present arrangement, the four papers in the combine were paying $2,500 in gold per month, or $625 apiece, for a daily news report of 1,000 words from Chicago to San Francisco, which was used by them in common. George's paper was paying $900 in gold for 500 words from New York to San Francisco, which were used by it alone. As now proposed, the combination was to take 2,500 words a day and pay $3,333 a month, "while you agree to charge the *Herald* $2,000 a month for its 500 words." To be sure, there was a proviso for the sale of 500 words daily to any paper willing to pay the insiders $1,000 a month; "this adds insult to injury," for "it would be 'rare old news' that the opposition paper would get for its share, even if it should consent to pay its rivals for 500 words of news more than they pay for five times the amount." Where the San Francisco *Herald* was paying 6.92 cents per word, "you raise this to 15.38 cents," leaving the others at a little over one cent a word, and, if it shut out the *Herald* altogether, the total revenue of the telegraph company would be actually lessened.

"Such a course," George persisted, "would disgrace and dishonor, among his fellows, 'a very shyster'; the lowest huckster would blush to be charged with it. What, then, shall be said of such a course on the part of the Great Western Union Telegraph Company, with its ramifications extending through all parts of the land, performing as it does the most delicate functions with which any corporation can be charged?" Incidentally, a gentle reminder was thrown in that the telegraph was not to be regarded as private property to be used "as whim, caprice or selfish interest may dictate," but was "a great public trust to be administered for the benefit of the whole community."

George had urged some plan that would charge each paper a definite price for its news, or be adjusted to a sliding scale, or impose the condition that the report, whether delivered to many papers or to a single paper, be available to any other publication willing and able to bear its proportion of the joint expense. Even while penning this outburst, the ominous handwriting must have been visible on the wall; Western Union directors were impervious to such pleas; the new rate schedule went into operation as per stipulation. Henry George, with salary and expenses in arrears, realizing that he could be of no further advantage to the paper there, instated Hasson as New York agent and started back by rail to California under the spell of the still reverberating hammer blows on the golden spike which had just joined the two oceans with bands of steel.

There is a postscript to the story. In February of the following year, Henry George became identified with the Sacramento *Reporter* and had only begun to warm his new chair when the old fight flared up again. The Atlantic and Pacific Telegraph Company had entered the field and the Western Union was faced with competition. Hasson had kept on the job in New York and had undertaken, with fair success, to develop an independent news agency, doing business as the Hasson News Association, now about to be transformed into the American Press Association. Was it surprising that Hasson should have asked George to serve as California agent? Or that George should have gone into the enterprise with enthusiasm and rallied a number of coast papers into the alliance? [6] The Franco-Prussian War was on, foreign news heavy, costs high. The assessment on the California territory was advanced and George put the entire increase on De Young's San Francisco *Chronicle*

---

[6] Henry George, Jr., *op. cit.*, p. 211.

as the journal which could best bear it and which benefited most from the service. When De Young made much ado in resistance, George called a meeting of all the interested publishers who, quite self-servingly, upheld his action unanimously, "De Young being so disgusted that he would not vote at all." The contest with the Associated Press and the Western Union continued, so far as George's participation was concerned, only until the spring of 1871, when he quit the Sacramento *Reporter*.

By this time, the American Press Association, managed through its first year with adroitness and vigor, had demonstrated its vitality and was purveying news to nearly one hundred publications in all parts of the country.[7] "Free trade in news" was its battle cry. Its ambition demanded the habiliment of incorporation which now, in June, 1871, was procured by grace of the lawmakers of Pennsylvania. Here is the list of papers whose publishers qualified as incorporators: the *Star*, the *Evening Mail*, the *News*, the *Journal*, the *Demokrat*, of New York; the *Bulletin*, the *Day*, of Philadelphia; the *Germantown Chronicle*, the *Mail* and the *Leader* of Pittsburgh; the Providence *Star*, the Boston *Times*, the Louisville *Ledger*.[8] The business of the association was "to collect, receive and distribute news to the newspaper press, and to such persons or corporations for public or private use, upon such terms as may be agreed upon"; and power was conferred "to print, publish, issue, and dispose of such newspapers, books, maps, pamphlets and literary productions as may be deemed expedient."

Membership required the investment of $1,000 in the stock, limited to a total of $200,000, and authority was expressly granted to make all needful rules and regulations

---

[7] Reid, *The Telegraph*, p. 831.

[8] *Laws of Pennsylvania*, p. 509.

and by-laws "for the well ordering of the business." The first official roster read: President, Francis Wells, Philadelphia *Bulletin;* Vice President, R. C. Dunham, Boston *Times;* Secretary, George Bartholomew, New York *News;* additional Directors, Joseph Howard, Jr., New York *Star;* Sidney Dean, Providence *Star;* Theodore Mierson, *New Yorker Journal;* and John Hasson, General Agent resident in New York. "The association, though young, is an infant Hercules, having furnished to its members many of the best news items that ever transpired, far in advance of the older press association. Its most notable beat was the capitulation of Sedan and the surrender of Napoleon." [9]

The activity of the American association did not pass unnoticed by the other organizations. Evidence of this stood out in the remonstrances pressed from time to time by the latter against its use of the wires at lower rates than accorded them and also against members continuing support of the opposition by taking, or paying for, both services.[10] The active management went in quick succession from Hasson to William Roche, and to William B. Somerville, an experienced telegraph man. Somerville's skillful guidance, credited with overcoming serious obstacles, greatly enhanced its prestige.[11] He had to utilize almost wholly the independent telegraph companies whose status was uncertain and changeable and with which definite or long-time contracts were rather hazardous. His arrangements, therefore, necessarily of a more or less temporary character, demanded unending watchfulness and were a cause of constant anxiety. The relatively small area reached by the independents, and the roundabout connections,

---

[9] *American Newspaper Reporter,* July 3, 1871.

[10] Western Associated Press Reports, 1878, 1879.

[11] Reid, *op. cit.,* p. 799.

forced the employment of several lines to secure the desired outlet. As a result of liberal agreements with these telegraph companies, by which they became news collectors and partners in the receipts, inducements were held out for a more effective cultivation of the news field. In the southern states covered by the new Southern and Atlantic Telegraph Company, for example, one of the measures "to organize success" adopted by George H. Grace, its president, was to appoint the local office managers as press agents, allowing them 10 per cent of the collections.[12] Pursuing this policy, the association, for a while on the verge of bankruptcy, soon proved profitable and could point to a fair measure of prosperity, the very condition contributing to the next developments, namely, purchase of control by other parties, a change of methods, a defection of dissatisfied members.

Withdrawal would have been dangerous were there not a ready haven. In this instance, the refuge was the National Associated Press Company. Though not actually chartered until 1877, the service of the National had been in process of formation and nominal operation for some time. Its pattern was not dissimilar to the rest; it contemplated sale of stock to members for franchises carrying absolute estoppal to sharing the news with other papers published in the same city or town except by consent. With its accessions from the American, the National soon took over and merged the former, to all intents and purposes, succeeding to its membership and its organization.

Somerville, finally, in 1879, went to the headship of a department of the Western Union entrusted with its relations with the press of the country and, on his retirement, J. H. Goodsell, as president, himself looked after its affairs. In

---

[12] *Ibid.*, p. 454.

practice, the serve-all policy continued. In the words of Goodsell, "the National Associated Press does not seek to monopolize the trade in news. All newspapers are freely admitted to its privileges on the same terms and conditions as the existing members and in no case has there ever been charged a bonus for membership." But when the Western Union swallowed the Atlantic and Pacific, transmission troubles multiplied. The special rates, "considered fair and the clear profit to the Atlantic and Pacific Company when made," were at once lifted skyward despite protests. The telegraph tolls on these reports had been aggregating from $60,000 to $80,000 for six or seven years. The papers supplied by the National had struggled with the inferior opposition telegraph concern all the while its wires were in poor condition and its connections confined to comparatively few news centers, had helped to build it up to a position where it could perform its service with a reasonable degree of efficiency, only to be at the mercy of the Western Union upon the absorption of its competitor.[13] Higher telegraph tolls meant either heavier expenses or more condensed dispatches, or both, inability to enlarge territory, even enforced denial of applications to join from newspapers not on existing circuits. Goodsell, however, managed the precarious business for several years and thus held the constituent journals together until they could be taken into another rival news association, projected to occupy the national field, and eventually to attain a high rank.

Responding to a call, a number of newspaper publishers, mostly affiliated with the National, dissatisfied with their telegraphic service, and driven to self-help by exclusion from the Associated Press and its allied groups, convened in Syra-

---

[13] "Hearing on Competing Telegraphs," Forty-fifth Cong., 3rd Sess., Senate Report 805, p. 57.

cuse in 1881. The summons, issued by Arthur Jenkins of the Syracuse *Herald,* procured a fairly good attendance. A decision was reached to organize anew, a charter was applied for in conformity with the laws of New York, and a corporate certificate was granted in 1882. The association purported to be nothing but a private venture of the incorporators, Walter P. Phillips, William L. Brown, and George H. Sandison, all of New York City, but the thirteen trustees, likewise designated in the application, identified the journals whose interests were to be subserved, namely, Charles H. Taylor of the Boston *Globe,* Robert S. Davis of the Philadelphia *Ledger,* Charles R. Baldwin of the Waterbury *Republican,* William L. Brown of the New York *Daily News,* Arthur Jenkins of the Syracuse *Herald,* John H. Farrell of the Albany *Times-Union,* Edward H. Butler of the Buffalo *News,* James W. Scott of the Chicago *Herald,* Isaac Dinkelspiel of the Louisville *Times,* James E. Scripps of the Detroit *News,* George H. Sandison of New York, and William J. Kline of Amsterdam. The defined purpose was "to carry on the business of receiving, obtaining, collecting and accumulating items and matters of news and selling, vending, furnishing and supplying the same." Capital stock in the sum of $20,000 was to be issued in 800 shares of $25 each. The corporation was to establish its principal office in New York City, but to have authority to transact business also in places outside the state. It took over the National Associated Press without much ado and, after absorbing its membership, instituted improvements in the service and began to enlarge its clientage. At the start, Francis X. Schoonmaker, previously connected with the National, officiated as general manager. After a few months of experiment by the organizers, the management passed to different control which set forth vigorously on a new path.

CHAPTER XVI

EXPANSION IN THE EIGHTIES

Charges of monopoly—Censorship and discipline—The second clash between East and West—The Joint Board of Control—Phillips of the United Press—The administration of William Henry Smith—The secret agreement: its exposure and termination

In the meantime, the Associated Press had not been stationary. By 1880, it was serving its reports to 355 members and clients, of which 228 were morning papers and 127 were evening papers.[1] This was out of a total of 971 dailies in the entire United States, increased from 547 in 1870. The Associated Press was paying the Western Union, for telegraph transmission, $392,800 of an aggregate $690,855 collected from the press by that company. It is worth noting that the largest amount paid the Western Union for telegraphing by a single newspaper in 1880, presumably the New York *Herald,* was $70,000. An enlightening account of the work performed by the Associated Press at this stage has been given by Simonton:

> In all sections other than those already named, (i.e. covered by affiliated organizations) the parent association makes its own collection of news. Though it pays for much of the telegraph service the same rate as the general public, it brings the news of the old world as liberally as the interest will justify from day to day. Confining itself to no arbitrary limit, its daily cable tolls are rarely less than $300, are not infrequently $500, and are sometimes even quadruple that sum. Its London offices are never closed. By means of a double corps of agents, the news of Europe, chiefly concentrated at the British capital, is forwarded at all hours as rapidly as received. By contracts with the great European news

[1] North, *The Newspaper Press,* p. 107.

agencies, including the well-known Reuter company, the Associated Press receives their news collections from every part of civilized Europe, Asia, Africa and South America. In sparsely settled districts, where news items are too infrequent to warrant appointment of regular agents, the telegraph companies, in order to earn the tolls, as well as for public accommodation, permit operators to act ex officio as agents for the press. So, too, the telegrapher's assistance is sought to improvise competent agents or reporters to visit scenes of sudden public calamity, disturbance, or other excitement, at points beyond telegraphic lines, to gather the facts, carry them to the nearest station and forward by wire.

Until recently, the Associated Press has relied entirely upon the Western Union Telegraph Company for transmission of its messages to and from all points in the United States; but now it has leased from that company, for its own special use, a wire between New York, Philadelphia, Baltimore and Washington, and employs its own operators to work it directly between Associated Press offices in the several cities named. This proves exceedingly convenient, though it would not be economical except for the very large amount of telegraphic service, 18,000 to 20,000 words daily, required by the Associated Press over that particular circuit. At Cincinnati, Detroit, Chicago, St. Louis, Milwaukee, and Memphis, condensed abstracts, known as pony reports, are made from the full one and promptly forwarded to smaller towns or outlying places in the respective districts whose journals can not afford to share the cost of the longer one. The cost of the news, laid down where published, every charge paid, ranges from $15 to $250 per week to each journal with the exception of those in New York City who rarely find their bills as low as $300, while sometimes they run up to $1,500.[2]

Relations of the New York association with the auxiliary groups had not been without occasional differences, principally as to service, costs, protection against competition, and extent of exclusive territory. Every time contracts came up for renewal with the news-supplying association or with the news-transmitting companies, concessions of one sort or another were at issue. The Western Associated Press endeavored vainly, in 1876, to have its daily report increased

---

[2] *Ibid.*, p. 108.

from 8,700 words to 10,000 words, and its annual payment at the same time reduced from $100,000 to $80,000. It was argued that this would do away with the separation into eastern and western reports, as provided in the then existing agreement, which prevented taking advantage of a paucity of news in one section to omit words in that report and add to the aggregate number of words in the other class for the month.[3] Two years later, the plea to the telegraph company for an abatement of $10,000 a year was buttressed by a showing that the value of the dollar in currency had risen, since 1869, from 75.2 cents to 99.5 cents.[4] Again, the following year, the directors dwelt upon three points of their program: first, lowered telegraph tolls, in which a reduction estimated at $10,000 had been obtained; second, a reduction of the amount paid the New York Associated Press, wholly unsuccessful, in which "we were not exactly treated with contempt but it amounted to the same thing"; third, protection against other news associations.[5]

The clashes over territory sprang from the hazy demarcations in the original contracts. It was disclosed, in 1876, that papers in northern Texas were being supplied by the telegraph company with the report made up in St. Louis by the agent of the Western Associated Press for the Missouri and Kansas papers. When objection to this proceeding was lodged, on behalf of the New York association, a letter written by Simonton was turned up which imparted the information that he was preparing to compile a report at St. Louis to serve to Texas papers. The conflicting claims naturally produced a sharp cross-fire.[6]

---

[3] Western Associated Press Report, 1876, p. 7.

[4] *Ibid.*, 1878, p. 10.

[5] *Ibid.*, 1879, p. 8.

[6] *Ibid.*, 1876, p. 16.

Almost concurrently came another move in California, when Simonton sought to have a copy of the report delivered at Chicago for the San Francisco *Chronicle,* which had arranged, so he advised, to receive its news both at New York and Chicago, "precisely as it is furnished at those points to the agents of the California Associated Press." In his words, "the *Chronicle* has become one of the customers of the New York Associated Press." Further explanation indicated that the effort of the *Chronicle* to capture a franchise had led to this compromise to which Simonton, himself, being a member of the California Associated Press through his proprietorship in the San Francisco *Bulletin,* was a party. "I must in good faith support whatever policy the association has determined," he wrote. "The California association is confident of its own ability, with fair play, to win its fight against the *Chronicle.* I fear the *Chronicle* will make its failure (to get its report at Chicago) its pretence for quitting the Associated Press and thus the California association will lose the moral effect to result from a square victory in an open fight." [7] The *Chronicle* actually built up a line of customers of its own among the Pacific coast papers to which it resold its Associated Press report and carefully stipulated, when it later obtained membership in the Western association, that its clients should continue to receive a report.[8] It particularly roiled the Western Associated Press people that the New York organization not only claimed ownership in the news collected by them as soon as delivered, and the right to sell the same in eastern territory, but also now sold that news in western territory without so much as asking leave. But the matter was adjusted for the time being, and again, when in 1879 the

---

[7] *Ibid.,* pp. 19-21.

[8] Young, *Journalism in California,* p. 129.

Colorado Press Association registered vigorous protest on service by the New York Associated Press to a paper in Colorado, not a member of their organization which was operating as an auxiliary of the Western Associated Press.[9]

Under these conditions, periodic renewal of attacks on the Associated Press as an oppressive monopoly would naturally arise; indeed, their absence would have been surprising. The Western association took under serious consideration, ten years after its incorporation, the question of applying to Congress for a Federal charter, but decided it inadvisable to proceed.[10] It was doubtful whether Congress possessed authority to pass a valid act of the kind suggested, which was ample ground for concluding to let things stand, not to stress the real reason, "the strong probability that it would be loaded down with amendments permitting all outside newspapers, irrespective of 'age, sex, or previous condition of servitude,' to become members of our association on their own terms."

Congress continued, nevertheless, the forum for discussion of the monopolistic features of the news-gathering machinery and its interlocking with the Western Union Telegraph Company. The subject emerged again and again.[11] The arraignment presented to a Senate committee in the winter of 1879 by Gardiner G. Hubbard, in advocacy of the construction of competing telegraph lines by the railroads, embraced these six counts:

1. Under agreements, either now or heretofore existing with the Associated Press, the other news associations are not allowed to use the wires of other companies than the Western Union.

---

[9] Western Associated Press Report, 1879, p. 18.

[10] *Ibid.*, 1876, p. 7.

[11] Forty-first Cong., 2nd Sess., House Report 114; Forty-second Cong., 3rd Sess., House Report 6; Forty-second Cong., 3rd Sess., Senate Report 242; Forty-fifth Cong., 3rd Sess., Senate Report 805.

2. By their contracts, on account of the low rates given them by the Western Union, they pledge themselves to oppose the opposition companies.

3. The New York *Evening Post* was not allowed to use special dispatches sent by its own correspondent about a disturbance in New Jersey until furnished also to the other papers connected with the Associated Press in New York City.

4. News at times is furnished by parties in New York to the agent of the Associated Press there and, instead of being distributed from New York where it originates, is forwarded to Washington and distributed from Washington all over the country, thus leaving parties to understand it emanates from Washington and not in New York.

5. The New York Associated Press has established a censorship over the papers of the country. It cut off a paper in Petersburg and subsequently threatened to cut off one at Savannah, "because it criticized the reports of the Associated Press."

6. The New York Associated Press, whether joint stock company or private co-partnership, is engaged in public business and, therefore, amenable to the laws governing corporations transacting public business.[12]

Besides voicing the contrary viewpoint of the press association, Simonton's testimony in rejoinder adds a touch of brashness:

The Associated Press is a private business, carried on under the same moral, legal and constitutional rights which permit any one paper, in a country village or in a metropolis, to collect and publish its local news. The charge of monopoly rests upon the single fact that here and there some newspapers, which did not share in the labor or risk of establishing the Associated Press, are not permitted to come in and share its facilities, now that the day of experiment and risk has passed. As well might they demand to force their way into a share of the already created business of any bank or dry goods house, or other mercantile establishment, which, like the Associated Press, had spent thirty-five years in perfecting its plans, securing its customers and their confidence, and creating its opportunities for doing business with profit. The profit of the

[12] Forty-fifth Cong., 3rd Sess., Senate Report 805, p. 37.

bank or mercantile business is in cash dividends; the profits of the Associated Press are in the use of the news which it collects, as the profits of the fisherman are in the fish which he captures and takes from the rivers and the sea, just as we take that in which we deal from the great ocean of human events.

Relations with the Western Union, Simonton asseverated, were simply those of carrier and customer. No pledge was involved to antagonize opposition to that company, and no privileges enjoyed not open to any and all parties desiring to do a similar business. He disclaimed knowledge of the mutual defense clauses of the Western Union contract with the Western Associated Press. Some concessions in rates, to be sure, were granted in return for conditions agreed on, such as to do a large business instead of a petty one, to do it all over the Western Union wires, and to accept a portion of it during those hours when the better-paying commercial messages did not crowd. The Associated Press and the telegraph company had united in arrangements whereby news reports could be delivered to many newspapers at very low rates in sections in which the population was sparse and the local papers struggled for existence. This was true of a large portion of the interior places, especially in the South, from which the Associated Press accepted much less than their fair proportion of the cost of the common service, and the Western Union made corresponding concessions. "By this means, and through our system of sending reports simultaneously to numerous places at a single wiring, we are able to supply many with daily reports at a total of from $10 to $15 a week each. Under this flexible system, the strong papers carry the heavy end of the load and, to the weak, the burden is made exceedingly light. The Press and the telegraph company both agree to give lower rates to the poor and recoup by higher compensation from the well-to-do." Such broad-minded policy could not be pursued by the government, should it operate the telegraph, because the government must treat all alike.

What warrant for suspecting monopoly when, with a few exceptions, the determination of who shall share the report was vested in the local associations? In New Orleans, for example, the local association was controlling all such questions for that area and, "despite our earnest efforts," keeping out one paper there "because its proprietor attempted to bribe its way covertly." Presumably, it should have paid up openly. Only two other southern cities had the right to restrict admission—Atlanta, where a newspaper must give security to take the reports for a reasonable time and pay a bonus of $2,500 to the paper then carrying the whole burden for that city since a previous publication dropped out; and Savannah, where a similar bonus requirement prevailed. In Massachusetts, embraced in the New England Associated Press, only the Boston *Globe* was being excluded. Any paper in New York State might join the State association on fixed terms, incidentally contributing a prescribed admission fee. The California association was governed under its own rules by its own members, bought news from the Associated Press at New York, provided for telegraphic transmission to the coast. The Western Associated Press exacted a bonus, of which a portion went to the local member, if there were such already in the same town.

As to the alleged censorship over the press, complaints referred merely to instances of disciplining for offenses against the rules and by-laws. The Washington *Post* had been dropped for permitting an employee to send dispatches to a subscriber to another news association. Yes, a criticism in a Petersburg paper had incurred the penalty of stopping the report. "I submit," contended Simonton, "that there is not a gentleman here who would sell dry goods, groceries, or anything else, day after day, to a man who told him every time he came in, 'You are a thief, a swindler and a liar.' You would very soon say, 'If you can't come in and behave yourself, I do not want your trade and you can go out.' This is the sort of censorship we exercise. When papers insist that they have grievances against us and give us an opportunity for explanation, they very often learn that they have been in error. But when papers will persist in abusing us for alleged grievances in advance of inquiry, we simply say to them, 'We do not want to serve you. If we can not be treated like decent men, you had better get your news-service elsewhere.' "

The ultimatum to the Petersburg paper had been reissued by Simonton as a circular in warning to members generally; it concluded: "While published assault is prohibited to those who desire our services, we earnestly invite private complaints and pledge ourselves to give them prompt and exhaustive attention." When an editorial paragraph in an inconsequential Savannah sheet had commented unfavorably on the report, intimation from headquarters quickly followed, as testified to, "that if any further remarks were made, we would be immediately stricken from the list of subscribers and no dispatches sent to us," and the owner was so frightened by the notice that the writer of the tabooed item found himself out of a job. A sudden cut-off of news supplies had been depicted by Simonton as "our readiest defense." Summarized by its general agent, the attitude of the Associated Press was presented in four propositions:

1. The Associated Press is not a monopoly. 2. It is a private business. 3. It is independent of the Western Union Telegraph Company. 4. It has no franchise from the government and no legislation within the power of Congress can take from it the tools of its creation.

The vigor with which Simonton battled for the Associated Press against enemies within and without was disproportionate to his bodily strength. The exacting demands of his key position undermined his health and hastened his retirement. His withdrawal, thought at first to be only temporary, from active direction of the machinery, which was carried along in the interim by Erastus Brooks and James C. Huston, proved to be permanent. The occurrence, however, was coincident with two significant events, the projection of the United Press into the arena, and the assertion by the Western Associated Press of full partnership rights. These shifts in the situation made the enforced change in management and methods opportune and were to mark another important turning point in the course of systematic news-gathering.

The western papers, never fully reconciled to even nominal servitude to New York, were showing new signs of restlessness. Their organization had not bettered its relative position materially in the fifteen years since the test of strength in 1866 when, as they believed, resort to stratagem alone had prevented them from attaining their objectives. "Is it not time," they were asking themselves, "to take the field again and either win the recognition we are entitled to or cut loose and arrange our own news service?" Some, doubtless, visioned other possibilities, some preferred readjustment, some would rather have independent action. The Associated Press offices in New York for the moment were in charge of substitutes or subordinates. Unaccustomed and emboldened competition was looming up. Differences between the New York Associated Press and the Western Union were causing friction between them. The opening was not to be ignored. As a preliminary move, resolutions were adopted at the annual meeting of the Western association to give the technically required notice for the termination of the contract with the New York Associated Press, to prepare to set up separate news-gathering and distributing agencies, and, glaringly inconsistent, to make "no new contract" that did not concede the long demanded territorial extensions southward and westward.[13] This was followed by a declaration of purpose to supply news to papers in Colorado, Dakota, California, Texas, and Louisiana. By way of strengthening the lines, it was also resolved to invite a representative of each of the Press Associations tributary to the Western Associated Press to attend the annual meetings, reserving the right to hold executive sessions whenever the exigencies of the case demanded. The outcome was to depend upon the measure of success crowning the efforts of the executive committee. An explanation of the rupture of 1882, written by William Henry Smith, who figured prominently in it, reads as follows:

The Western Associated Press had now reached the limit of its growth unless it could make a new and better arrangement with the New York Associated Press. Opportunity offered in 1882, when a quarrel arose between the association and the Western Union, which was promptly embraced by our board. In May of that year, I was invited by the managers of the Western Union to take charge of a large news service designed to supplant that of the New York Associated Press to all of its clients. There was no doubt this invitation involved two things: First, the breaking up of the New York Associated Press, and, second, great personal advantage to me. I felt the true interests of the American press required union between the associations and, upon placing before Mr. Richard Smith and Mr. Haldeman the proposition of the telegraph company, I declared my intention to waive all personal advantage involved in it. Thereupon, I received instructions to go to New York and work out the problem. To advance the power and influence of the Western Associated Press, while effecting a reconciliation between the tele-

[13] Western Associated Press Report, 1882, p. 3.

graph company and the New York Associated Press was the aim. A five months campaign saw alliances made in Texas, Colorado and California and in New England; preparations for an independent Washington and a new cable service; and a compact with a majority of the New York members with the help of the telegraph company, out of which union, peace and prosperity were to come.[14]

But the break was not permitted to reach a stage of open hostilities; in fact, the severing of joint service was wholly superficial. Committees of the two associations took up the task of perfecting a more satisfactory working agreement and were by no means guided by a single hand in the negotiations. Calling representatives of the Western Union also into the conference, the various suggested solutions were subjected to many-sided scrutiny. All plainly saw that some form of combined management held the only way out.[15]

One proposal would set up a joint board of control of seven members of each association "with entire charge of the business of collecting, transmitting and selling news for the two associations and to make any contracts desirable for the conduct of the business for this period which shall be binding upon both associations." Charles A. Dana wanted to substitute a pooling arrangement on the basis of existing receipts and expenditures, administered by an executive committee of two from each association and a chairman chosen by the New York association. At a subsequent session, the western spokesman expressed willingness to accept either a division of territory, or a pooling arrangement, the status quo to continue, pending agreement on details. Another plan would constitute the prospective joint executive committee of three members from the New York Associated Press, two from the Western Associated Press, two from the New Eng-

---

14 *Ibid.*, 1891, p. 27.

15 Memorandum of Joint Executive Committee Contract, 1882.

land Associated Press, one from the New York State Associated Press, and one from the Baltimore and Philadelphia associations, the arrangement running from year to year. Finally out of the labors of a special committee headed by Erastus Brooks, a five-year contract was evolved and approved for union under one joint committee, made up of two members from the New York Associated Press, two from the Western Associated Press, and a chairman chosen by the former, with a general manager to be commissioned by this committee as the active executive. The several reasons for adopting the plan were enumerated by Brooks:

> To avoid conflict. To maintain the New York Associated Press in its existing arrangements with other clients. Non-interference with our territory, excepting Colorado and California relinquished to the Western Associated Press. No pecuniary sacrifice is involved. No admission of new partners is called for. Maintenance of existing contracts.

The New York Associated Press designated the *Sun,* the *Herald,* and the *Tribune* for its representation on the Joint Executive Committee, which invested Dana with the chairmanship. The Western Associated Press named Walter N. Haldeman, of the Louisville *Courier-Journal,* and Richard Smith, of the Cincinnati *Gazette,* and the announcement was made of the appointment of William Henry Smith as general manager, a promotion from the position of general manager of the Western Associated Press rendered easier by the vacancy left by Simonton. The business relationships between the two associations, with reference to exchange of news, payments toward the cost of European news, Washington service, exclusive control in respective territory, etc., were to be substantially unchanged.

Again the confederated associations faced an era of livelier activity, the auxiliary associations accepted their alignment as tributary organizations, the telegraph company resumed harmonious coöperation, even the opposition press served by the rival news agency seemed less resentful of their exclusion. This rival, the United Press, after re-forming its administrative set-up, had replaced Schoonmaker in the position of chief responsibility, with Walter Polk Phillips, and was laying the foundation for a news service ignoring geographic divisions. It was to be dominated soon, if not already, by three men of force and ambition, a triumvirate of Phillips, Laffan, and Walsh, personalities rising in the horoscope of journalism. Of the three, William M. Laffan was the business manager of the New York *Sun,* having had his first connection with the paper as its dramatic critic, and enjoying the full confidence and support of Charles A. Dana, its distinguished editor, while John R. Walsh was the principal proprietor of the Chicago *Herald,* in conjunction with James W. Scott, not to mention his holdings in numerous financial and business enterprises.

Phillips, till now, had played rather inconspicuous parts. When a mere lad, at the age of fifteen, while the guns fired at Sumter still rang in his ears, he had secured employment as a messenger for the American Telegraph Company at its office in Providence. He was born in 1846 in the near-by village of Grafton, Massachusetts.[16] Permitted to practice on the clicking instruments, he was pronounced an expert operator before a year had passed. As winner of a speed contest in receiving messages by sound, he once received a testimonial gold pencil from Professor Morse. From time to time afterwards, he utilized his skill as a telegrapher to perfect means of repeating by sound. He was the author of the "Phillips Telegraphic Code," a list of code words for

---

[16] Reid, *op. cit.,* p. 802.

the rapid transmission of press reports and other messages. He also devised a complete system of punctuation by which every symbol known to typographical art could be readily sent over the wire and delivered in better condition than the ordinary edited copy.

Attracted to journalism, Phillips, in 1867, began to devote his nights to reporting for the Providence *Journal*. In 1868, he became, first, city editor, and then managing editor, of the Providence *Herald*. In 1871, he was a reporter on the staff of the New York *Sun* and, before long, went into the office of the Associated Press under Simonton. His aptitude, here displayed, caused his transfer to Washington, where he directed the work of the Associated Press during the administration of President Hayes. Upon his return to New York, the organization of the United Press, in which he participated, sent him back for a brief service as Washington agent of that association, whence he was soon called to be business manager of the home office and then to the management of its affairs generally. Phillips brought his indefatigable energy and resourcefulness at once to the development of a scheme of leased wire distribution. He worked this out with the Mutual Union Telegraph Company and, when its wires succumbed to the Western Union, he let the contract lapse and transferred the business to various opposition companies. In due time, the patronage of the United Press was sought by all the telegraph companies. By 1885, three wires, radiating from the New York headquarters, were dropping his report simultaneously to seventy cities and towns; the average number of words transmitted daily was 17,500. Instead of uniform assessments, the charges were carefully rated according to the capacity to pay; the returns were well in excess of the annual expenditures of $250,000, and, even more to the point, substantial amounts were collected as the condition precedent to a service.

Phillips' previous connection with the Associated Press had taught him that its foreign news had always been its best card. He undertook to match its cable messages. Schoonmaker, his predecessor, was given charge of a separately constituted "Cable News Company," with an alliance with the Central News of London, and essayed to supply members and clients of the Associated Press as well as of the United Press. This was in 1883. The Chicago *Tribune,* peremptorily notified that it was violating the rules by taking the Cable News Company's service, "which is only an annex of the United Press," and that continuance invited stoppage of the news reports, protested strenuously. Short and ugly words passed on both sides. Schoonmaker categorically denied the charge and insisted that his was a distinct organization and that he was providing two foreign news services, that going to Associated Press papers being entirely different from the one going to United Press papers. The Western Associated Press directors resolved against this contention and all Associated Press papers dropped the Cable News Company's service. Within a few months, so it was later asserted, the very same cable report was obtained for the Associated Press, in whose service it constituted for years an important part, while Schoonmaker went upon the Associated Press payroll at a handsome salary.[17] Such, in those days, were the sudden turns and counterturns, shall we say, the tricks of the trade. Afterwards, Phillips exploited these side lines through other subsidiary concerns under various names, such as the International Telegram Company, the Telegram News Company, the Pan-American News Association.

---

[17] Correspondence in Relation to the Cable News Company.

And who was the new chief factotum of the Associated Press? For over twelve years, William Henry Smith had been the general agent of the Western Associated Press and, in that capacity, had acquired a familiarity with the business transacted. Born of colonial stock in up-state New York in 1833, he had been raised in Ohio, where his parents located in 1836.[18] His education looked to the law, but he manifested a literary bent. He began with a weekly paper at Cincinnati and, at the outbreak of the Civil War, was on the editorial force of the Cincinnati *Gazette*. In 1863, he was made private secretary to Governor Brough. The following year, he was chosen Secretary of State in the same election that seated Rutherford B. Hayes in the governor's chair. His close association with Hayes led political opponents to caricature him as the governor's conscience-keeper.[19] Smith was reëlected, but resigned to resume journalistic work in Cincinnati. A physical breakdown drove him to a rest, lasting to 1869, when he went to Chicago to open offices there for the Western Associated Press. From his own pen, we have a glimpse of his initiation:

> When I took charge, the headquarters, which were removed from Cleveland to Chicago at the instance of the telegraph company, comprised a desk in the third story of the *Tribune* building. There was neither clerk nor book-keeper, messenger nor devil of any kind. When the general agent locked the door and put the key in his pocket, the headquarters were closed until he appeared on the scene again.

A menacing accumulation of debt had awaited his assumption of his duties. By constant economy and sagacity in widening the field of operations, the burden was shortly rolled off and a balance began to appear on the other side.

---

[18] Reid, *op. cit.*, p. 797.

[19] Adams, "The Two Smiths," pamphlet, 1880, p. 6.

When President Hayes came into power in the White House, he conferred on Smith the sinecure collectorship of the Port of Chicago, whose stipend he drew in addition to his $5,000 salary as agent of the association. Needless to say, the dual job again made him the target for political sharp-shooters. He lost the appointive position after the death of President Garfield. Inherently a student, he was the author of several scholarly volumes of American history and biography, published at intervals during all this time, and he left unfinished, when he died, the work he was engaged on as the literary executor of President Hayes, to which he devoted his closing years.[20]

In the exercise of his wider powers, now, Smith applied himself to a firmer integration of the associations and to betterment of the news-collection and distribution. The account of old-world happenings, coming through the exclusive exchange contracts with the Reuter Company, which included the Wolff and Havas bureaus, its German and French allies, remained the mainstay of the foreign service. The London and Liverpool offices were put in the charge of experienced journalists instructed to cover European events more thoroughly. Reuter strengthened his representation in Asia and Eastern Europe, bringing those remote lands into closer touch. With the extension of the lines of the Mexican Central and South American Telegraph and Cable Company to Chile and Brazil, the Associated Press service also followed, and its news from South America was as fresh as that from Europe. The Associated Press Washington staff was enlarged with good effect on the report out of the national capital. These features of the service could not be matched or replaced within the resources of any rival news association or the enterprise of any single newspaper. They made

[20] Reid, Introduction, in Smith, *Political History of Slavery*, p. xii.

the Associated Press service, in whole or in part, almost indispensable to the journal having any pretensions as a newspaper.[21]

About 1884, the typewriter was introduced and employed for receiving the report. The operator, to universal wonderment, took the message directly from the sounder without confusing the tapping of the two machines; he was able, after sufficient practice, to write from 40 to 50 words a minute, and with code, up to 60 to 70 words a minute. Thus, clean printed copy was produced, and a full set of carbons at the same time.

Authority to lease a wire, or wires, of the Western Union or the Baltimore and Ohio Telegraph Company, voted on motion of Melville E. Stone at the 1884 meeting of the Western Associated Press, marked the introduction of the leased wire system in the western territory.[22] It is barely possible that the credit for this stroke of enterprise should be divided. According to Colonel Charles S. Diehl, at the time news editor in the Chicago office and subsequently in higher executive positions, it was he who made the initial suggestion to set up an exclusive wire between Chicago and New York, and Smith, at first, was unresponsive, saying that the telegraph company would not consent to let the press association have a wire, because "the theory was held by the telegraph people that such an innovation would cause the large daily newspapers to stop sending special telegrams." The records show, however, that the leased wire had already been employed by the New York Associated Press between New York and Washington for five years, and also by the United Press in the East, so that it could not be hailed rightly as an innovation except by its intro-

---

[21] Reid, *op. cit.*, p. 796.
[22] Western Associated Press Report, 1884.

duction to a new area.[23] Regardless of these considerations, the move to obtain a wire ran against no serious obstacles and turned out to be the forerunner of the system of leased wires carrying the reports over the length and breadth of the land. What had been going out as a skeleton report of the markets and general news, narrow in scope and incomplete, was thereby steadily broadened and enlarged and speeded up, was redistributed from various radial centers to permit of selection better suiting the demands of the particular papers served, in some cases, notably the Pacific Coast, of an extra report obtained through a special news-collection bureau supported by an additional assessment covering the tolls.

The amplified facilities permitted a deviation from the stereotyped handling of routine news to which the reports had been confined. Between mechanical market quotations and dull congressional proceedings, a real "story," displaying initiative and individuality, sometimes came forth. It was an Associated Press dispatch that, despite all avowed neutrality-in-politics policies, spread the startling "Rum, Romanism, and Rebellion" speech of the Reverend Dr. Burchard on the eve of the balloting, and overwhelmed Blaine and elected Cleveland. To the same reporter was credited a beat on the death of General Grant at Mount McGregor a year afterwards. The old play of flag signals, which antedated the telegraph, was resurrected; by prearrangement, one of the attending physicians promenaded the porch, slowly drew a handkerchief from his pocket, and wiped his hands; the reporter deciphered a death message, wired it to the main office, scored a great scoop. In 1885, a devastating tropical hurricane afflicted the Samoan Islands, isolated in mid-Pacific. An Associated Press man by accident happened to

[23] Diehl, letter dated April 9, 1928.

be in Apia; three American war ships, a British cruiser, and a number of German craft rode at anchor in the harbor; all the American and German vessels were shattered on the coral reefs at a cost of 150 lives; the British boat alone escaped serious injury. A graphic account, mailed to San Francisco, a month later riveted attention of readers of Associated Press papers. Alas for John P. Dunning, the journalistic hero of Apia, that subsequent clouds should have dimmed a well earned literary fame! [24] For the most part, however, the report was made up of news gathered in first instance by the local staffs of the member papers.

Before the end of the Smith era, this exhibit of progress for the period could be made: [25]

> The leased wire system now [1891] covers New England, the State of New York, the Atlantic seaboard as far as Norfolk, to the South West as far as New Orleans, West as far as Denver, and North West to St. Paul and Minneapolis and a recent extension to Omaha and Grand Rapids. Two wires extend from New York to Washington and from New York to twelve of the principal Western cities. Neatly printed copy is now supplied directly from Morse instruments by means of type-writers manipulated at the rate of 40 words per minute, a revolution in the method of handling the report.
>
> The report shows increase in quantity of domestic and foreign news, greater rapidity in handling, and a notable improvement in character. In addition to the services of foreign agencies, representatives have been placed recently at Paris, Rome and Berlin, and it is in contemplation to have others at St. Petersburg, Copenhagen and Stockholm.
>
> Some 62 contracts have been made with the Western Union, with co-operating associations, and with individual clients.
>
> Of the total annual revenue of the New York Associated Press and the Western Associated Press aggregating $1,170,204, members pay only $359,566 and clients pay $810,638.

---

[24] Stone, *Fifty Years a Journalist*, p. 211.

[25] Western Associated Press Report, 1891, p. 20.

The just apportionment of expenses among the beneficiary papers was a problem changing as conditions changed. While deficits were the rule, occasional special levies by percentage of regular dues answered the purpose, but, when mounting current income or increasing admission fees produced a surplus, it became necessary to redistribute in some way. For the New York Associated Press, a sevenfold partnership, the situation resolved itself with ease. For the Western Associated Press, consisting of corporate members supposedly enjoying equal participating rights, and clients who were served merely as customers, other considerations had to be taken into account. Just what was done to meet the "equities," came out in an answer by Smith to specific complaints of unfair treatment in the allotment of surplus collections:

The Joint Executive Committee considered it important that the impression should not get abroad that the Western Associated Press were paying dividends to their members and, therefore, their action was to direct the refunding of money beyond what was required to carry on the business.

It was very difficult to determine how this should be done so as to meet the equities of the case. I use the word equity because it is certain that it was upon that ground, and not upon the legal claims of the members, that the committee acted.

The New York members received on the basis of their direct payments. Thus the *Mail and Express* paid into the treasury $200 a week and each of the morning papers $300 a week, and they received in return at the same pro rata respectively.

In the West, it was much more complicated because the membership was of different dates and the organization was of unequal growth and the widely different services rendered made it impossible to determine in all cases what, if anything, was really in excess of cost. Indeed, in some cases, the cost of delivering a report was in excess of receipts. The Committee did not expect to be able to decide correctly in every case, although they conscientiously attempted to be just and equitable. The refunds in the West to most of the members were made on the same principle as in the case of the New York members; in a few other cases, where there was no balance on the side of receipts, or where it was uncertain, or where there was really a deficit, the Committee directed arbitrary amounts to be sent, if there was money to warrant it. This will explain the yearly differences in this class of cases.

The total amount refunded to Western members up to the close of the year 1891, was $331,876.22.[26]

Despite a dissent, now and then, the Joint Executive Committee plan apparently gave measurable satisfaction for nearly ten years. The fact that the personnel of the committee stood practically unchanged, testified approval of the service supplied and of the general management of affairs. Charles A. Dana, of the *Sun,* filled uninterruptedly the position of chairman, with Whitelaw Reid, of the *Tribune,* and either Bennett, of the *Herald,* or Brooks, of the *Mail and Express,* acting for the New York Associated Press; and Richard Smith, of the Cincinnati *Gazette,* and W. N. Haldeman, of the Louisville *Courier-Journal,* for the Western Associated Press. The five, aided by William Henry Smith as general manager, held the master key to the Associated Press edifice.

The five-year contract, entered into in 1882, was to terminate in 1887. More than six months before its expiration, it was renewed, without a word of discussion, for another five years. The excuse for early action, as imparted to the western membership, was a desire to avoid possible complications growing out of threatened trouble with the telegraph company.[27] In reporting the renewal to the New York Associated Press, President Stone declared that "the new arrangement had worked much better than had been anticipated."[28] This was all that appeared on the surface.

[26] *Ibid.,* 1892, p. 81.
[27] *Ibid.,* 1887.
[28] New York Associated Press *Minutes,* June 4, 1887.

American journalism was now supporting two full-fledged news-gathering associations, the Associated Press and the United Press, duplicating each other's activities, to a large extent paralleling each other's territory. The Associated Press papers held the more fortified position but had to defend themselves constantly against invaders. They were eager, naturally, to keep to themselves all the benefits, and reluctant to share with competitors. As a consequence, each new publication, coveting a telegraphic report for a city or town in which an established journal was being issued, had either to make terms with the Associated Press member, or negotiate a contract with the United Press. In the way of drumming up new customers, the United Press was hampered by fewer entanglements and made more noticeable advance, enrolling many papers shut out by the Associated Press. The availability of the United Press news service was, moreover, a constant stimulus to the projection of papers in competitive territory; it was even charged that United Press influences procured the launching of new journals to add to that organization's patronage, or to fill in gaps in its circuits. The inevitable next step was to contract to existing Associated Press papers the control of the United Press service for their respective territories as immunity from competition. The United Press thus collected revenue from Associated Press subscribers for not furnishing its service to any one in the same locality. In such operations, the line between the straight and the devious path is likely to become extremely hazy; nor should the United Press be posted as the sole offender, for it was not altogether a newly invented practice. The Associated Press and affiliated associations could themselves furnish examples of arbitrary exactions for supplying reports to papers unable to deal elsewhere, although bona fide and uninterrupted publication was invariably a condition of continued membership, and no contracts in evidence indicate payments for merely suppressing service to a rival.

There is testimony, for example, that when Mr. Dana decided to start a daily paper in New York, he had been compelled to pay for the franchise a bonus of between $100,000 and $150,000; that the Chicago *Inter-Ocean* had paid the *Republican* $25,000; that the *Globe*, in St. Louis, obtained the rights of the *Staats-zeitung* for $47,500, only to buy a law suit, pending which it took over the *Democrat;* that, in Cincinnati, the *Chronicle* had paid $6,000 for a franchise which soon lapsed with its demise.[29] Delving into the past? Yes, but in 1884, Joseph Medill estimated a morning paper service to the Chicago *Daily News* to be worth $50,000, and accepted $10,000 in payment for the one-fifth-share consent on the part of the *Tribune;* William Penn Nixon, at the same time, was talked into acquiescing for the *Inter-Ocean* without any money consideration and, after learning how the *Tribune* was won over, complained of having been misled into the belief that all five waivers were to be made on the same basis, and that his stockholders had been unfairly deprived of their due. But his appeal produced no result beyond a report from the association's attorney that the contract for service to the *News* had been legally executed and was not subject to reopening. The Los Angeles *Times* paid the Western Associated Press $6,000 for a perpetual franchise, and the Sacremento *Bee* paid $4,000. In 1892, $1,000 was demanded for starting service to a paper in Devil's Lake, North Dakota; $5,000 was exacted from the Duluth *Evening Herald;* a bonus of $20,000 was asked for a service to Tacoma, Washington, or $25,000 for a full

29 Hearings on Competing Telegraph Lines, Forty-fifth Cong., 3rd Sess., Sen. Doc. 805, pp. 77-91.

membership.[30] These bargainings often provided for deferred, or serial, payments. Between 1883 and 1893, the aggregate amount of such bonuses for Western Associated Press franchises totaled $118,410, of which $85,294 had been collected.[31]

Competition was emphatically the life of trade in the realm of journalism. Here, more than elsewhere, unrestrained rivalry, however calculated to sharpen wits and energize zeal, must prove costly to all concerned. But how keep up a show of uncompromising opposition and at the same time escape excessive outlay of money and effort to beat one another? Whether a state of nonaggression is deliberately concocted by previous combatants, or is a situation attained by a sort of mutual gravitation, is not always readily determined. In this instance, a relationship of amity and intimacy evidently soon developed, though long effectually concealed. In time, the true inwardness of affairs was bound to come to light. With the conclusion of the second five-year period of the Joint Committee arrangement drawing near, growing rumor and gossip, and intermittent rumblings, presaged trouble. Members of the Western Associated Press, made suspicious by discovering that news supplied by them to their association was brought back to their competitors in the reports of the United Press, or resentful of the dubious methods of disposing of franchises, against which they had believed themselves to be protected, began to talk out loud. Before long, then, the mystery was unraveled and the amazing story heralded in the open.

What started inquiry upon the right track was the adoption by the Western Associated Press, at its 1890 annual meeting, of this resolution, offered by E. W. Coleman, of the

---

[30] Western Associated Press Reports.

[31] Cornyn, "Press Associations," *Encyclopedia Americana*, XXII, 556.

Herold, a German language newspaper published in Milwaukee:

> That the Board of Directors shall report at a special meeting of the Western Associated Press, within 90 days, the relations now existing between the Western Associated Press and the United Press and what, in their opinion, will be the ultimate outcome of these and similar arrangements to be entered into in the future by the two associations.
>
> Also how newspapers belonging to the Western Associated Press shall be protected from those receiving the reports of both associations in view of the fact that the United Press receives the report of the Western Associated Press and gives nothing in return.

Narrated in successive reports of special committees, what had taken place was unfolded in several chapters. As the United Press had gained ground, despite an uphill climb, its commercial possibilities had loomed larger and larger. It became clear, moreover, to those in charge, that the revenues could be immensely expanded, and the expenditures greatly curtailed, by harmonious relations with the Associated Press. The idea was "sold," to use a modern phrase, to the members of the Joint Executive Committee administering the machinery of the Associated Press, and a policy of reciprocity inaugurated. The effective part of the understanding consisted in an exchange of news between the two ostensibly "opposing" associations. Competition, henceforth, was to be limited to enlarging the number of members and clients and, inferentially, getting out of them all the traffic would reasonably bear. At first but a working plan, legal form and binding obligation were added by execution of a trust agreement, dated October 1, 1885, over the signatures of Walter P. Phillips and others, as controlling stockholders of the United Press, and John R. Walsh, of the Chicago *Herald,* as "trustee."

By this instrument, 480 shares of the stock of the United Press of New York, out of the 800 representing its total capitalization, were pooled in the name of John R. Walsh, of Chicago, as trustee. The parties to the agreement were Walter P. Phillips, of New York, Robert S. Davis, of Philadelphia, Charles R. Baldwin, of Waterbury, Connecticut, James W. Scott, of Chicago, and John R. Walsh, of Chicago, all members of the United Press; and the trustee was to deliver to each, "or such person or persons as they may direct," certificates representing the deposited stock. Certificates for half of these pooled shares were bought and paid for at par by Charles A. Dana, Whitelaw Reid, Richard Smith, and W. N. Haldeman, members of the Joint Executive Committee. In the delivery, one-third of the shares bought by Smith and Haldeman were issued at their request to William Henry Smith, General Manager of the Associated Press. The remaining half continued in the ownership of the original proprietors of the United Press. "Shortly thereafter, a 100-per cent dividend was declared and paid to these individuals on this stock." [32]

The harvest must have exceeded all calculation, not only for the United Press, but especially for the Associated Press, participants. In fact, too big a business was being done for the small capitalization which stood as a stumblingblock to large-scale operations. The lawyers thereupon proceeded to draw up articles for a new United Press to be chartered under the laws of Illinois, where application was filed and granted August 16, 1887. The powers of the corporation were greatly enlarged. Its purpose was now "to buy, gather and accumulate information and news; to vend, supply, distribute and publish the same; to purchase, erect, lease, oper-

[32] Western Associated Press Report of Special Committee of Conference, 1890.

ate and sell telephone and telegraph lines and other means of transmitting news; to publish periodicals; to make and deal in periodicals and other goods, wares and merchandise; to acquire, hold and deal in securities and shares of other corporations." The Board of Directors was to comprise, at first five, then seven, still later, eleven, members. The president was John R. Walsh, and the secretary, Azel F. Hatch.

A second trust agreement followed, of date September 29, 1887, bearing the names only of Walter P. Phillips and John R. Walsh. The stock involved was now 6,000 shares, amounting to $600,000, out of 10,000 shares representing the capitalization of $1,000,000 of the United Press of Illinois. The beneficiary stipulations were substantially the same as before. The new corporation entered into a contract with the United Press of New York, by which the stock of the latter received the guaranty of a 6 per cent annual dividend, and the work of collecting and distributing tne news was undertaken for it by the United Press of Illinois. The new United Press then bought at par the pooled 480 shares of the old United Press and interned them in its treasury. By this purchase, it was pointed out, the holders of the original pooled stock were paid back their entire investment a second time. The United Press of Illinois next issued to the members of the pool, without further consideration, its own stock in the proportion of fifty shares to one, so that, of the 6,000 pooled shares, the members of the Joint Executive Committee, together with the general manager and the business manager of the *Sun*, received one-half, of par value of $300,000. The report listed the holdings as follows: Charles A. Dana, $72,500; Whitelaw Reid, in the name of Henry W. Sackett, $72,500; W. N. Haldeman, $50,000; Richard Smith, in the name of

J. D. Hearne, \$50,000; William Henry Smith, \$50,000; William M. Laffan, \$72,500; total, \$367,500. All these shares, it was disclosed, were held individually and not as trustees for the Associated Press. Regular quarterly dividends of one per cent had been paid since January, 1889, eleven dividends in all, and each of the Western Associated Press holders had therefore received altogether \$6,500. The late H. H. Byram, of the Pittsburgh *Chronicle-Telegraph*, member of the Western Associated Press and of the United Press, had been also a stockholder to the amount of \$17,500. The trust agreement was to run to September 19, 1898.

While this complicated scheme was being developed, and in anticipation of it, a so-called tripartite agreement for reciprocity had been negotiated between the New York Associated Press, the United Press, and the New England Associated Press. And now followed a more specific, but still secret, triple alliance between the New York Associated Press, the United Press, and the Western Associated Press. Formally signed at Cincinnati, May 28, 1888, the contract avowed its purpose "to harmonize conflicting interests and end a useless and expensive competition between the United Press and the Associated Press and to improve the services of each for the common benefit of American newspapers," and made clear and specific the working arrangements between the New York Associated Press and the Western Associated Press, on the one side, and the United Press, on the other. The main items mutually agreed to were:

1. That both parties shall have representation in a corporation, organized August 16, 1887, known as the United Press of Illinois, each party preserving the same relations in the control as in the United Press of New York, the number of directors to be seven and selected by the owners of the stock placed in trust.

2. That the Associated Press continue to supply the United Press with the news of New England, as provided in the tripartite agreement with the New England Associated Press executed May 1, 1887; Congressional reports, and reports of legislative proceedings at Albany, as heretofore, and with cable news as at present.

3. That the United Press will not furnish any clients, now, or recently, receiving the news of the Associated Press, with a substitute service, unless at a higher rate, and not without the consent of the Associated Press.

4. That the United Press will not render service to new newspapers in cities or towns where the Associated Press has franchise members or clients for a less sum than is charged for a corresponding service by the Associated Press without consent of the Joint Executive Committee.

5. That the United Press, on request of the Joint Executive Committee, will furnish any news that it uses out of the reports received from the Associated Press to such members or clients of the Associated Press as may be designated simultaneously with its own members or clients in the same cities or towns, free of charge.

6. That the United Press will collect news from points on leased wires not covered by the Associated Press and deliver same at either New York or Chicago for use of the Associated Press.

7. That where the United Press has sold, leased or granted to a paper, or papers, of the Associated Press, the control of its news reports, or has agreed with the Joint Executive Committee to refrain from entering any section of the country in competition with the Associated Press, the Associated Press shall supply the United Press with its news originating in such city, or section, laid down at New York or Chicago.

8. That other exchanges of news shall be made as agreed on from time to time.

9. That in cases of disagreement, H. H. Byram, of Pittsburgh, be referee and his decision final.

10. That the arrangement be effective the first Monday in June and continue during the life of the trust agreement.

The special committee which first gave definite information of this contract, judging by its report, saw extenuating circumstances for it.[33] It dwelt on the inducing causes, the

[33] Western Associated Press Report, Special Meeting, 1890.

conflicting interests, the competition to be harmonized. At that time, it recalled, on consolidation of the *Chronicle* and the *Telegraph* in Pittsburgh, that the combined paper had been permitted to keep both news services, "the by-law being waived by general consent"; in the East, the New England association was negotiating with the United Press and, to meet the emergency, the tripartite agreement had been put through; in New York, the *Sun*, an Associated Press paper, began to issue the *Evening Sun*, March 17, 1887, with United Press service in violation of obligations existing between the Western and New York associations; individual members of the Western Associated Press had bought franchises in the United Press to protect themselves against competing papers in their respective fields. Under these circumstances, an understanding was brought about which would cause the United Press "to cease aggressive opposition, cease starting new papers against Associated Press papers, cease under-bidding for business with clients of the Associated Press, on condition of being permitted to sell reports to Associated Press papers and receive news reports from those points which it had surrendered to the Associated Press." The accruing advantages were outlined in detail:

In the West, retention of the sub-associations as clients of the Western Associated Press.

The making of contracts with these associations at higher rates.

The making of long-time contracts with individual newspapers at an advance in rates.

Exclusion of the United Press from territory west of the Missouri river.

Protection of members and clients from the competition of new papers supplied by an efficient competing news organization.

Expressed in figures, the receipts of the Western Associated Press had been: in 1888, from members, $234,096, and from clients, $233,088; in 1888, from members, $237,905, and from clients, $228,384. Without the contract, the revenue received from clients would have been open to competition and the Western Associated Press would have lost at least a part of this annual revenue of $230,000.

To the New York Associated Press was preserved the New England Associated Press without competition. The United Press had been retired from New England and Pennsylvania, except Philadelphia, and the threatened loss of New Orleans averted.

Jointly, the New York Associated Press and the Western Associated Press had been enabled to put the business on a solid basis, and to destroy the California Associated Press which was preventing receipt of legitimate patronage and which, if attached to the United Press, would have given the latter a permanent foothold on the Pacific coast.

The only disadvantages the committee could discern were, in the first place, the larger payments for news service by those Associated Press papers as had bought United Press franchises, and, secondly, the supplying of a considerable part of the Associated Press report to United Press papers. "It would be useless to now attempt a complete separation of the Associated Press and the United Press."

To be entirely candid, we should note that the special committee responsible for the quoted report, of which Victor F. Lawson, of the Chicago *News*, was chairman, included in its membership William Henry Smith, the general manager, a beneficiary under the trust agreement, and that the trust agreement, itself, was still reposing among the hidden archives.

CHAPTER XVII

THE NEGOTIATIONS FOR READJUSTMENT

Proposed tripartite contracts—Decline and fall of the New York Associated Press—Formation of the Southern Associated Press—Plans for a federation into one national association

When the additional documents in the case were brought to light, a second special committee, consisting of Lawson, again as chairman, and Frederick Driscoll, of the St. Paul *Pioneer-Press,* and Robert W. Patterson, Jr., of the Chicago *Tribune,* on behalf of the Western Associated Press, engaged in a series of conferences with the representatives of the New York Associated Press to iron out the strained situation.

Right at the outset of the negotiations, an unexpected and disturbing factor was injected, when Irving F. Mack, of the Sandusky *Register,* who happened to be president of the Western Associated Press, endeavored to discredit the authority of the committee to act. Appearing without notice at the initial conference, Mack assumed to present officially a copy of a resolution adopted by the association reaffirming the unchangeableness of the contract of 1882. This, he insisted, was voted to show complete acquiescence in what had been done by the Western members of the Joint Executive Committee and to nail any rumors tending to create in their colleagues a different belief.[1] It was agreed that a joint committee of three from each association should investigate and report upon relations between the Associated

[1] Western Associated Press Report, 1891, p. 9.

Press and the United Press. When Lawson, as chairman, suggested recognition of his special committee for that purpose, it was discovered that President Mack was figuring on himself naming other and more tractable members to represent the Western Associated Press. Mack's peculiarly inspired efforts to obstruct were in evidence further at various stages of the proceedings.

After hearings and examination of the records, the special committee submitted a statement to the members, under date of New York, June 5, 1891. It found that the original contract creating the Joint Executive Committee vested in it power to control the distribution of news collected by the two associations but expressly limited "to the papers now entitled to receive it." Since the United Press was not at the time entitled to receive the news of either association, the action of the Joint Executive Committee exceeded its powers. "We, therefore, hold the contract in question is illegal and recommend notice to the United Press of abrogation at a certain date not later than October 10, 1891." Accompanying this recommendation went another, that the negotiation of a new working agreement with the United Press be authorized, "all the terms of which shall be submitted to the two associations for approval."

A month later, the same special committee reported progress toward a new working plan: The New Yorkers had appointed three members to act in conjunction with the western representatives. They had joined in the judgment that the contract with the United Press was illegal. The New York Associated Press had served the formal notice for the abrogation of this contract and had appointed a committee of three to confer with the United Press. The execution of a new contract was recommended but, if to be negotiated by the Joint Executive Committee, the representatives of the

Western Associated Press should be asked to resign from it. Furthermore, if the legal status of the United Press stock held by the members of that committee, or by the general manager, were established as calling for its surrender to the Western Associated Press, steps should be taken to recover the stock and all dividends paid on it.

Much discussion ensued, with a variety of proposals: that no further exchange of news be made with the United Press by purchase, sale or otherwise; that no person be eligible as director, who, individually, or by his paper, held stock in the United Press; that the directors be instructed to look into and report on the inequalities and departures from the organic law of the association. Only the last was adopted. Orders went to the Executive Committee to take advice on the validity of the contract in question, to abrogate it if illegal, to act with the New York Associated Press to formulate a new contract with the United Press in place of it. Events were fast coming to a head and demanded fully empowered handling. The Executive Committee took hold with decisive assurance.

What was happening seemed to spell the end of the New York Associated Press, notwithstanding its distinguished career. The *Sun* and the *Tribune* had announced their secession and adhesion to the United Press, which it was planned to reorganize on an all-comprehensive scale. "The difficulties here in the New York Associated Press," so read a contemporaneous report, "are local and based very largely on personal differences between the members. The *Tribune* and the *Sun* have withdrawn and are out to remain. There is a by-law which requires six months' notice which delays action but does not change the aspect of affairs. The re-establishment of harmonious relations, or any relations, that would enable the New York Associated Press to proceed as heretofore, is out of the question." This was part of an explanation of a dispute over a telegraph bill between the allied associations, resulting in cutting off service to the western papers which was restored only after payment under protest.[2] The National Associated Press, by which title the new organization was to do business, was to be backed by the two recalcitrant New York papers, and got so far as to initiate a wire service, but only for a single day. An interested southern journalist, who happened to be on the ground, has also described the affair:

> The breach in the New York Associated Press is a serious one and can only be healed by one faction or the other clearly showing the greatest strength. On the one hand is the *Mail and Express, Journal of Commerce* and the *Times;* and on the other, the *Sun* and *Tribune;* the *Herald* is neutral, and the *World,* while acting against the *Sun* and *Tribune,* may change position when it comes to the test; Mr. Bennett and Mr. Pulitzer are expected from Europe next week, and the situation will then be made clear.[3]

Yet, a few days later, the representatives of the Western Associated Press felt warranted in reporting "very satisfactory adjustment of recent differences," and further:

> The attempted withdrawal of the *Sun* and the *Tribune* from the New York Association was not in legal form and there is every possibility it will never be practically executed. The return of Mr. Bennett and Mr. Pulitzer and the firm stand each has taken in favor of a maintenance of the New York Associated Press has not only dispelled all uncertainty but tends greatly to insure the continuance of the *Sun* and the *Tribune* in the association. The New York Association is in fact intact and six out of seven of the members have participated in meetings this week.[4]

---

[2] *Ibid.*, 1891, p. 37.

[3] Message signed Adolph S. Ochs, dated New York, October 24, 1891.

[4] Confidential Circular Letter signed by Lawson and Driscoll, October 31, 1891.

The picture had been painted in too glowing colors. With the beginning of 1892, the *Sun* and the *Tribune* were at outs with the Associated Press, and out for good, casting lot with the United Press. Finality was added, if need be, by editorial announcement in italicized letters, the customary way of accentuating, as follows:

Those journals of the Associated Press that are distressed by reason of the superior and more accurate news that is regularly supplied by the United Press are hereby informed that there is no necessity for their remaining in such a state of unhappiness.

The United Press is prepared to furnish the news, foreign or domestic, to any newspaper that is ready and willing to pay a reasonable rate for the same; and that without discrimination on account of race, complexion or previous condition of servitude.[5]

In the meantime, the interchange of news between the New York Associated Press and the United Press had been discontinued except for meeting the requirements of the tripartite agreement with the New England Associated Press. The Western Association had asked such modification of the expiring contract with the New York association as would permit of equal representation on the Joint Executive Committee. Notice had been given Messrs. Richard Smith and Haldeman that their services and salaries as members of that committee would cease October 15, and quite a flare-up had followed their refusal to resign or yield their authority. The rules against Associated Press papers furnishing news to agents of other news associations were tightened, and orders promulgated for absolute separation of telegraph lines and operating offices. Especially important was the appearance of a new factor to be reckoned with, the Southern Associated Press, which was to have a short but an eventful history.

---

[5] *Sun,* March 11, 1892.

The very message, from which quotation has already been made, constituted a call on the part of Adolph S. Ochs, as secretary of the Southern Press Association which he had served in that capacity for years, for its members to meet in New York, October 29, 1891, "to put the association in shape to control the Associated Press news of the South."

> It behooves the Southern Press members to keep out of the fight, array themselves with neither faction but stand together and act in harmony. United, the Southern Press Association will become an important factor, and may be able to settle the trouble to its everlasting gain. We should be in position to form an alliance with the strongest. We can dictate our own terms.

As perhaps indicating what was in mind, he added:

> The interest of all Associated Press papers is that there be but one association and it is possible that, in accomplishing this, the Southern Press will be in it in terms better than they now enjoy. A plan of settlement suggested by a man well posted in the controversy is that the clients of the New York Associated Press—the New England, New York State, such of the New York City papers as will enter into the agreement, the Philadelphia, Baltimore, and Southern papers,—each in their separate organizations, form one association; that one representative of each meet in a congress once a month for conference as to service of news; that each organization maintain its autonomy and transact its own financial business, but act in harmony for the improvement of the news service, and in making rates with the telegraph companies for its transmission.

The meeting was duly held. Since the Southern Press Association had functioned merely as a fellowship society, a form of organization similar to the auxiliary associations in the other sections was by necessity the next step. Articles of agreement were thereupon signed on the spot by all present, thirteen in number, each subscribing to $500 worth of stock. The books were to remain open to any member of the Southern Press Association, but not more than $1,000, nor less than $100, allotted to one city or town, except New Orleans with limit of $2,000. "The purposes of this organization," it was proclaimed, "are to buy and sell news, and to contract with individuals, firms, associations and corporations for its collection, editing, transmission, sale and exchange." There was to be the usual board and officers; "the manager shall be the only salaried officer the first year, and his compensation shall not exceed $1,200 per annum." No new member, not already a member of the Southern Press Association, would be eligible "without the joint consent, in writing, of three-fourths of the Executive Committee, and the nearest shareholder of the Southern Associated Press to the applicant." The directors chose Evan P. Howell, of the Atlanta *Constitution,* to be president, and Adolph S. Ochs, of the Chattanooga *Times,* to be secretary, treasurer, and general manager.[6]

By the time the southern papers reassembled in January to go on, there was no concealment that they sought to deal as a group with the rival news associations and to turn the best bargain they could extract. The distinguished presence in Atlanta of William M. Laffan and Walter P. Phillips, the vice president, and the general manager, of the United Press, respectively, and also of William Henry Smith, the general manager of the Associated Press, was noted. The former were ready with a proposal on behalf of the United Press, embracing these points:

1. The United Press agrees to furnish at Washington a complete daily service of about 40,000 words.

2. The Southern association may include in the 40,000 words news of such character, or from such point, as desired, if obtainable by the United Press.

---

[6] Southern Associated Press Official Documents.

GERARD HALLOCK

HORACE GREELEY

WILLIAM COWPER PRIME

DAVID M. STONE

3. The Southern association to deliver at Washington news of the South to the United Press.

4. The Southern association to pay the United Press $25,000 per annum.

5. The United Press to surrender complete control of its news service in this territory, *i.e.*, Virginia, North and South Carolina, Florida, Georgia, Alabama, East Tennessee, and Mississippi and Louisiana, and also protect the Southern Press in this control, "should the United Press enter into any alliance or amalgamation with any other news service."

6. The contract to run to January 1, 1900.

7. The Southern Associated Press to elect one of the seven directors of the United Press who shall be on the Executive Committee.

8. All existing contracts and revenues of the United Press in defined territory to be given over to the Southern Associated Press; same at present is $36,528 of which $4,504 is being paid by Associated Press papers to hold franchise.

9. Texas is to be included, if the Southern Associated Press elects, but, if done, the net additional revenue is to go to the United Press.

10. The United Press to serve no papers or associations in Southern territory, directly or indirectly, without written consent of the Southern Associated Press, nor the Southern association serve papers outside its territory without written consent of the United Press.

When the United Press spokesman was advised that the New Orleans members were tied to the Associated Press in binding obligations terminable only by six months' notice, he withdrew the proposition, but later presented it again, stipulating a price for the service of $20,000 a year, to be raised to $25,000 with New Orleans included. No definite proposal being obtainable from the New York Associated Press, a committee of ten was deputed to go to New York with authority to conclude the negotiations. It was April before the conference materialized, but real competition had been provoked. As a counter to the United Press, President

Stone, for the Associated Press, offered to recognize the Southern Press as an organization and treat with the papers solely through their association. The news report delivered at Washington in exchange for news from the South would be available on this basis:

1. That all papers within Southern limits now served by the Associated Press be satisfied with the new report.
2. That neither the Southern association, nor any of its members, receive news of any rival news association or furnish to it any local news gathered by them.
3. That recognition be made in the contract for prospective growth of the South with corresponding increased payment.
4. That the contract run for five years, if desired, at $25,000 a year for three years and $30,000 a year thereafter, New Orleans excluded.
5. That payment be increased by $10,000 a year if New Orleans joins.

Various matters seemed to block agreement, especially the price, which the southerners wanted reduced to $25,000 a year for five years, including New Orleans. So the conference ended, after three days of wasted effort, with a parting communication addressed to William Henry Smith as general manager of the Associated Press:

> We are now confronted with two difficulties, one to make a contract with the United Press, or to let matters remain as they are. We have concluded to put ourselves in your hands and to ask your assistance to solve the complication. We give you full power to handle our case, looking to the further improvement of our news service, protecting our franchise, and putting us on an independent basis where we cannot be raided by rival news companies in the future and squeezed out of improper charges for the service we get.[7]

---

[7] Southern Associated Press, p. 22.

Invaluable experience had been gained, including a start toward collective bargaining, but the hoped-for independence had to be foregone yet a while in the distasteful tenure of clients, tempered only by a fair prospect of ultimate recognition similar to that accorded in other geographical areas.

The scene of action now veered to the West. The Western Associated Press and its so-called tributaries were being more closely welded. Objections in the way of complete amalgamation were being gradually overcome. The Northwestern Associated Press, the oldest and most important of these auxiliaries, had modified its position, along with a change in its official roster. For years, under the lead of its president, James S. Clarkson of the Des Moines *State Register,* a jealous guard had been maintained over its autonomy as the best leverage for concessions, and all overtures threatening its separate existence were unceremoniously repelled. Distracting duties for the Republican National Committee and subsequently in the Post Office Department under the Harrison administration, led to Clarkson's resignation and to his replacement by Dennis R. Richardson of the Davenport *Democrat,* who was ardently in favor of consolidation and bent himself to winning the membership to his view.[8] Other associations working with the Western Associated Press were going through the same process.

Generally speaking, a radical rearrangement of the whole machinery of news-gathering was "in the air." With its auxiliaries absorbed, the Western association was to become federated in "one grand national organization," an ideal constantly held in view, as we are aware. Keeping this in mind, the tardy and reluctant offer of the New York

[8] Clendenin, *Autobiography,* p. 146.

Associated Press to yield three members of the Joint Executive Committee, still entitled to only two votes, was politely declined and determination announced not to renew the expiring contract.[9] But the notice was not accepted as conclusive. "I presented your letter," wrote President Stone to President Nixon, "notifying us of your desire to terminate the existing contract between the two associations on the first of December next ensuing. I cannot but regret that an arrangement which has worked so harmoniously for so many years should be terminated for any cause. I do not know, of course, what 'material modifications' your association desires but I trust they are not such as are likely to disturb the friendly relations which have been so long maintained between us. I suggest that the changes you propose be submitted to us at an early date that we may give them that consideration which their importance may demand." Even as late as the middle of October, President Stone repeated the wish "to continue news relations with you," adding, "We feel confident a mutually satisfactory basis for a renewal of our contract can be agreed upon." Hope of healing differences might persist but was hardly warranted in full knowledge of what had already occurred.

Another shift of scene. Meeting in New York, September 20, 1892, a combination for working purposes of the New York State Associated Press, the New England Associated Press, the Southern Associated Press and the Western Associated Press had been virtually decided upon. Articles of agreement were actually signed by the officers of the two first named associations. Participating in the conference, in addition to the principals, were John M. Dickinson of the Binghamton *Republican,* John H.

[9] Western Associated Press Report, 1892, p. 87; 95.

Holmes of the Boston *Herald,* Evan P. Howell of the Atlanta *Constitution,* and Adolph S. Ochs of the Chattanooga *Times.* Only a few trifling details remained open to tie in the Western association, and these were to be attended to at an adjourned meeting in Chicago the next week.[10] The reconvening in the western metropolis disclosed that the Western Associated Press, also in session, was divided in sentiment. The latter went to the point, however, of resolving "that it is the sense of all present that a National Associated Press should be organized," but the discussion discredited probability of immediate agreement; in fact Lawson, for the Executive Committee of that association, declared it could not then be considered because of pending negotiations with the United Press, "which were near completion."

How far plans had been developed, together with their precise purport, was indicated by the confidential digest distributed to those present: Two great news-gathering concerns, the United Press and the Associated Press, the latter formed out of the Western Associated Press, were to be joined in a treaty of perpetual peace and amity. As surety, each was to exchange one half of its capital stock with the other, turned over to the custody of trustees. Each was to name three members of the other's board of directors. An executive committee of six, equally divided, was to be in supreme command, being the six chosen as members of both boards, an arbitrator to decide in case of disagreement. The United Press was to withdraw from territory west of the Alleghanies and north of Virginia and transfer its business there to the Associated Press. The Associated Press was not to be restricted to any particular territory. There were mutually protective measures against outside

[10] Southern Associated Press, p. 25.

papers and news agencies. The United Press was to collect foreign and Washington news, as well as the news of its territory, and exchange for the Associated Press news. The Central-Reuter contract was to be made in the name of the two corporations. The contracts with the Southern Associated Press, the New York State Associated Press and the New England Associated Press were to be made with the two corporations jointly. Local boards and complete veto on new franchises were to be granted to members. This was the pompous program. Another sitting the next month was to put it through. Again, those interested assembled, everything appeared to be smooth-running, every one impressed that nothing more was needed but the legal formalities.

In the language of the report, "We were informed that a contract had been consummated between the United Press and the Western Associated Press. In substance, this contract is an equal co-partnership between the United Press and the Western Associated Press. The United Press capitalizes at $2,000,000 and is to deposit one-half of its capital stock in the hands of a board of trustees for the benefit and use of the Western Associated Press. The Western Associated Press, on the other hand, is to be reorganized as the Associated Press with a chartered capital of $30,000. One-half of this capital stock is to be put in the hands of a trustee for the benefit of the United Press. The agreement was signed by the United Press, by all the members of Chicago newspaper organizations, the St. Louis *Republic,* Cincinnati *Enquirer,* Cincinnati *Commercial,* Louisville *Courier-Journal,* Pittsburgh *Commercial-Gazette,* Cleveland *Plaindealer,* Milwaukee *Wisconsonian,* St. Paul *Pioneer-Press,* Nashville *American,* Memphis *Appeal-Avalanche,* Galveston *News,* Indianapolis *Sentinel* and a number of other newspapers." Further, "we were informed that the combination of the United Press and the Western Associated Press virtually made one organization; that they have the exclusive control of the Reuter European News Service, also the foreign news service of the Central News Agency of London; that provision had been made to admit the New York City Associated Press papers on an equitable basis in the new organization. Whether or not they avail themselves of this privilege was a matter of no concern to the western papers. They were assured at any rate of the withdrawal of the New York *Tribune* from the New York City Associated Press and that through the United Press they had the New York *Evening Post, Commercial Advertiser, New York Press,* and *New Yorker Staats-zeitung.*"

The southern papers, unquestioningly, proceeded to qualify for a place in the combination. A definite proposition was before them. In its consideration, several points were emphasized; each party would share in control instead of being dependent upon the will or selfish caprice of another; the news of the South, coöperatively collected, would be had at a minimum of cost and might be sold elsewhere at a profit; the combination, covering almost the entire area of the United States and Canada, would be "the most powerful organization in the world, an organization that it would be impossible to duplicate or to compete with"; each constituent association would have a monopoly of its respective territory and the support of all in its defense; a fixed and increasing value would be secured for Associated Press franchises. Under the arrangement contemplated, a report equal to the full Associated Press service would be delivered to the Southern association at Washington and Memphis for $20,000 a year for an exclusive territory embracing Virginia, North and South

Carolina, Florida, Georgia, Alabama, East Tennessee, Mississippi and Louisiana, except New Orleans, and all the patronage of the United Press surrendered. This was hailed as the delivery of all the news of the world "absolutely free of cost," because the $20,000 annual payment in consideration would be more than offset by the $35,000 then being collected by the United Press in southern territory. "There is no reason why the sale of news to franchise holders and others, not members of the association, should not be a source of great profit and pay a handsome dividend on the capital stock, besides reducing the assessments to a minimum."[11] Wire service was to start November 1, 1892. There was a supplemental agreement, owing to retention of New Orleans in the exclusive southern territory, despite the desire evinced by the papers there to hold membership in the Western association, that any question of assessment on New Orleans be referred to specifically designated arbitrators, a stipulation fraught with trouble for the future.

The renewed counter-proposal of the old New York Associated Press to accord recognition as an organization and finally to lower the consideration for the service to one-half of the $25,000 previously demanded, thereupon was firmly rejected. These negotiations, carried on for that side by George F. Spinney of the New York *Times,* and Henry W. Odion, general eastern manager, marked the last activity of the New York Associated Press, which soon after lost its identity by the admission of all the remaining members into equal rights with their former associates in the United Press. In fact, within the next month, the step was taken by the New York Associated Press. "It is the sense of this association that the United Press should give

---

[11] *Ibid.,* p. 55.

to the *Times*, the *Journal of Commerce*, and the *Mail and Express*, the same amount of stock, to wit, $72,500, as held by the *Herald*, *World* and *Tribune*," as part of the terms of consolidation. Thus vanished the historic pioneer news-gathering association which had ruled supreme for nearly half a century.

The Southern Associated Press now perfected its re-incorporation. At a meeting held in Atlanta, November 16, 1892, nearly a score of the important newspapers became subscribers to the capital stock, which was limited to 300 shares aggregating $30,000 par value. Officers were chosen as follows: Evan P. Howell, President; Frank P. O'Brien, Vice President; Frank P. Glass, Secretary; Patrick Walsh, Treasurer; Adolph S. Ochs, Chairman Executive Committee.

The original subscribers comprised the Atlanta *Constitution*, Augusta *Chronicle*, Birmingham *Age-Herald*, Charleston *News and Courier*, Chattanooga *Times*, Columbia *Register*, Columbus *Enquirer-Sun*, Jacksonville *Times-Union*, Knoxville *Journal*, Knoxville *Tribune*, Mobile *Register*, Montgomery *Advertiser*, New Orleans *Picayune*, New Orleans *Times-Democrat*, Savannah *News*, Shreveport *Times;* the Richmond *Dispatch* and Norfolk *Landmark* were given additional time to come in. A contract for wire service, entered into with the Western Union, called for payment of $105,000 a year.

Viewing all the arrangements as settled, permanency and protection were to be provided for. No director was to have a vote in assessing the tolls on his own paper. The executive committee might coöperate with any of the various news organizations and sell the news to, or admit to membership, any newspapers printed in another language in the same places as present members, "but it shall not serve any paper not now served without the consent of the holder of a franchise for the same class of publication in the same place." A forfeited or lapsed franchise could be replaced only if a remaining paper did not take it over for self-protection, paying tolls for both. Each member or client was to be in duty bound to furnish the news of his district, and also forbidden to furnish news to, or receive news from, "any newspaper member or client of a rival or competing organization, except where the Southern Associated Press has agreements permitting such exchange or sale of special news." Although the last to pool their news-gathering facilities, the southern papers were fully organized for businesslike efficiency.

CHAPTER XVIII

THE ASSOCIATED PRESS OF ILLINOIS

Organization and membership—Expected alliance with the United Press—Miscarriage of negotiations—Melville E. Stone at the helm—The Reuter contract—Deal with the United Press reopened—The armed truce—Its breach and mutual recriminations

BACK-TRACKING a bit chronologically, a survey would show the Western Associated Press being meticulously transformed into the Associated Press, the "Associated Press of Illinois," in contradistinction to its successor, known as "The Associated Press of New York." Application for the charter of incorporation had been made November 10, 1892. "The object for which it is formed is to buy, gather and accumulate information and news; to vend, supply, distribute and publish the same; to purchase, erect, lease, operate and sell telegraph and telephone lines and other means of transmitting news; to publish periodicals; to make and deal in periodicals and other goods, wares and merchandise." The first meeting of stockholders was held in Chicago, December 13, 1892; an elaborate array of by-laws was adopted; William Penn Nixon, of the Chicago *Inter-Ocean*, was elected president, Charles P. Taft, of the Cincinnati *Times-Star*, vice president, Delavan Smith, secretary, and Victor F. Lawson, of the Chicago *Daily News*, Charles W. Knapp, of the St. Louis *Republic*, and Frederick Driscoll, of the St. Paul *Pioneer-Press*, the members of the all-important executive committee. Sixty-five daily newspapers were listed on the original printed roll as entitled to stock-holding memberships:

Chicago—*Tribune, Times, Inter-Ocean, News-Record, Herald, Journal, Daily News, Evening Post, Staats-zeitung*
Milwaukee—*Sentinel, Wisconsonian Herold*
St. Paul—*Pioneer-Press, Globe*
Minneapolis—*Tribune, Journal*
Kansas City—*Journal, Times*
St. Louis—*Globe-Democrat, Republic, Post-Dispatch, Anzeiger, Amerika, Westliche Post*
Nashville—*American*
Louisville—*Courier-Journal*
Cincinnati—*Commercial Gazette, Enquirer, Times-Star, Volksblatt, Volksfreund*
Denver—*Times, Republican, Rocky Mountain News*
Omaha—*Bee*
Indianapolis—*Sentinel, Journal, News*
Pittsburgh—*Commercial Gazette, Chronicle-Telegraph, Post, Dispatch*
San Francisco—*Chronicle*
Portland—*Oregonian*
Galveston—*News*
Wheeling—*Intelligencer, Register*
Sandusky—*Register*
Cleveland—*Leader, Plaindealer*
Toledo—*Blade, Commercial*
Detroit—*Tribune, Free Press*
Evansville—*Journal*
Oil City—*Derrick*
Terre Haute—*Express, Gazette*
Dayton—*Journal*
Columbus—*Journal, Dispatch*
Memphis—*Appeal-Avalanche*
Seattle—*Post Intelligencer*
Springfield—*Illinois State Journal*

The pressing business in hand was to get under way the new alliance on which all moves were focusing. The draft of the proposed "General Contract" was approved, and its execution authorized, along with the collateral trust agreement to insure fulfillment. The provisions disclosed in the draft contract were most comprehensive. Though this document was executed December 23, 1892, it went back to October 15, the date of the provisional compact, as its starting point, and was to continue, by its terms, for a period of ninety-three years, unless modified by mutual consent. So important is it to an understanding of events to follow, that its stipulations must be set forth in some degree of fullness:

1. The United Press "will vacate all the territory covered on the 15th day of October, 1892, by the Western Associated Press, confining itself to Canada and points east of the Alleghany mountains and north of Virginia" and will not hereafter "gather, buy, sell or transmit news within the territory so vacated otherwise than as the agent and at the request of" the Associated Press to which it will "turn over its business and revenue in the territory vacated."

The Associated Press "shall not be restricted to any particular territory in the collection or sale of news" and will hold all United Press papers in the vacated territory "on a basis as to service and tolls equal to that which they enjoyed on the 15th of October, 1892."

The Associated Press shall "have the use of all the leased telegraph wires of the United Press in the territory vacated by it, as well as those connecting the East therewith, on the same terms as the United Press has them under its contracts with the telegraph companies."

2. The United Press will "collect the foreign news, news at Washington, New York City, and all territory covered by it," and "exchange for the news of the territory west of the Alleghany mountains and south of the northern boundary line of Virginia," delivered in New York City or Chicago.

3. "The scope, character and management of the news service so exchanged shall be subject to the direction and supervision of the board of control, composed of the executive committees of the two corporations, each committee being entitled to one vote on all questions at issue, and the orders of the board of control shall be final." In case of disagreement an arbiter shall decide.

4. "The Reuter contract shall be made in the name of the two corporations," all expenses and payments arising therefrom borne by the United Press.

5. The contracts with the Southern Associated Press, together

with the profits and expense, are allotted to the Associated Press; the contracts with the New York State Associated Press and with the New England Associated Press to the United Press.

6. The Associated Press shall assume the contract of the United Press for the plate business at Pittsburgh, Cleveland, Cincinnati, Chicago, St. Louis, Omaha and St. Paul.

7. Neither shall furnish news except under a contract in writing "which shall require the party receiving such news report to take the same for a stated period, to publish the same, and to pay therefor stated weekly assessments" and "to furnish to the corporation furnishing such news report all the news, local and telegraphic, or for specified districts."

"Said contracts shall also prohibit the party receiving news thereunder from furnishing, or permitting any one to furnish, its special or other news to any person or corporation engaged in the business of collecting or transmitting news, except upon the written consent first obtained of the Board of Directors" and shall prohibit "furnishing or permitting any one to furnish its special or other news to, and from receiving news from, any person or corporation which shall have been declared to be antagonistic to said corporation."

Enforcement shall be by "suspension of the news report thereby agreed to be furnished and the termination of said contracts." Moreover, notice that the board of one of the associations has declared a person or corporation antagonistic shall be followed within thirty days with a declaration of the same purport by the other. But no news required to be furnished shall be supplied to any other newspaper published in the district of the paper furnishing it.

8. Obligation is expressly disclaimed "to print or publish any credit or copyright notice in the name of either party," for news coming from the other party.

9. Each shall provide satisfactory office room to the representatives of the other in their respective quarters in Chicago, New York and Washington.

By a separate indenture, ninety-six shares of Associated Press stock and 10,000 shares of United Press stock were to be deposited with and held by trustees in guaranty of "performance of said contract." Still another agreement was to provide for a jointly owned subsidiary, "Telegraphic News Association," to serve limited news reports to publications not eligible to their regular memberships. Surely, so much thought, time, and effort would not have been devoted to the formulation of these intricate documents had there been no genuine desire to push on to the goal. For the United Press, the names proposed for directors were submitted at once for approval of the Associated Press, and the list of the board of the Associated Press promptly furnished in return.

But now the unforeseen snag was struck. A letter, signed by Laffan as vice president of the United Press, submitted for consideration "some minor amendments" to the proposed contract, particularly elimination of the clause leaving the Associated Press unrestricted in the collection and sale of news in any territory, "the purpose for the attainment of which it was originally introduced no longer existing." The Associated Press spokesmen had lodged an informal protest against the inclusion of a representative of the Southern Associated Press in the United Press directory. They positively declined to accept the suggested modifications of the contract, and shut the door to argument by insisting that they possessed no authority to do so. Shortly afterward came information that, at the instance of the New York *Times,* a restraining order had been issued which prevented the United Press from proceeding with the contemplated exchange of stock involved in the trustee plan. Negotiations lagged. Mutual suspicions multiplied. When the Associated Press committee repaired to New York for conference, ready and authorized to waive the matter of depositing stock as security for observance of the contract, the situation was visibly changed. Demand was made upon the members for payment forthwith of a bill for $3,500 for the services rendered by the United Press during the month of January, and one-half of the collections from the Southern Associated Press, under penalty of a stoppage of the report. Until this money was forthcoming, no further discussion could be had. On compliance, professing to speak for President Dana, Laffan announced that they would not again take up the provisional contract for consideration, though offering to continue the service pending different arrangements. There was no alternative but to accept under protest the proposition and its terms. Request for reasons brought only a curt note of regret, "that at the moment it is not in my power to impart to you any additional information."

What had produced the change? Were there hidden moves and motives behind it? There must be two versions of every such controversy. The explanation of Laffan was set forth at length in a letter which he addressed the very next day to John R. Walsh to correct misstatements and make "our position" available for reference, in which, among other things, he said:

> We went, in October last, Mr. Phillips and myself, to Chicago and there, after considerable discussion, entered into a provisional agreement with the representatives of the Western Associated Press. That agreement was of such a nature that it made us in all particulars the equal partners in the news-gathering business of the Western Associated Press. Our revenues were to be divided, our purpose was to be common, and our joint management was to be unified in the hands of Mr. W. P. Phillips. All negotiation was based upon the fundamental principle that our common interests were to be confided to Mr. Phillips' administration, and therein reposed all merit that such combination might imply.
>
> We stood, therefore, with a tacit understanding and a sealed document between us. The Western Associated Press never recognized either the understanding or the document as anything but a temporary expedient thereby to gain its own ends. Although we were its equal partners in absolutely every particular that constitutes

partnership, its deliberations were secret; we were never invited to one of its meetings; and in all the conferences that ensued no modification was suggested that had not been thought out with reference to in what degree it might prove detrimental to our interests. At no time was it admitted or recognized by the Western Associated Press in any of its proceedings that the partnership was anything more than a channel whereby the United Press should be belittled, restricted and ultimately destroyed.

We, on our part, regarded it as an agreement made in good faith, whereby our interests were to be absolutely mutual, and we so bore ourselves through all the negotiations and transmutations of that trying period. When finally we had made concession upon concession, and the spirit of the original agreement had been changed and impaired, we ascertained only by a mere accident that the fundamental and tacit understanding that Mr. Phillips was to be the general manager of the united concern, had been furtively set aside without a word of warning to us or of consultation with us. In fact it was studiously concealed from us, and it was only too apparent that the design of the Western Associated Press was to secure our signatures to the agreement and then open their ambuscade upon us when we were no longer in a situation to defend ourselves.

After the Detroit meeting, Mr. M. H. de Young, of the San Francisco *Chronicle,* was deputed a committee of one to proceed to New York and take into the Western Associated Press those members of the New York Associated Press with whom we had been so long in antagonism. Mr. de Young unconsciously and unintentionally illustrated the spirit by which our equal partners in the West were acting toward us. He notified us—and he was fully sustained in doing so by the tenor of the resolutions of which he was the bearer—he notified us that we were to go out of business; that the appearance in the news business of the United Press as a potential element would not be tolerated. In detail he explained to us what was to be our lot, and how complete were the plans of our Western partners for our humiliation and extinction. Not only did Mr. de Young fully inculcate this view upon us, but he secured its publication and coming as it did from him, with the authority with which he was vested, it was sufficiently official to complete our conviction as to what constituted an equal partnership in the eyes of the gentlemen with whom we had been negotiating in Chicago.

It was only this week, in Chicago, that members of the Kansas and Missouri Press Association were advised by Mr. Delavan Smith of the complete absorption and subordination of the United Press and its assimilation by the Western concern.

When we left Chicago in December, we agreed with the Executive Committee of the Western Associated Press that, until such time as re-adjustment could be had, we would continue to them the service they had had from the New York Associated Press, upon the same terms as those understood to exist. When we presented our bill for the month's service during January, the Executive Committee of the Western Associated Press repudiated it. They also refused payment to us of any money on behalf of the service to the Southern Associated Press, even going so far as to return to the Southern Associated Press the cheques that had been forwarded to the order of our general manager, instructing the treasurer of the Southern association to make them out in favor of the Western Associated Press and return them. On Wednesday, the 15th inst., the Executive Committee of the Western Associated Press called upon me, and I informed them that unless the money were forthcoming at once, we would promptly discontinue all service to the Western Associated Press and have no further relations with them of any sort whatever. After some few minutes deliberation among themselves, they agreed to pay and they telegraphed to their general manager in Chicago a peremptory order to transfer the amount involved to our credit.

We have since advised them of our willingness to continue the present arrangement and serve them the news in New York, upon the terms heretofore agreed between the Western Associated Press and the New York Associated Press, until such time as an adjustment of our interests and a better understanding of our affairs and prospects would justify us in reaching a conclusion which we could hope would be permanent, satisfactory and beneficial. This proposition they have accepted. Such is, in outline, the existing condition.

Neither the existing condition nor the outlook was reassuring to the western papers. The United Press was apparently in possession of all the available news sources of Europe, in fact had previously sent notice that the "Reuter Contract," which was to have been negotiated jointly, had been executed with the United Press for a period of ten years. "We shall hold it," wrote Laffan, "for the strict account of ourselves and the Associated Press of Illinois until such time as you decide to have it redrawn in the name of both associations."[1] Could dependence be placed on a promise made before any sign of rift? Could a right to share this contract be legally enforced apart from other features of the old agreement? Furthermore, the United Press was in undisputed control of all territory east of the Alleghany Mountains and north of the city of Washington. The dissemination of news in the West was being conducted under a temporary and altogether unsatisfactory arrangement for an exchange of reports in New York City and the payment of a bonus of $42,000 per annum to the United Press.

The instinct for self-preservation seemed to force the effort to obtain an independent service at whatever cost. For this, some offsets were to be counted to the good. The members and clients constituted a compact body solidified by common grievances. On moral grounds, they could rally popular sentiment to their support. As a whole, they were resourceful and enterprising. They commanded certain strategic points of news collection and transmission which rendered large stretches almost immune to attack. They had the too-little-appreciated advantage of the name, Associated Press, and the prestige attaching to it in the public mind as a standard of authority and reliability, an element of value in every franchise for Associated Press news service. Selection of the right man to take the lead was the first prerequisite.

The calendar proclaimed the month of March. The directors of the Associated Press were in thoughtful con-

[1] Associated Press Report, 1894, p. 10.

sultation. "A prolonged discussion was had over the existing relations between the Associated Press and the United Press." They voted to secure new quarters in the city of Chicago for their association. They pledged to the Executive Committee "cordial support in the future in the conduct of our business and the defense of our franchise rights." They directed the president to notify the president of the United Press of their desire to have the contract with the Reuter Telegram Company redrawn in the name of the two associations, "as provided in the agreement made by the vice president of the United Press in his acknowledgment of 1892." They authorized the Executive Committee to confer with Melville E. Stone "with reference to his engagement as general manager of the Associated Press and if, in their judgment, such engagement be for the true interests of the association, to consummate the same at a salary not to exceed $12,000 per annum."[2] The newspaper emissaries came upon Stone, not exactly like Cincinnatus at the plow, but in the rôle of a retired journalist turned bank president. "All I could say was, in the phrase of the young lady, that their proposal was 'rather sudden.' There were things to think of." But he was persuaded. The bank directors were impressed, and consented to a leave of absence for their president. For something like five years he held both offices.[3] The move to draft Stone in this emergency was to be ascribed unquestionably to Lawson, with whom he had been formerly in partnership in the publication of the Chicago *Daily News*.

For a full quarter of a century, for a period longer than Craig, longer than Simonton, longer even than William Henry Smith, Melville Elijah Stone was to be the guiding

---

[2] *Ibid.*, p. 74.
[3] Stone, *Fifty Years a Journalist*, p. 214.

spirit of the Associated Press. Born in the little country town of Hudson, Illinois, August 22, 1848, the son of a poor, circuit-riding Methodist preacher, he had learned to set type at the age of ten, had removed with his parents, after sojourns in various small towns, to Chicago where he had a brief term of public school training, had earned money occasionally by delivering local papers to subscribers, and by a try-out at reporting. At twenty, he had published his first newspaper, the *Sawyer and Mechanic,* "the only paper in the United States devoted to Saw and Flour Mill Work," followed soon, on its demise, by embarkation in an iron foundry and machine shop which foundered in the distress in the wake of the Chicago fire. Daily journalism had then claimed the young Stone, yielding him a taste of life in various cities throughout the country, including the national capital and Chicago. Entranced by the idea of establishing a one-cent paper, undismayed by the abortive first attempts, he finally put out the initial issue of the Chicago *Daily News* in January, 1876, which achieved an immediate triumph. More capital was quickly needed, with the result that Victor F. Lawson, once a schoolmate, was introduced as a partner, who, in turn, bought out his associate's interest in 1888 and made it possible for Stone to become a banker. These years had brought him many vitalizing contacts. He had talked with Greeley and had worked under Dana and Storey. He had done local reporting and field writing, had composed leading editorials, had occupied a seat with the corps of Washington correspondents. He had perpetrated "detective journalism." He had covered national conventions of the great political parties. He had a goodly number of journalistic exploits to his personal credit. Both at home and abroad, he had acquired valued friends and acquaintances: Mark Twain,

Bob Ingersoll, and Roscoe Conkling; Grant, Arthur, Cleveland, Logan, McKinley; Parnell, Dillon, Davitt; T. P. O'Connor; Gambetta, Clemenceau, Porfirio Diaz. He had learned to know "big news" from handling it, he knew the notables figuring in current events, he knew the geography behind the news, and the economic interests likely to be affected by it. Except for lack of a more robust health, he was equipped as no man in the position before him to become the active head of a great news-gathering organization.

It required no "thinking over" to realize the next imperative move. From its nascent days of harbor boats and news schooners, the unshakable strength of the old New York Associated Press lay in its secure hold on the foreign intelligence. When telegraph and cable supplanted steamer and carrier pigeon, exclusive access to the news collected abroad by the great European agencies, that had developed along the same lines, rendered its grip still firmer. The special representatives subsequently commissioned to act for the Associated Press abroad depended on these connections, whose reports they supplemented, or amplified, or speculated about. The foreign news was no less the key to the then existing complication. Possession of the transatlantic news gateway might well be decisive. But was the asserted claim of the United Press to the Reuter contract well grounded? Rumor persisted of a vulnerable spot in the transaction. At this critical moment, definite information regarding this point was received. William Henry Smith, who in the interval had been designated temporary treasurer, turned over a letter from Walter Neef, once his assistant in the Chicago headquarters and afterwards his chief of European staff in charge of the London office, containing the surprising but welcome word that the contract negotiated with the American representative of Reuter's had never been completed. Mr. Neef wrote:

I had a long talk with Herbert de Reuter and, after I explained the situation, he expressed himself as fully recognizing the importance of the Western Associated Press and said he would sign no contract which did not include it as a contracting party. Moreover, that he regarded the West as the more important connection of the two. Up to the present time, no contract at all has been signed.

Herbert de Reuter, as you perhaps know, is the managing director of his concern and, in these negotiations with America, has full power from Wolff and Havas. The old baron pays but little attention to this company and spends most of his time abroad. I have always had somewhat intimate personal relations with Herbert de Reuter, which have continued since I left the office here, so that we are able to talk freely and confidentially to-day. I learned that the draft agreement which Reuter prepared and which they sent over to the United Press in December for execution provided that the agreement should be between the three agencies and the United Press and the Western Associated Press. This is distinctly provided. Not long after this arrived in America, the United Press wrote that Laffan was coming over here soon and would then execute the contract and asking that in the meanwhile the news be turned over to them. To this Reuter agreed, and thus the matter stands to-day.

Reuter expressed some surprise that, throughout the negotiations, he had never heard anything from the Western Associated Press, but supposed that Laffan was fully authorized to represent both associations. Laffan, who is now in Nice or on his way there, is expected in London in about six weeks' time, and if the Western Associated Press has not a draft of the proposed contract, and desires to see it, I would suggest that you cable to Reuter asking that a copy be sent you at once, and it can be returned here with any comments and instructions the Western Associated Press may have in regard to its execution before Laffan arrives here.[4]

Here, in the language of the turf, was a horse of a different color. Without a moment's delay, a message was

[4] Associated Press Report, 1894, p. 75.

dispatched to Neef by cable: "You are commissioned agent Associated Press. Reëstablish relations and protect our interests. Forward copy Reuter contract immediately." It was also resolved that the whole subject matter of the foreign service be left to the chairman of the Executive Committee and the general manager with power to act, and that it was their judgment that the latter should go abroad at once to make such arrangements as might be necessary to safeguard their interests.

Within twenty-four hours, the new general manager was on his way to London, where he arrived on the eve of St. Patrick's day. It was all unnecessary, for there was nothing for him to do. Neef, alert, able, prompt, had already executed his commission to perfection. "I called on Mr. Herbert de Reuter, the managing director of the Reuter Telegram Company," reported Stone, "and I learned from him, as well as from Mr. Walter Neef, our very efficient agent in London, that the agreement between the two had been concluded on the 7th day of March." Affixing his signature in ratification of the agreement, Stone confirmed the covenant executed by Neef and took passage for home. The main provisions of the document, which should be noted, are as follows:

> On behalf of the Agence Havas of Paris and the Continental Telegraphen Compagnie of Berlin, as well as on behalf of Reuter's Telegraph Company, Limited, of London, and on behalf of the Associated Press, it is hereby mutually agreed.
>
> In the event of the United Press failing to come to an arrangement with the Associated Press, and of the United Press not adhering to the said treaty and duly ratifying the same by the 16th day of May, 1893, the contract shall take effect in its entirety as between the three European agencies and the Associated Press.
>
> Reuter's Telegram Company shall supply to the agent of the two associations in London a copy of all telegrams furnished by it to the London papers, and simultaneously therewith, the Agence

Havas to the agent at Paris all telegrams furnished by it to the Paris papers.

The three agencies shall not supply news directly or indirectly to any person or newspaper in the United States or British North America.

The two associations shall furnish to the correspondents of the three agencies in New York, for the exclusive use of the three agencies, all American or other news obtained and received by them, and as early as possible, provided always that the three agencies shall not, directly or indirectly, furnish the same to any person or newspaper in the United States or British North America.

The two associations shall not directly or indirectly by their agents transmit, nor suffer or permit their members, subscribers or clients to transmit, their intelligence outside the continent of North America, nor to carry on any business of telegraphic intelligence outside the continent of North America, except by and through the three agencies.

All telegraphic expenses for transmitting intelligence from Europe to the United States, or direct to their London office, shall be borne and paid by the two associations, and all telegraphic expenses for transmission from North America to Europe or elsewhere shall be borne by the agencies by whose order the news is transmitted.

Any of the contracting parties shall be entitled to call upon the others for any telegraphic news analogous to, but not comprised in the ordinary services, and to have such news solely on payment of the telegraphic tolls to the point of delivery and any extraordinary expense of obtaining it.

If any question, dispute or difference arise on any matter in any way connected with these presents or the operation thereof, it shall be referred to two arbitrators, one to be chosen by each side, or to an umpire chosen by such arbitrators, whose decision shall be final and conclusive.[5]

"A close alliance for the exclusive interchange to each other, outside their respective territories, of all telegraphic news received by them"—so it was characterized. In addition to the exchanged news, the Reuter Company was to be paid, for and on account of the three agencies, a yearly sum

---

[5] *Ibid.*, p. 77.

of 3,5000 pounds sterling, clear of all deductions, in equal monthly installments. The agreement, effective June 1, 1893, ran for ten years, self-renewing for another ten-year period unless terminated by twelve months' notice in writing.

On his home-coming, the general manager repeated the detailed story of his excursion to the Executive Committee, but the satisfaction which it inspired was carefully concealed behind a formal approval entered on the minutes. "We were ready for a fight," said Stone in retrospect. Eagerness for the fray, however, was bridled to await resumed negotiations for adjustment. A specific proposition had come from the United Press to retire from the western field, relinquish all rights to serve newspapers in the territory of the Associated Press, and exchange reports, for a consideration of $2,000 a week to be paid continuously during the term to be agreed upon. In the correspondence, Phillips struck the ledger balance succinctly in this fashion:

Our gross revenue from all points reached by your leased wire system is $300,000 per annum.

United Press Business

Of this $300,000, we collect from newspapers and the plate industries at points reached by your leased wire system	$101,000
The above item of $101,000 I count as net to you, and there is in addition:	
Net revenue from the Western Union pony circuit, extending from Chicago to Sioux Falls	4,200
Net revenue from United Press papers served by the Postal Telegraph Company	11,000
Net collections from United Press papers at miscellaneous points where the Associated Press is now rendering an abridged service	3,000
	$119,200

Regarding the first item, we have underestimated it, if anything. Moreover, you must take into account that our prices at several points are susceptible of re-adjustment. The minimum is $101,000. This figure should be improved. The other items could probably be improved somewhat in your hands by combining the business and conducting it on one circuit. But even if it were conducted on the present basis, the minimum net is fully $18,200.

ASSOCIATED PRESS BUSINESS

Duplicate service, or keeping franchises alive — members, including California	$75,292
Duplicate service, or keeping franchises alive—clients, including morning service at Detroit	47,116

It seems to me that out of the $300,000 we are collecting, the net to you on United Press business ought to be got up considerably, so that even if you remit the $75,292 paid by your members, the money advantage to you in our proposition should be fully $170,000. Add to this the $42,000 formerly paid to the New York Associated Press, and we have a total benefit to you of, say, $212,000. We started out to divide profits equally with you, and though we are now working on a different plan than we were last autumn, I have kept that object in view. This leaves out of the account altogether any saving that may come to you from the use of our leased wires, if you wish to use them; and there are several other advantages that will probably occur to you and to which I need not refer.[6]

The Associated Press was quite willing to treat with the United Press but felt itself entitled to more favorable terms. So a counter-proposition was authorized to pay the United Press $75,000 a year for seven years, "conditioned upon the absolute and permanent abandonment by each association of the territory of the other, upon an exchange of gathered news by the two associations in New York, i.e., the United Press to deliver to the Associated Press all news gathered by it in foreign countries or in its territory, and the Asso-

[6] *Ibid.*, p. 82.

ciated Press to deliver to the United Press in New York, in like manner, all news gathered by it in its territory; and upon the right of each association to serve its own news, or that of the other contracting association, to any one outside of and beyond the limits of the territory of the two associations." To this, the further stipulation was added "that the United Press should assign and turn over all telegraphic and other valuable contracts it might have, directly affecting the territory of the Associated Press," and the whole proposition predicated upon the accuracy of the United Press statements as to its revenues and business advantages in the western territory.

As bearing on these provisions, it was pointed out that the seven years were coterminous with the United Press' preferential wire contracts, of which the Associated Press was to benefit; that the right to serve news beyond defined territorial limits was necessary, because each must deliver a complete American report to its foreign connections; that the price exceeded by $7,000 the present $42,000 bonus and the $26,000 net profits from western clients accruing to the United Press, to which the Associated Press must add $17,500 to be paid Reuter, and $2,000 expense in preparing the news after its receipt by cable. "In other words," ran the accompanying communication, "the proposition on the one hand guarantees you for a term of seven years a larger net revenue from this territory than you are now in the enjoyment of, and gives it to you without any of the care and risk of doing business in the territory; and on the other hand increases our annual expenditure from $42,000 to $94,500, or more than doubles it. For these reasons, it seems to the committee that its proposition is an equitable one—in fact, a generous one." Ten days were allowed for acceptance.

The generosity of the offer somehow failed to impress those representing the United Press. Parleys were broken off and renewed several times with a final tender by the Associated Press of $95,000 a year for ten years, but all to no result. The Associated Press thereupon proceeded with the absorption of the Western Associated Press which had been continuing nominally to function. After due notice and preliminaries, the news report was distributed as the Associated Press service, beginning August 1st, the change being chiefly in the label rather than in the substance. The newspapers, with few exceptions, acquired membership contracts, and the client associations went along as before. As in all such mergers, the personnel and mechanism of the organization transferred themselves almost automatically. The general manager was empowered at the same time to invite applications and to make contracts for service with any newspaper "entitled to a service of news from the United Press on the 15th day of October, 1892."[7] It is of utmost importance to keep this date in mind with reference to later developments.

Stirring events were now confounding the industrial and financial world. The paralyzing panic of 1893 had broken in uncurbed fury, with disastrous effect on the business of newspaper publication. With fear of threatened shipwreck, mutual interest cautioned both associations to keep their craft close to shore and for that purpose to preserve the status quo. One of the big three of the United Press, John R. Walsh, of the Chicago *Herald,* happened to be engaged extensively also in banking, over which ominous clouds were hovering. Stone, too, was occupying a dual position, combining journalism and finance.

---

[7] *Ibid.,* p. 92.

"You and I must attend to our banks," Stone quoted Walsh.

"Not at all, I have no concern about the panic."

"But," persisted Walsh, "what will you do if they start a run on you?"

"Then I laughed at him," said Stone, "and explained: As treasurer of the Drainage Canal Board, I have several millions on deposit in yours and other banks of the city. I will withdraw this, deposit it in my own bank, and pay on demand."

"Oh," he replied in alarm, "we can't stand that."

"Then we arranged a truce." [8]

What Stone called a truce was evidently open to two interpretations. As recorded by Walsh in a letter to Lawson, dated July 22, 1893, he merely confirmed the willingness of the United Press "to let its present temporary arrangement with the Associated Press continue, either until November 1, or December 31, as your association may desire, thus giving all parties more time and better weather in which to negotiate a permanent contract."

Stone, a week later, endeavored to induce Walsh to incorporate this assurance in a written stipulation, but the latter declined to sign any definite agreement and held himself to verbal reiteration. The incident might have been unimportant but for the issue soon to be raised as to which first broke faith and transgressed the proprieties. Every great conflict at arms, as we know, is a war of aggression and a war of self-defense on the part of both contenders at one and the same time.

"It did not surprise us that the United Press violated the truce. Such a course was to be expected." In saying this,

---

[8] Stone, *op. cit.*, p. 216.

Stone explained that the change to the United Press of the Chicago *Tribune,* which had hung back from signing a membership contract with the Associated Press, had been the subject of a tacit understanding. But when, three weeks later, a message arrived, signed by W. N. Haldeman, directing discontinuance of reports to the Louisville *Courier-Journal* in view of arrangements with the United Press for service hereafter, Stone wired: "Am greatly surprised at your telegram." Why surprise? Was it not common knowledge that Haldeman had been for years, as member of the Joint Executive Committee, intimately co-operating to the limit with the United Press, a stockholder in it, and in sympathy with its management? A forced choice on his part would naturally incline to the United Press. Stone invoked the obligation of the *Courier-Journal* contract of membership, which was at once repudiated as having been signed with express notice that authority was lacking and that it was subject to ratification which had not followed. The contract was referred to counsel to take measures for its enforcement. And now came the proclamation of war:

Resolved, That the truce between the Associated Press and the United Press, which was agreed upon by the general manager and Mr. John R. Walsh, treasurer of the United Press, having been violated by the United Press furnishing its report to the Louisville *Courier-Journal,* the general manager is instructed to notify Mr. John R. Walsh that the Associated Press holds the truce terminated.

Resolved, That the United Press, the Telegram News Association, and the International Telegram Company, and all allied associations, are hereby declared associations antagonistic to the Associated Press within the meaning of the by-laws.

Resolved, That the New York *Sun,* the Chicago *Tribune,* the Chicago *Herald,* and the Chicago *Post,* be and they are hereby declared antagonistic and in opposition to the Associated Press, and the president is instructed to notify all members and clients that they are prohibited from furnishing, or permitting anyone to furnish, special news to, and also from receiving news from, the papers herein declared antagonistic.

The signal for mobilization of forces was hoisted. But after spreading these bristling resolutions on the record, the more pacific motion was unanimously voted:

That the following gentlemen, I. F. Mack, W. A. Bunker, Richard Smith, and D. M. Houser, be invited to act as a special committee to make one further attempt to negotiate an honorable adjustment of the relations between the Associated Press and the United Press, with a view to the retirement of the United Press from the Western field.

The peace commissioners met at Cincinnati, September fifth, present Smith, Houser, Bunker, Haldeman, Laffan, Walsh, Phillips. At the session, the United Press, through its spokesman, stood ready to give each member of the Associated Press a franchise in the United Press to run five or ten years, at option of holder, absolutely binding on its part, yet with privilege to the member to withdraw at any time; each to be charged the same amount then paid to the Associated Press, thus saving members of both associations from double payments; five years' notice requisite for increase of price; an executive committee to include two in the East, one from St. Louis, one from Cincinnati, and one from Chicago. But it would yield no farther. "We had a long conference. They absolutely refused to confer on the basis of an exchange of news with the Associated Press and would not consider figures at all. Thereupon your committee considered its mission at an end." [9]

[9] Associated Press Report, 1894, p. 100.

CHAPTER XIX

WAR OF THE NEWS GIANTS

War taxes and war chests—Invading the enemy's country—Premature self-congratulations—Re-alignment of the Southern Associated Press—Futile peace moves—Position of the United Press—Foreshadowing the end—Collapse of the United Press

THE war was really on at last. It was to be a war to the knife, and knife to the hilt. Independent news service by each association to all members and clients commenced immediately. Intercourse between the combatants had to cease at once. Alliances with banned newspapers must be ended regardless of unexpired contracts, regardless of loss of valuable features to hated rivals. "No aid to the enemy" was to be the rule. The westerners decided on a campaign of aggression. They were convinced that they had good prospects to win the support of prominent journals in the East. To take in converts with full rights of membership, additional capital stock would be necessary. Summoned to a special meeting for this purpose, despite the significance of certain absentees, those present voted to increase the capitalization to $100,000, "to the end of nationalizing the proprietorship of the association by the admission of leading newspapers in all sections of the country to stockholding in the association in individual amounts not exceeding the holdings of the present stockholders; provided, this shall not impair the existing rights of members." By-laws were amended to conform. Unanimously adopted resolutions voiced determination to sustain officers and directors in their purpose to build up a national, mutual news-gathering association for the benefit of its members and the public thus served, and also a pledge of continued loyal support. By way of emphasis, signatures were attached and the instrument widely broadcasted.

That war would cost money was fully appreciated. The general manager had a financial statement and estimate of needs ready. For the month of August prior to the hostilities, the deficit had been $4,152. Offsetting new outlays by deducting the $3,500 paid to the United Press, and adding $2,000 returns from three new services just put on, the monthly shortage was whittled down on paper to $1,282. "It will not be possible for the general manager to submit any absolutely accurate estimates for the future beyond the foregoing but it is believed that the statement fairly represents the probable expenses, unless extraordinary news events should involve temporary additional outlays. The existing cable service is of large volume, and has easily demonstrated its superiority in all its features to the service heretofore obtained through the Eastern alliance. The Washington bureau is well equipped and is supplying the best service had for many years from the National capital." There was but one way to maintain the standard and meet all exigencies. The budget must be better balanced. Revenues must be increased. Reserves must be built up. Assessments were lifted 30 per cent. Since a war chest must be provided, a binding legal form was prepared. "In consideration of one dollar," we agree to pay, as called for, "our several pro rata shares of the cost of such service, over and above its current income, for a period of two years, the total liability of any subscriber not to exceed the sum set opposite his name," with this further condition, "the amounts so advanced to be repaid without interest when and as soon as said Associated Press shall have surplus funds on hand available for such purpose and not otherwise."[1]

The paper was dated Chicago, October 4, 1893. More signatures were appended from time to time, until the total reached $550,500. For moral effect, this formidable guaranty pledge was spread upon the minutes, printed in a special circular, and published far and near.

In due time, the United Press, not to be outdone, sought similarly to impress the publishers of newspapers and the public with its substantial backing and stability. "We pledge ourselves and our associates to leave nothing undone to promote the interests of the United Press and strengthen its position in the several places in which we respectively conduct business, believing as we do that it is to the interest of every one of us to protect to the utmost of our power the integrity of the news service." This carried another imposing array of names: Charles A. Dana, New York *Sun;* Whitelaw Reid, New York *Tribune;* Beriah Wilkins, Washington *Post;* L. Clark Davis, Philadelphia *Ledger;* William M. Singerly, Philadelphia *Record;* Barclay H. Warburton, Philadelphia *Telegraph;* Charles H. Taylor, Boston *Globe;* Stephen O'Meara, Boston *Journal;* F. B. Whitney, Boston *Transcript;* R. S. Howland, Providence *Journal;* W. F. Balkam and Norman E. Mack, New York State Associated Press; A. D. Shepherd, New York *Mail and Express;* C. R. Miller and George F. Spinney, New York *Times;* Samuel Bowles, Springfield *Republican;* John H. Holmes, Boston *Herald;* Gardiner G. Howland, New York *Herald;* and George W. Turner, New York *Recorder.* Incident to the fray, Beriah Wilkins, one of those subscribing this pledge, afterwards took his Washington *Post* over to the Associated Press and drew from Dana a vitriolic denunciation of the backslider.

---

[1] Associated Press Report, 1894, p. 110.

Let us look at Lawson and Stone setting out bravely upon their expedition into the enemy's country. It happened that three of the big New York dailies were being directed by wise men out of the West, formerly associated with the Western Associated Press, friendly disposed. Horace White, at the head of the New York *Evening Post,* recalled his earlier experience with the Chicago *Tribune.* Joseph Pulitzer, new master of the New York *World,* owned the St. Louis *Post-Dispatch.* John A. Cockerill, managing the New York *Advertiser,* had come not so long before to the metropolis from St. Louis. "The *Evening Post* will join your company. But I am under pledge to make no move in the matter without consulting my friends of the New York *Staats-zeitung* and the Brooklyn *Eagle.*" [2] The *World* was averse to running needless risks. Pulitzer wanted to know in advance how he was to stand. The proposition, submitted to him in writing, embraced these items:

The New York *World* and the New York *Evening World* are invited to become members of the general association, with the understanding that each is to hold eight shares of the stock of the Associated Press.

The members holding certificates of the "A" class constitute the local board in each city. These holders have the right of veto of any new member; that is, the association binds itself that it will admit no new members without the unanimous consent of the members of the local board.

The local board in New York is to have, in addition to its veto power as to the admission of new members in New York City, a like veto power in the city of Brooklyn. But it is proposed that the Brooklyn *Eagle* shall be given a veto power in Brooklyn, which is not extended to New York; that is, should a paper desire service in Brooklyn, it would require the assent not only of the New York local board, but also of the Brooklyn *Eagle.* This in no way affects the present status of the Brooklyn editions of the *World,* and before

---

[2] Stone, *Fifty Years,* p. 217.

any contract is signed with the *Eagle*, the rights of the Brooklyn editions of the *World* will be protected.

The New York local board is to consist of the New York *World*, the New York *Evening World*, the New York *Herald*, the New York *Telegram*, the New York *Evening Post*, the New York *Staats-zeitung*, and the New York *Tribune* or *Times*, or both, as the New York *World* may elect. In case the *Herald* and *Telegram* should not join immediately, it would be within the power of the *World*, after a reasonable time, say three months, to say that they should not come in as holders of certificates of the "A" class.

The Associated Press is to give proper and adequate representation to the Eastern papers on its Board of Directors. We have a vacancy in the board to-day, which, in case the *World* joins, will be filled at once by the election of any qualified person you may name.[3]

The *World* thereupon came in and, as its representative, S. S. Carvalho became a member of the directing board. The *Evening Post*, the *Advertiser*, the *Staats-zeitung*, the Brooklyn *Eagle*, came too, but not the other New York papers.

Worthwhile accessions were soon gained in other eastern territory. A number of up-state New York publishers, either outsiders altogether, or desirous of more ample service, became early recruits: in Buffalo, the *Express*, the *Commercial*, the *News*; in Rochester, the *Post-Express*; in Syracuse, the *Herald*, which had been the prime mover in organizing the United Press. A little later, the Philadelphia papers transferred their allegiance almost in a body to the Associated Press, the *North American*, the *Inquirer*, the *Times*, the *Press*, the *Demokrat*, leaving out the *Ledger*, the *Record*, the *Telegraph*.. The advent of the *Traveler* permitted the leased wire to be extended to Boston, then to Maine. By the end of the year, the Washington *Star* and the Baltimore papers, the *Sun*, the *American*, the *News*, had crossed the bridge. The United Press instituted suit against the Baltimore papers for $50,000 damages for breach

---

[3] Associated Press Report, 1894, p. 125.

of contract. Their defection was laid by Dana to the personal efforts of Frank B. Noyes, of the Washington *Star*, whom he violently assailed and upbraided editorially in the *Sun*. Libel suits were started, but eventually dismissed before trial of the issues upon withdrawal by Dana of his charges against Noyes. "The article was written under a misapprehension as to the facts in the case and we regret its publication as doing a grave injustice to a gentleman whose character is above reproach."[4]

In the realm of the old Western Associated Press, numerous accessions were brought in and a few errant papers recovered. "Meanwhile the United Press was utterly unable to break our lines in the West. Only four papers of standing joined that organization. The members of the Associated Press stood like a rock unmoved by the specious and alluring offers made them." As a final stroke, opening the year, all the United Press papers in Chicago, the *Tribune*, the *Herald*, the *Post*, the *Staats-zeitung*, simultaneously abandoned the United Press and joined the Associated Press, so that Chicago presented a solid phalanx of Associated Press papers in welcome to the annual meeting there in February, 1894, which chose Lawson president in appreciation of his work. "The contest has cost not only strenuous exertion, but also a very large expenditure of money. While the increased assessments on the old members, and the added revenue from the steadily growing number of new memberships, have contributed very materially to meet the increased cost of the service, there has remained a considerable additional amount to be provided to meet the heavy cost involved in the contest. In view, however, of the fact that the members of the association have provided

---

[4] *Sun*, April 17, 1897.

an ample guarantee fund for the emergency, the management has conducted the contest on a broad basis, in confidence of complete ultimate success, and has not hesitated to maintain the highest standard of excellence in the news service, and the most aggressive manner of warfare against its adversary." Indeed, the message went on to congratulate one and all, "upon the happy issue of this contest," concluding:

> It is now practically ended, and our memberships and alliances extend to every city of consequence in the country. Tried in the hot fires of the past months, this association, devoted to the principle of the independence of the American press, comes purer and stronger from the ordeal, and with the brightest possible promise for the future. If the members but continue true to themselves, mindful of their highest interests, liberal in the exercise of their rights and privileges, and vigilant in the discharge of their duties, we may reasonably expect the growth and development of this association to the full ideal at which we have aimed.

Premature self-congratulations! The fight was by no means yet won. It was to go on, with bad blood on both sides, now at furious pace, now with unfeigned signs of weariness. The zeal of the leaders kept at white heat, and they carried on like crusaders fired with a holy mission. Though some began to talk of compromise, informal overtures by individual members of the United Press, looking to termination, were declined because, in each instance, based on a territorial division between the two associations. "This has been deemed impossible in view of our obligations, moral and legal, to our eastern members, unfair to our western members in view of their right to some voice in the determination of the character of their eastern and cable news, and unwise as respects the true interest of the entire press of the country in that it would destroy the national character of the Associated Press as an organization." [5] There was to be no turning back of the clock, no return to the *statu quo ante.*

The Southern Associated Press had held aloof and had notified both associations that it abided by the tripartite contract jointly executed, although the dominant members manifested a sympathy for the cause of the United Press. Knowing this preference, the Associated Press offered the New Orleans papers full membership, which offer was at once snapped up. The attempted secession naturally met resistance. Their association refused to accept resignations which would cut a main artery of communication. Unwilling, or unprepared, to extend the line of battle at the moment, the Associated Press prevailed on the New Orleans papers to hold the matter in abeyance, remain with the Southern Associated Press, and pay to that body the charges on the news and the tolls for the leased wires.[6] A demand for revision of the assessment on New Orleans followed and was pressed to arbitration under the supplemental agreement to the contract. When the judgment was rendered in November, 1894, by representatives of the Associated Press, it decreed a reduction of the charge on New Orleans. The Southern association angrily repudiated the finding. It issued an ultimatum to the papers at New Orleans to pay at the old rate or be cut off. The Associated Press started its report to the city on the Gulf, and the Southern Associated Press threw its fortunes with the United Press. The coup netted the latter forty papers in one haul.

Explanations were the order of the day. As president of the Southern organization, Colonel Estill, of the Savannah *News,* insisted that the arbitration agreement applied

---

[5] Associated Press Report, 1895, p. 10.

[6] *Ibid.*, p. 76.

only to an attempted increase of assessment on New Orleans, that it was intended solely to protect the papers in that city against a raise and not to lower the cost of their service at the expense of their associates.[7] For the Associated Press, Lawson retorted that there was room for difference of opinion as to the meaning of the contract; that, conditioned as it was on the then pending agreement between the Associated Press and the United Press, it was legally unenforceable; that a voluntary observance had been undertaken but, "feeling it could not safely assume that the Southern Associated Press would voluntarily continue the contemplated relations," all being equally free to act as they pleased, the Associated Press "deemed it the part of ordinary business prudence to take into membership such papers of the South as could be immediately reached. The New Orleans papers were, in this way and under these conditions, at once taken into membership." "The Associated Press," as Lawson put it, "while considering itself no longer under obligations to do so, still stands ready to abide by the whole contract with the Southern Associated Press as it understands its obligations expressed therein and its report is still being tendered your agents as per the provisions of the contract and this notwithstanding that the report of the Southern Associated Press to the Associated Press has been discontinued."[8]

It was too late to retrace steps. To the invitation to join the Associated Press as individuals, only one or two responded, most outstanding among them, Adolph S. Ochs, of the Chattanooga *Times,* himself the leading figure in the original organization of the Southern Associated Press. Imbued with a deep sense of fairness to his colleagues, he

[7] *Ibid.,* p. 81.
[8] *Ibid.,* p. 83.

expressly stipulated that the same door be kept open for them, that the other papers of the South be accepted on equal terms, should they elect to adopt his course. He had cast the single vote against the exclusive alliance with the United Press which was then being acclaimed by the latter as insuring the downfall of its western rival. There were no indications of yielding, much less of surrender, and both combatants continued to parade their "beats" and to boast their superiority louder than ever.

Soon, new pressure spurred new efforts to secure mutual understanding. Another conference, held this time in the neutral atmosphere of the executive offices of the Western Union, faced the altered status. Tentative plans prepared by the two general managers, Stone and Phillips, were offered for consideration, then other plans. The first scheme submitted laid down these aims:

1. To maintain the integrity of both the Associated Press and the United Press organizations.
2. To perfect a working arrangement between the two bodies so as to save the duplication of expense.
3. To establish the relations of the two concerns by specific contract for a term of years.
4. To put the administration of the joint organization thus created into the hands of a joint board of control.
5. To obligate the joint board to carry out faithfully all existing contracts of both associations.[9]

Though Stone presented the proposal which he had helped to draft, he simultaneously withdrew his endorsement of it. "I am utterly unable to see how the Associated Press could adjust the relations of its members in New England, New York state and the South to these minor organizations." The obstacles were pictured as almost insuperable. "The

[9] *Ibid.*, 1896, p. 103.

inviolability of contracts, both in letter and in spirit, is and must be of the highest importance in all of this business. The Associated Press has contract obligations which it must be mindful of and which seem to me to absolutely forbid the adoption of this plan. Therefore, I feel bound to say that, unfortunate as is the present situation, I can see no way out except for the United Press members and clients to join the Associated Press wherever it may be possible and for those left to carry on their own service."

Two days later found the conference committee sponsoring still another program which it had worked out:

1. A working arrangement in accordance with powers given by the by-laws of each association.

2. A simple contract for a specified period.

3. A board of control of five members, two each from the Associated Press and the United Press, and a fifth chosen by the United Press from three names submitted by the Associated Press of its members east of the Alleghanies.

4. Board members to have one-year terms, but each association to have power of removal and substitution; the board to have full control of assessments, disbursements, news report and other business pertaining to the joint organization.

5. A guaranty to United Press members and clients of present contract service and assessments, except in certain cases to be scheduled.

6. Surplus revenues to be devoted to: (*a*) repayment of advances to cover expenses and losses during the last two years; (*b*) accumulation of a reserve fund; (*c*) reduction of assessments on an equitable basis.

7. Incorporation of a New York Associated Press out of the membership of the United Press and its subsidiary associations.

8. Contract to run until terminated by six-month notice by one of the parties.

9. On adoption by both the Associated Press and the United Press, a joint committee to put the plan into execution.

The United Press agreed, but the attorney for the Associated Press blocked further progress by questioning the power of his corporation to give the authority proposed to a joint board of control. "Having spent five days in earnest consideration of the various plans and suggestions offered, the representatives of the Associated Press feel bound to advise the representatives of the United Press that, in their judgment, the only feasible method of settlement must contemplate the maintenance of its news service throughout the entire country by the Associated Press. We, therefore, beg to invite you to give consideration to some plan looking to the admission of the United Press members to the Associated Press."

Receiving the report of the stalemated proceedings, the directors of the Associated Press noted their approval. The peace project "disregards obligations which this board holds as inviolable." The question of disregarding inviolable obligations of the United Press seems not to have been raised. So far as the Associated Press was concerned, all were specifically advised that no terms but these would be entertained:

1. A working arrangement with the United Press covering news service only.

2. The Associated Press must hold the entire reins.

3. The Associated Press to gather all the news and supply it to the papers of both associations where its contract obligations do not prevent.

4. A subsidiary association to be formed which shall furnish news to the existing papers which the Associated Press contracts prevent it from serving.

5. The Associated Press to sell and furnish such news to subsidiary associations as may be deemed wise and which will give the Associated Press an excluding vote where new papers apply for service from the subsidiary association.[10]

"Your proposition is received and rejected. We regret that your committee has so singularly misunderstood the

---

[10] *Ibid.*, p. 130.

meaning of the resolution presented on behalf of the United Press conferees at the meeting of May 24, 1895." So read the curt reply.

"The real difficulty in the way of a settlement of the contest," declared Lawson in a confidential letter to the members, "was the fact that the four New York newspapers are individually under legal obligations, which they cannot escape if they would, to provide an adequate news service to certain papers throughout the country, some of which obligations the Associated Press is unable to assume without the consent of those of its members who hold exclusive rights as to the delivery of the service to new papers in the cities affected."[11]

The United Press could not rest silent under these imputations of weakness. Its answer took the form of an interview with Phillips, the general manager, published and republished in friendly journals.[12] Among the newest recruits, Phillips let it be known, were the *Tribune* at Cincinnati, and the *Chronicle,* the morning daily just established at Chicago. The United Press was serving 100 more papers in the whole country than the "Chicago Associated Press," as the adversary was flippantly designated. The United Press had recently captured three of the principal papers of the Pacific coast, the San Francisco *Call,* the San José *Mercury,* the Sacramento *Record-Union.* During the two years of warfare, it had never raised its price to customers. "The character of the organization can be judged from the class of men who are associated in its management. Its president is Charles A. Dana of the *Sun,* the recognized dean of American journalism. Among the

---

[11] *Ibid.,* p. 138.

[12] Louisville *Courier Journal,* June 17, 1895; San Francisco *Call,* June 30, 1895.

directors are James Gordon Bennett, proprietor of the New York *Herald;* George F. Spinney, publisher of the New York *Times;* Whitelaw Reid, owner of the New York *Tribune;* John H. Holmes, proprietor of the Boston *Herald* and president of the New England Associated Press; Evan P. Howell, proprietor of the Atlanta *Constitution* and president of the Southern Associated Press; George Bleistein, proprietor of the Buffalo *Courier* and president of the New York State Associated Press; Milton A. McRae, general manager of the Cincinnati *Post* and St. Louis *Chronicle;* L. Clarke Davis, of the Philadelphia *Ledger.*" The smaller papers could see how much more advantageous "our plan" was for them. About 70 per cent of the aggregate cost of the news was met by a few papers in the large cities and it was but natural and just that the management should be in their hands instead of being scattered among a number so large that it could not work coherently. "Any client of ours can become a stockholder in the United Press and thus have a voice in its management and at a nominal cost."

More than three years had passed since the parting of the ways, with no cessation of the struggle. The Associated Press now felt it necessary to call for payments on its guaranty fund in order to reduce floating debt and strengthen its financial fortifications. The United Press, despite a bold front, was clearly taking the heavier punishment. The New York dailies which had to bear the brunt of it were wincing. One of them, the *Times,* had actually collapsed under a weight of which its news-war tax had been no small item. James Gordon Bennett, in his Paris palace, was showing an annoyance and a desire to be relieved of it. The omens looked more favorable to peace maneuvering. After consulting with President Lawson, General Manager Stone sailed for Europe for the one purpose of discussing the possibilities with the proprietor of the New York *Herald*. He found Bennett, possessing interests in common with Dana, reluctant to act by himself. He advised offering Dana an Associated Press service for the *Sun*. Stone returned, he prevailed upon the *World* to yield its consent, he asked Dana by letter for an appointment, "for the consideration of a plan for the settlement of the existing press war." Dana referred him to Laffan, expected to be back from Europe in two weeks. Bennett, when informed of this, cabled Stone "to write Mr. Laffan a polite and friendly letter." Stone followed the suggestion. "In my present state of health," was the word from Laffan, "a conference is not possible but Mr. Stone may put what he proposes in writing." The written memorandum was submitted under date of January 28, 1897:[13]

I propose: (1) That the Associated Press take over such United Press papers as may be served by it without infraction of existing contracts between the Associated Press and its own members. This I assume will provide for a vast majority of the United Press papers. (2) In the exceptional cases, the differences be composed by mutual effort.

The following day brought a reply that left no doubt as to its finality:

NEW YORK, January 29, 1897

Melville E. Stone, Esq.

DEAR SIR: Your proposition can not be entertained by us and any conference about it would be useless. The only proposal from you that we would be willing to consider would be one offering to withdraw entirely from the eastern field and hand it over to us just as it was before you began business; and then we might be prepared to discuss with you the terms of any subsequent dealings that might become convenient between the parties.

Yours truly,

W. M. LAFFAN

---

[13] Associated Press Report, 1898, p. 161.

The serious nature of the situation was no secret. It was heightened by the defection from the United Press of the Boston *Herald,* whose editor, John H. Holmes, had long been president of the New England Associated Press, a director of the United Press, an active proponent of its claims. The principal owner of the paper now delivered it into the camp of the Associated Press. When efforts to stop the move in the courts failed, members of the New England Associated Press forthwith called for a general meeting of all the various organizations affiliated with the United Press to ascertain the facts and discuss their news relationships. Their action was set out in the communication, of February 10, 1897, presented officially by the chairman, General Charles H. Taylor, to President Lawson:

At a meeting held to-day by the representatives of the various press associations making up the United Associated Presses, the chairman was requested to notify the various members and clients that the United Press was in better and stronger condition, financially and otherwise, than it has been at any time during the past three years.

Resolved, That we have every confidence in the ability of the United Associated Presses to successfully conduct their affairs.

Resolved, That we pledge our united support to maintain the integrity of our respective associations and our contract relations with the United Press.

Resolved, That it is the sense of the representatives of the different associations present at this meeting that we act as a unit in the matter of any possible settlement of the differences between the United Associated Presses and the Associated Press.

Resolved, That a committee consisting of a representative of each of the four New York newspapers, which are a party to the contracts between the New York State, Philadelphia, Southern, and New England associations, be appointed to confer with the officers of the Associated Press with a view to the settlement of differences existing between the United Associated Presses and the Associated Press, said committee to report at as early an hour as possible.

The conference concerned itself with a proposal to take United Press papers into the Associated Press, "as far as possible," and to assume a part of the United Press debt. No way could be devised to compose an agreement acceptable to the *World* providing for the Hearst New York publications on equal terms. It was disclosed that the four New York newspapers had made a contract the preceding year with Hearst to protect the New York *Journal* and the San Francisco *Examiner* in the same rights and privileges, in any new combination, as they were enjoying in the United Press, and to continue with the United Press for a period of eighteen months from the date of the agreement, of which only five months had expired. Without a moment's vacillation the *Sun* announced its irreconcilable position:

> Our associates in the conduct of the United Press, the *Tribune,* the *Herald,* and the *Times,* having entered upon negotiations for the surrender of the United Press to the Chicago Associated Press, without consultation with the *Sun,* and without even asking our consent, it becomes proper that we should now give public notice to whom it may concern that the *Sun* has no part in these negotiations, but firmly rejects them, believing them to be conceived in bad faith, and conducted in folly. Furthermore the *Sun* makes known that thirty days from the date hereof, it will cease to be a member of the United Press.
>
> The *Sun* will also continue to collect the news for itself and to discharge all obligations imposed upon it through the confidence of its contemporaries, now or hereafter.[14]

Again, not so fast. Another day's prints were to proclaim failure of the negotiations, the return of the *Sun,* the continuation of the United Associated Presses.

Five weeks of rumors and uncertainty ensued. Finally, March 27, the *Herald,* the *Tribune,* the *Times,* and the

---

[14] *Sun,* Feb. 19, 1897.

Telegram, were taken into the Associated Press, leaving out, in New York City, only the *Sun,* the *Evening Sun,* and the *Journal.* Two days later, an assignment in bankruptcy of the United Press was filed by President Dana, and Frederick G. Mason named as receiver. Liabilities were scheduled at $129,415 and assets at $38,040. Service of news by the United Press ended April 7. In a few months, Dana was dead, having been ill a long time. Laffan succeeded to the management of the *Sun* and its news-gathering activities. Walsh, ere long, was in financial difficulties that eliminated his interest in journalism. Phillips became one of the executives of the Columbia Graphophone Company, with which he was identified for more than fifteen years; he was prominent in the National Red Cross and, for a time following the Spanish American War, was one of its Board of Control; the last six years of his life were spent in retirement at Vineyard Haven, Massachusetts, where he died in 1920 at the age of 73.

CHAPTER XX

BINDING UP THE WOUNDS OF WAR

The set-up of the victorious Associated Press—Conditions imposed upon the vanquished—Survey of the news situation—Underlying principles of the association—Excluded papers forced to self-service

THE long-lasting, bitter, stubbornly fought struggle had been hard on the victors as well as the vanquished. The Associated Press board was convened in New York. It ordered immediate discontinuance of the voluntary increase in assessments paid for nearly three years by about ninety stockholding members. These payments had amounted to $283,393. Guaranty fund subscriptions had been collected in the sum of $159,712. The aggregate of these advances figured $442,105, "which it is the purpose to refund to the contributors." With the original reserve gone, the grand total chargeable to the conflict had mounted well over $500,000, probably nearer to $1,000,000.[1]

Since all opposition forces were shattered, the Associated Press was at length the undisputed overlord in the domain of news in the United States. The next task was to pick up the broken fragments, to fit them together in an all-inclusive nation-wide organization, to smooth out the rough places, to repair its own spent strength, to make the future secure against recurrence. From very inception, the incessant demands of the fight had consumed every energy and distracted all attention. It was time to turn to introspection and to inquire what sort of edifice had been

[1] Associated Press Report, 1897, p. 3.

erected in which all must find a home and live together. How had the principle of a self-governing coöperative news-gathering association been worked out? What did the charter and by-laws contemplate?

The Associated Press was a stock company, incorporated under the laws of Illinois, with its capital stock limited originally to $100,000 in shares of $50 each. The stockholders chose the directors for overlapping terms of three years, and the directors annually elected the officers. All proprietors of papers served with news were members of the association, but only those holding stock had votes in the annual meeting and were eligible for directors. Stockholdings were in blocks of no more than eight shares. So there could be at most 250 stockholding participants; the actual maximum attained was 184. Nearly 700 papers were to be served with news reports. Two-thirds of these must be content with non-voting, "B" membership, contracts. No new member might be admitted in any district except by consent of the "A" members, unless within the further specific exemption whereby papers entitled by contract to Western Associated Press or United Press service on October 15, 1892, were not to be considered new members. The district was not to exceed 60 miles in radius and, within each such area, "A" members composed a local board possessing unconditional veto power. Each news report delivered was to be published in but one paper, and in but one language, as specified in the contract. All members were obligated to maintain uninterrupted regular publication, to take the service for a stated period, to publish the same in whole or in part, to pay weekly assessments in advance, to furnish all news of the district spontaneous in origin, such news, however, not to be supplied by the Associated Press to other papers in the same district. To safeguard the report, news must not be given to any outsider ahead of publication, nor news to another member which the association was debarred from serving. No one receiving the report might furnish, or permit another to furnish, its news to, or obtain news from, any person, firm, or corporation, declared to be "antagonistic," nor pay money to an antagonistic association, nor furnish news to any news agency except with the written authority of the board. Members must print credits to the Associated Press, or other paper, as required. Violating a nonintercourse order following an antagonistic declaration would risk suspension, or fine up to $1,000, after a hearing, in case of suspension, subject to appeal to the annual meeting. Penalties of suspension and fine attached also to premature publication of any document confided to the association for use on a designated date, "however said member may have secured said document."

Post-war reconstruction raised many fine questions. Associated Press memberships must be held for the papers individually, with no more bulk service to auxiliary associations. In preliminary parleys, a broad and liberal policy of admission for United Press papers had been pledged and it was believed this pledge contributed materially to the outcome. When termination of the opposition service precipitated a flood of applications from nearly every publication thus affected, the promise was construed to mean admission for all, unless "some conclusive objection" were presented by the local board involving the interests of the association as a whole. Complications arose, nevertheless, in numerous cities, particularly where the contest had been relentlessly waged to the finish. Should a paper which had done all it could to destroy the Associated Press, which had stood out to the end, perhaps a deserter from original

Associated Press ranks, which had refused persistently every overture and inducement to come in, which had saved money by taking the cheaper United Press report and thereby imposed extra costs on its loyal competitor, be now placed in as good a position as if it had been a faithful member all the time? Should the consent given to facilitate the scheme for division of territory as at first proposed, and then renewed only as a war measure to help save the day, avail the enemy after peace had been so dearly won? What would have been the reprisals were the United Press the master? What consideration would have been accorded Associated Press partisans left similarly at the mercy of their opponents?

This much, at least, was settled—the sectional associations must go out of active business. Furthermore, unless by special dispensation, the outcasts from the United Press camp must accept "B" memberships without stockholding privileges. In different places, limitations of various kinds were inserted in the contracts. In New York, admission of the *Mail and Express,* for example, was subject to a proviso, exacted by the *World* as condition precedent to waiver of its supreme prerogative, which read:

> Should the said *Mail and Express,* or its successor or assign, or newspaper amalgamated or consolidated therewith, or said newspaper under other name, or the majority of the capital stock of the corporation publishing the said paper, or its successor or assign, or newspaper consolidated therewith, or said newspaper under other name, pass into the hands of one William R. Hearst, or any corporation which he shall own or control, directly or indirectly, or in the event of this franchise being used in any manner whatsoever in connection with the publication of an evening edition of the *Journal* in New York City, or any successor thereof, then, [etc.], this franchise ceases and shall be void.[2]

---

[2] *Ibid.,* 1898, p. 342.

Admission of the New York *Times* was likewise made contingent on a conditional clause against its passing into possession of "one William R. Hearst, or Charles A. Dana, or William M. Laffan, or two or more of said persons," to be used "in any manner whatsoever in connection with the publication of an edition of the *Journal* or New York *Journal*, or the *Sun* or the *Evening Sun*." In Buffalo, the *Times* had to submit to a definite stipulation covering change of management or sale. Contracts with each former member of the Trans-Mississippi Press Association required execution of a waiver for an additional afternoon paper, whenever the population of the city or town should increase 50 per cent, and providing for the issue of a new contract in its place should such member at any time cease publication or surrender its contract.[3] Still other papers were compelled first to relinquish and assign to the Associated Press whatever damage, or other rights, they might have claimed under certain unexpired contracts with the United Press. The covenants in question had been guaranteed by the four New York dailies, the *Herald*, the *Tribune*, the *Times* and the *Sun*, which had been given assurance by Lawson of this measure of protection.[4]

For the four papers owned by the Scripps interests, the Cleveland *Press*, the Cincinnati *Post*, the St. Louis *Chronicle* and the Kansas City *World*, the beginning of our great newspaper chains, a combined application was presented. "Let me say that, unless all can be admitted, I should want to withdraw the application of all."[5] The Kansas City *World*, founded only the preceding year, could not come under the exemption accorded to publications

[3] *Ibid.*, p. 378.
[4] News Publishing Co., *versus* Associated Press, 114 Ill. App., p. 241.
[5] Associated Press Report, 1898, p. 318.

receiving a press service in October, 1892, and William R. Nelson, proprietor of the Kansas City *Star* and possessed of protest rights, could be induced to consent to a contract for the *World* for one year only, to cease then unless further consent were given. Nelson insisted the paper could not long survive, a prediction eventually vindicated, and was not to be budged an inch even by a bombardment lasting till 4 o'clock in the morning.[6] Consent for Cleveland territory had been secured on express condition that all four applicants passed muster; and, in St. Louis, the *Post-Dispatch* declined to concede an equal-term franchise. On disclosure of this situation, the request was recalled, an incident fraught with far-reaching, and at the time unsuspected, consequences.

Regardless of the record as here set forth, it has been stated repeatedly that the Scripps papers declined to enter the Associated Press when the opportunity to do so was within their grasp.[7] Such assertions rest upon a version of Edward W. Scripps, which described the conditional application submitted to the Associated Press over the name of Milton A. McRae, to whom the rôle had been assigned, as merely a feint to compel its rejection and thus to forward a project, long in mind, for launching a new news agency. Desiring to bring his associates, especially his brother, George H. Scripps, to his way of thinking, the application purposely incorporated the stipulation for admission of all four papers or none, and also a verbal requirement that full "A" membership contracts be granted to each, the last demand surely known to be impossible of fulfillment. By artfully impressing the desperate and help-

---

[6] Noyes, *Battle for a Free Press*, p. 10.

[7] Howard, "United Press," *Publishers' Guide*, XXI, 31; Irwin, "United Press," *Harper's Weekly*, April 25, 1914.

JAMES W. SIMONTON

ERASTUS BROOKS

HENRY GEORGE

THOMAS W. KNOX

less position of the journals in question upon the representatives of the Associated Press dealing with the matter, an appearance of arrogance and condescension on their part was utilized to win adherence to the independent news project, nurtured by Edward W. Scripps, as their sole alternative. So, when it transpired that no place remained open to them except "as humble clients," the determination not to submit to this indignity and subordination was strengthened, and unanimity attained for the Scripps group to go it alone; in fact, there is evidence to the effect that the working details of the scheme, including even the outline of the announcement to be sent out to all clients of the defunct United Press soliciting their patronage, were formulated in advance and immediately set in motion.

In some localities, litigation alone could determine the respective legal rights of old and new members, resulting frequently in adjustments, sometimes in the form of bonus payments. In such cases, differential assessments over a fixed period were to equalize previously paid bonuses or other reimbursable items. These payments by the United Press papers included $2,775 in Springfield, Massachusetts, $3,000 in Hartford, $8,370 in Omaha, $26,016.67 in Milwaukee. Other bonuses were to be applied to reduction of the association's indebtedness.

The Associated Press was now delivering news to 708 papers, and its expenditures were running over $1,500,000. As stable conditions were restored, improvement of the service called for greater attention, the effort being unhindered by the old fear of an overdrawn bank account. The leased wire circuits were largely extended, reaching, in 1897, a total of 26,798 miles. The extra outlay entailed by the exciting presidential campaign of 1896, lasting through six months, had been held down to $37,328 for wires, tolls, operators, salaries, travel expense, etc., including $9,212 for the Republican convention, $12,691 for the Democratic convention, $5,618 for the Populists and Silverites, $3,820 for the Gold Democrats, and $5,985 for the campaign.[8] With the war with Spain, all precedents were thrown to the winds. To meet the expected demands, assessments were increased at the first war signal by 25 per cent on all leased wire members, and 10 per cent on pony papers.[9] Before the treaty of peace was ratified, the war news had cost the Associated Press $274,514.[10] The job was done with infinite industry and expedition. Sixteen men were taken from the offices at Albany, New York City, Washington, Buffalo, St. Paul, Chicago, and San Francisco for the work in and about Cuba. Five dispatch boats were chartered to speed the news of land and sea engagements to cable stations in Jamaica, Haiti, San Domingo, and the Virgin Islands. The difficulties and dangers were many and severe, tropical tangles, fever camps, disputes with harbor officials, watching battlefield scenes, hovering over hospitals. It was a definite test of the art of news-gathering and transmission. The same could be said of the work in the Philippines, where the war moves were covered in all detail, and what once would have been prohibitive cable tolls had no deterrent effect on the transmission of big stories from the other side of the globe. In a little while, an expenditure of $18,697 simply to cover an international yacht race was not considered extravagant, $28,000 was to be paid later to report the Martinique disaster, over $300,000 to get the news of the Russo-Japanese War.[11]

---

[8] Associated Press Report, 1897, p. 34.

[9] *Ibid.*, 1899, p. 134.

[10] *Ibid.*, p. 38.

[11] *M. E. S.*, p. 184.

It is not always easy to reconcile ideal and actuality. The ideal of the builders of the Associated Press had contemplated a single, nation-wide, non-profit, coöperative news association, controlled by the papers served, yet protecting each member from the menace of new competition. The concept, as a practical guide, was neither unchangeable nor clear-cut. At times, the paramount issue seemed to be mainly one of control.

Shall the news-gathering business be permitted to fall into the hands of a syndicate of mercenary sharks who will use it simply to plunder the press of the country, or shall the newspapers continue, as in the past, to coöperate in the collecting of their own news and to enjoy both the advantages of controlling the service and getting it at actual cost? [12]

It is a monstrous absurdity to think of two great press associations, each paralleling the lines of the other with a net-work of wires from the Pacific to the Atlantic and from the Lakes to the Gulf, expending every day a vast amount of energy and money and taking a double force and a double equipment to do what could be done just as effectively, if not more so, by one well-organized, concentrated national organization.[13]

It is the theory of the Associated Press that there should be but one news-gathering association of the first class and that, if conditions compel the existence of a second organization, it should be one in which the stockholders of the Associated Press are stockholders, and controlling stockholders.[14]

The issue was this: Shall the newspapers of the United States be at the mercy of a privately owned news-collecting and distributing organization, at its mercy not only as concerns a money tribute, but, of much more importance, at its mercy as to the news received, whether it would be honest or perverted, whether it should be impartial or biased, whether it should be influenced by the interests and opinions of its owners, and the press of the United States and the people of the United States be subject to the unrestrained will

[12] James E. Scripps, circular letter, Sept. 1, 1893.
[13] E. P. Howell, in Associated Press Report, 1896, p. 55.
[14] Lawson, Associated Press Report, 1897, p. 75.

of individuals, or an individual, so far as press association news was concerned.[15]

Opportunism, however, had more often prevailed. Demonstrably, negotiating at the outset turned, not on the matter of coöperation or self-government, but upon a proposed division of territory between the Associated Press and the United Press, and the amount of bonus to be paid to one side by the other in addition to the exchanged news. More than half the country was to be left to the profit-seekers. Later adjustment on the original lines was frustrated more than once only by contract obligations to protect exclusive franchises in enemy territory. The final terms in themselves contemplated, not a single nation-wide organization, but a controlling association and one or more subordinate associations to which the less favored newspapers were to be relegated. Inability or indisposition to take in all was sure to force some to depend on other news springs. The very structure of the Associated Press, forbidding and penalizing commerce with "antagonistic" agencies, recognized and made necessary alternative news arrangements, even while proclaiming the goal of all-inclusive relations. So, though the United Press had been smashed, a guerilla warfare upon the scattered remnants of the former foe persisted.

Abandoned by previous allies, outlawed from every contact with Associated Press members, compelled to rely wholly on its own resources, the New York *Sun,* uncompromising and undaunted, held aloft its motto, "The *Sun* Shines for All." Since the late eighties, the *Sun* had been maintaining an extensive corps of special correspondents, whose characteristic treatment of current happenings was

---

[15] Noyes, *op. cit.,* p. 7.

placed at the disposal of other papers through the Laffan News Bureau. Upon this Bureau now devolved the task of providing an adequate general news service. "I have just torn up my Associated Press franchise. We've got to have the news of the world to-morrow morning and we've got to get it ourselves," is the way Dana is said to have called the Bureau to action when he first broke from the old combination.[16] The *Sun* at once fell back again upon its own organization and provided a shelter, at the same time, for many of the papers set adrift by the disintegration of the United Press. The Laffan Bureau became a commercial news mart, the clearing house of the *Sun's* news; it bought and sold to customers; the number of its patrons, never great, varied from time to time, but it kept going nearly twenty years, until 1916, when the *Sun*, purchased by Frank A. Munsey, secured Associated Press service by merger with the New York *Press*, which he had previously picked up. In the beginning, however, the *Sun* and the Laffan Bureau held stellar places on the Associated Press blacklist of "antagonistic" organizations, with which members were forbidden to traffic under threat of severe penalties.

A difficult position also confronted the Hearst papers, especially in New York. There, the *World* and the *Journal* were at grips in a combat without quarter for the coign of vantage in their competitive field. Pulitzer evidently believed that he had the whip hand and that he had effectually shut out this opponent by the conditions exacted for his consent to admission of the other dailies. Such was the charge, at any rate, preferred by Hearst, when he executed a flank movement and suddenly bought the *Commercial Advertiser* and united it with his morning paper. The

[16] O'Brien, *The Story of The Sun*, p. 373.

Advertiser had been one of the original Associated Press recruits in the metropolis, and the membership contract granted Colonel Cockerill, in the meanwhile deceased, contained no clause voiding it in case of transfer. But the proprietor of the *Journal* was soon to print papers also in other cities, some entitled to Associated Press service and others excluded from it. His nonmember publications were prohibited, not only from using information received by their sister journals from the Associated Press, but also from sharing the news gathered by the Associated Press members of the group. It would be a matter of life and death for these papers to have the news of the day. The exchange arrangements, at first a sort of family affair, developed in due course into a separate news bureau which afterwards was to become a dual agency, the International News Service for evening papers, and the Universal Service for morning papers. Their news was similarly sold to customers not included in the Hearst-owned chain. Lest the patronage of Associated Press members contribute to building up a rival, these news exchanges were branded "antagonistic."

The four Scripps-McRae publications, as just explained, constituted another combination which had to make sure of a dependable supply of general news in consequence of inability to obtain admission to the Associated Press for all of them. Since all four were evening papers, it was feasible for them to pool their news. By taking on other papers as customers, they succeeded in extending their coverage and sources and began to look forward to making news-vending yield a profit. Thus, the Scripps-McRae Press Association entered the field as a news agency on strictly commercial lines. Interlocked with the Publishers' Press in the East, and with the Scripps News Association on the Pacific coast, it had drawn the ban of being "antagonistic" to the Associated Press.

Upon the passing of the old United Press from the scene, and during the years immediately following, a recrudescence of the early régime of independent reporters was visible, especially in New York. Various more or less impressive titles were adopted to elevate their standing in the eyes of possible clients, such as Globe Press Association, National Press Association, Consolidated News Service, etc. Their activities were devoted principally to querying for special dispatches on order, supplying news tips out of the early editions, furnishing by mail rewritten foreign news letters for Sunday release. Special agencies sprang up, offering reports covering limited fields, insurance news, financial news, marine news, sporting news, verging on the feature syndicates, and also for supplying the foreign language press with material, usually translated from the English dailies or compiled from the latest-received European papers.

CHAPTER XXI

LEGAL ENTANGLEMENTS OF THE ASSOCIATED PRESS

Dangers inherent in the existing contingency—Nonintercourse order on the *Inter-Ocean*—Court maintains that the association is impressed with a public interest—Missouri court rejects Illinois precedent

WHILE these opposition or independent organizations could not be regarded as formidable, they carried a threat to the protective aspects of Associated Press membership; they held out possibility of service encouraging establishment of new papers in any locality which invited. Such conditions meant danger to the Associated Press both from within and without. An insistent journal, proscribed by refusal of consent to its admission by an Associated Press competitor, might challenge its exclusion and attempt to crash the gate. In fact, legislation to facilitate this very aim, by establishing a status of common carrier, was being proposed in a number of states and actually passed in Kentucky, Tennessee, and Texas.[1] Again, some disgruntled newspaper, already a member of the Associated Press, called to account for subscribing to an interdicted service, might resist discipline and defy all power to curb its action. Both of these tests were bound to come, and soon came. In St. Louis, the *Star* essayed to assert a legal right to admission to Associated Press membership, resulting in full vindication of the association's contentions. In Chicago, the *Inter-Ocean* resorted to the courts against an order suspending service for violation of an "antagonistic" bull, and evoked

---

[1] Associated Press Report, 1899, p. 3.

a drastic judicial declaration that the Associated Press came within the rule of a public utility required to furnish its service on fair and equal terms to all applying.

The nonintercourse question had been up before. Some years earlier, the Washington *News* was enjoined from furnishing news to the United Press, although the court refused to interfere with its receipt of dispatches from that source. "I can see no objection in the world on the score of public policy, or any other ground, to this part of the contract," declared the deciding judge. "By virtue of the contract, that news became the property of the complainant and the defendant had no right to deliver that news to any other organization."[2] The New York *Sun* had instituted suit in equity and for damages by reason of the blacklisting, which suit was still pending but destined never to reach a decision on the merits. The same fate, for that matter, awaited similar actions subsequently initiated on the part of other publications.[3]

So far as surface indications showed, therefore, no serious alarm was caused by the filing, in January, 1898, of an injunction petition likely to project this point anew. In this case, the Chicago *Inter-Ocean*, cited for supplying news to and receiving news from the New York *Sun*, "antagonistic to the Associated Press," moved for restraining orders against interruption of service and expulsion from membership. The preliminary ruling favored the Associated Press, whereupon, early in March, the report going to the *Inter-Ocean* was unceremoniously discontinued. The appeal from the decree of dismissal started the customary train of time-consuming docketing, briefs, motions, arguments, and consideration in chambers. Not for two years was the final

---

[2] *Ibid.*, 1895, p. 42.
[3] *Ibid.*, 1898, p. 49; 1900, p. 103.

adjudication announced. On February 19, 1900, it fell like a thunder-clap on the camp of the association. What had caused the bolt, apparently, stood in the stated purpose of the corporate charter of the Associated Press, "to erect, lease, or sell telegraph and telephone lines," incidental to its mission of collecting and distributing current news, which statement the court construed to stamp its character, even though it had never actually engaged in the telegraph or telephone business. Pursuing this line of reasoning, the opinion went on to say:

> The organization of such a method of gathering information and news from so wide an extent of territory as is done by the appellee corporation, and the dissemination of that news, requires the expenditure of vast sums of money. It reaches out to the various parts of the United States where its agents gather news which is wired to it, and through it such news is received by the various important newspapers of the country. Scarcely any newspaper could organize and conduct the means of gathering the information that is centered in an association of the character of the appellee because of the enormous expense, and no newspaper could be regarded as a newspaper of the day unless it had access to and published the reports from such an association as appellee. For news gathered from all parts of the country, the various newspapers are almost solely dependent on such an association and, if they are prohibited from publishing it, or its use is refused to them, their character as newspapers is destroyed and they would soon become practically worthless publications.
>
> The Associated Press, from the time of its organization and establishment in business, sold its news reports to various newspapers who became members, and the publication of that news became of vast importance to the public, so that public interest is attached to the dissemination of that news. The manner in which that corporation has used its franchise has charged its business with a public interest. It has devoted its property to a public use and has, in effect, granted to the public such an interest in its use that it must submit to be controlled by the public for the common good to the extent of the interest it has thus created in the public in its private property. The sole purpose for which news was gathered

was that the same should be sold, and all newspaper publishers desiring to purchase such news for publication are entitled to purchase the same without discrimination against them.

The by-law of the appellee corporation [the "antagonistic" order] is not required for corporate purposes, nor included within the purposes of the creation of that corporation. To enforce the provisions of the contract and this by-law would enable the appellee to designate the character of the news that should be published and, whether true or false, there could be no check on it by publishing news from other sources. Appellee would be powerful in the creation of a monopoly in its favor and could dictate the character of news it would furnish and could prejudice the interests of the public. Such a power was never contemplated in its creation and is hostile to public interests. That by-law tends to restrict competition because it prevents its members from purchasing news from any other source than from itself. It seeks to exclude from publication by any of its members news gathered from any other corporation or source than itself which it declares antagonistic. Its tendency, therefore, is to create a monopoly in its own favor and to prevent its members from procuring news from others engaged in the same character of work, and such provision is null and void.[4]

Upon confirmation of the decision in April, 1900, the *Inter-Ocean* asked for reinstatement to membership, for a receiver for the association, for indemnification of losses during its suspension, for an injunction to prevent a dissolution of the Associated Press that would enable it to evade the result of the litigation.

In the St. Louis case, the facts were simple enough and not disputed. The *Post-Dispatch* enjoyed a contract investing it with exclusive rights to the Associated Press service in that city for evening publication. It refused to share these rights with the *Star*, which thereupon invoked equitable relief, alleging that it was a victim of an unlawful monopoly. After another dilatory course of legal sparring, during which the decision in favor of the *Inter-Ocean*

[4] Inter-Ocean Publishing Co., *versus* Associated Press, 184, Ill., p. 439.

was rendered, the petition filed on behalf of the *Star* was denied. In the accompanying opinion, the Missouri judge definitely declined to be governed by the Illinois interpretation of the law, stating his views, in part, as follows:

> In so far as relates to respondent being possessed by its original charter of a right to conduct a telegraph and telephone business, it never exercised that authority and therefore did not acquire the right of eminent domain; that right lay dormant. But whether exercised or not, the charter having been so altered by amendment to eliminate those rights, the case stands here as if such rights had never been existent.
>
> The controlling element which gave origin to the opinion relied on seems to have been that of a monopoly, but of course, that element can have no place in the present instance because respondent has been granted no special or exclusive right or privilege by the state nor has it received any benefits from that quarter. Nor has the respondent acquired any additional right by reason of its incorporation to that it possessed before. Every one is at liberty to gather news; and the fact that one has greater facilities or finance for gathering and transmitting news, or that the business has grown into one of great magnitude, widespread in its ramifications, or that mere incorporation has been granted a company organized for the purpose of gathering news, does not, and can not of itself, give the state the right to regulate what before incorporation was but a natural right.
>
> The business is one of personal service; an occupation. Unless there is "property" to be "affected with a public interest," there is no basis laid for the fact or the charge of a monopoly. Nor is there any more "property" in "news," to wit, "information," "knowledge," "intelligence," than there is in the "viewless winds," until the "guinea stamp" of copyright is impressed upon its external similitude.[5]

The opinion further recited that, according to the testimony, other news agencies possessed the same facilities over the wires, that the terms for the use of the telegraph were uniform, that hundreds of daily newspapers in every

[5] Star Publishing Co., *versus* Associated Press, 159, Mo., p. 410.

quarter of the union were supplied by some other agency, that some publishers had discontinued relations with the Associated Press and gone to a competing organization, and that the spokesman for the applicant paper had claimed that it printed a better budget of news than any of its rivals, all supporting a conclusion against the charge of monopoly. Missouri was at variance with Illinois, but it did not matter because it was too late.

CHAPTER XXII

THE ASSOCIATED PRESS OF NEW YORK

Invitation to join the new organization—Objects to be achieved—The old Associated Press merged and discontinued—Structure of the successor association—Validity of the transformation upheld

SOMETHING had to be done to save the situation. If the Associated Press were to be at the beck of all who might wish its news service, and on equal terms, then the long costly war to win supremacy was fought in vain. Must the structure reared with so great pains fall to pieces? The jibes of the New York *Sun* were most exasperating, for it ascribed the new troubles of the Associated Press to its keeping up the fight on the *Sun* after the United Press had gone to ruin.[1] To cripple the *Sun*, so that paper affirmed, the Associated Press had forbidden all dealings with it, no employee of an Associated Press member might transmit news to the *Sun*, every intrigue was resorted to to exclude the *Sun* from the chambers of the House and Senate at Washington, members were enjoined from buying a single line of news from the *Sun*, and the *Sun* was formally declared "antagonistic." "It was an *Inter-Ocean* contract with the *Sun* for its service that caused cutting off the *Inter-Ocean* 'without warning and at midnight,'" resulting in the sad dilemma.

It was quite evident that it would be idle to bandy words and that prudent counsel, resourcefulness, determination and concerted action were needed to provide the remedy.

---

[1] *Sun*, June 7, 1900.

The first thing was to adopt such amendments to by-laws and contract forms as would bring the corporation into conformity with the law. The recommended changes were debated at the annual meeting which, by chance, was just impending, but voted down according to tacit understanding. The officers forthwith declined reëlection while Charles W. Knapp, of the St. Louis *Republic,* was chosen president, and Charles S. Diehl secretary and general manager, clearly foreshadowing a program already in hand. There was talk of reorganization which, however, was pronounced impracticable. Other states might not recognize the same rule of law as Illinois, but no corporation could escape the application of the statutes of the home state in which it was chartered. Exclusive rights had been, in the main, the inducement to membership contracts, whose binding nature might now be questioned, as well as an important factor in the price paid for the service. The association, too, might be held pecuniarily liable to shut-out newspapers. The lawyers surely could discover a feasible plan; they must already have done so, for further talk hinted that the state of New York offered a hospitable and safe field of operation.

By a quick move, in less than a week, a certificate of incorporation was issued to "The Associated Press of New York," under the laws of that commonwealth, the names attached to the application being all of men previously prominent in the Associated Press of Illinois: Frank B. Noyes, of the Washington *Star;* Stephen O'Meara, of the Boston *Journal;* A. H. Belo, of the Galveston *News;* St. Clair McKelway, of the Brooklyn *Eagle;* Adolph S. Ochs, of the New York *Times;* William L. McLean, of the Philadelphia *Bulletin.* Identified with them was Melville E. Stone, who sent out the invitation to join.

NEW YORK, June 7th, 1900

MY DEAR SIR:

As you know, a new Associated Press has been formed by our friends who are not content to longer operate under the Illinois association because, under the decision of the Supreme Court of Illinois, it cannot carry out its contracts with them. All of the lawyers consulted, after careful consideration, have agreed that the "Membership Corporation Law" of the State of New York was best adapted to our needs, and the incorporation was therefore effected under this statute.

This is not a re-organization of the Associated Press of Illinois, as all our counsel advised us that a re-organization was impossible. It is a new organization, intended to carry out the purposes for which the Illinois association was originally incorporated. Under this new corporation, the proprietor of every newspaper taking the service, must be a member and will have one vote in the annual meeting. There will be no stock, but, in lieu thereof, members may subscribe for bonds, which carry with them the right to vote for directors. The face value of each bond is $25.00 and no member can vote upon more than forty of them, costing an aggregate of $1,000.00.

The members must all be natural persons, so that newspaper corporations or partnerships cannot be members as such, but must name some individual, either an executive officer or co-partner, to be a member.

By order of the Board of Directors, I send you herewith the following papers:

1. Application for membership.
2. Certificate of the Secretary of your corporation that you are an executive officer of your company, and therefore qualified to be a member.
3. Proxy authorizing some one here in New York to sign the By-laws and accept membership for you.
4. Bond subscription.
5. Copy of By-laws.
6. Explanatory address of the incorporators.
7. Opinion of counsel.

I think you will find no difficulty in filling out the blanks. It is desirable that they be returned at once.

I may say to you that this scheme of organization has been the result of an exhaustive investigation of the subject, by a large number of our friends under the guidance of the ablest lawyers we could secure, and it meets the approval of all to whom it has been submitted. You will observe there is no contract, but that each member may withdraw upon six months' notice.

The purpose, as you understand I think, of this whole operation, is to protect our friends in their rights. Membership is to be offered only to newspapers which have been heretofore co-operating and it is proposed to maintain the relations of such newspaper proprietors intact. That is, this is simply an effort to preserve rights which it was sought, but unsuccessfully, to establish and maintain through the instrumentality of the Associated Press of the State of Illinois.

Please fill out and sign the enclosed papers and return as soon as possible, and oblige,

Very truly yours,
MELVILLE E. STONE

Certain problems seemed still to puzzle confused publishers. "Assurances are both publicly and privately made that the promoters of the new corporation project nothing hostile to the interests of the newspapers now receiving their news from the Associated Press [of Illinois] but propose to take every member of that association into the new corporation with rights and privileges as nearly as possible exactly the same as those heretofore enjoyed but now seriously endangered by the decision of the Illinois Supreme Court in the *Inter-Ocean* case." That unquestionably was the sticking point. Before abandoning the old news service, each publisher wanted to be certain of what he was to have instead, and what his position in the new association was to be. Animated by this desire, the stockholder members convened in Chicago in September and appointed a committee to represent their interests, three each from the eastern, southern, central and western divisions, with Harvey W. Scott, of the Portland *Oregonian*, as chairman and V. S. McClatchy, of the Sacramento *Bee*, as secretary. After accumulating suggestions, the committee repaired to

New York and went into session with the directors of the new Associated Press and returned these detailed findings:

1. That the most important elements of value in a news service could no longer be maintained under court decisions, through membership in the Associated Press of Illinois.

2. That, while it would take a longer time to legally wind up the existence of the Associated Press of Illinois, it could be done without imposing further stockholders' liabilities; and that the interests of members, as regards a news service, could meanwhile be protected by co-operation in a new organization.

3. That under the laws of New York an association could be formed which would protect news rights better than could be done in Illinois, and as well as could be done in any other state.

4. That the Associated Press, organized under the laws of New York, is a legal corporation but that the committee had not been enabled to make such examination of its By-laws as to judge whether news rights could be properly protected thereunder.

After repeated conferences and more careful deliberation, the committee recommended unanimously that the Illinois association be disincorporated, since joining the New York association offered the only way to restore and maintain former advantages. The most radical change was the conversion of the unqualified veto power on new admissions into a right of protest which might be overruled by the vote of four-fifths of all the members, "the extreme limit," so counsel warned, "to which an embodiment of the old veto power could be safely attempted in the new organization." Attention also was invited to the proviso enabling the Board of Directors to elect to membership the proprietor of any newspaper which was entitled to a service of news under an existing contract with the Associated Press of Illinois on the 13th day of September, 1900, assuring admission to all so qualified. The committee, without dissent, approved of the conversion of the veto power into this conditional right of protest. So far as known, no newspaper among the 670 members of the Associated Press of Illinois now had grounds for dissatisfaction with the new arrangement as finally perfected.

The record of the Associated Press of Illinois waited only for the official finis. The resolution to terminate its activities and dissolve the corporation had been adopted. The controversy with the *Inter-Ocean* had been amicably arbitrated, and a payment of $40,500, voluntarily discounted 25 per cent from the award, accepted by the *Inter-Ocean* in satisfaction of its claims and dismissal of the suits brought by both it and the *Sun.* The property and business were transferred to the Associated Press of New York, along with the liabilities. The last wire service of the Associated Press of Illinois was dated September 30, 1900. One more stockholders' meeting was to have been held in December following but, as no quorum responded, the final report of the officers went to them by mail in March, 1901. It reads much like a self-written obituary:

> Appreciating the regret every member of the Associated Press felt when compelled to abandon the splendid organization built up under the Illinois charter, the directors believe that there is none the less occasion for congratulation in the matter of the Association's final dissolution in two important particulars. It has retired from active life with an absolutely clean balance sheet, evading no obligation, of law or honor, paying every debt and fulfilling every service for which any one had a right to ask.

As the lineal descendant of the first of the name, and as the successor to all the news-gathering agencies that had that designation before, the re-formed New York corporation could now assume the sole right to inherit the title and to be known henceforth as the "Associated Press." The report already quoted has disclosed the adroit devices introduced to avoid the difficulties created by the decree in the *Inter-Ocean* case and, at the same time, to accomplish as far as possible what was prohibited by that decree. The new association was not an ordinary business corporation. On the contrary, it came within the general laws providing for the legal status of social clubs, charities, agricultural societies, and stock exchanges. It was a strictly membership association, an association of persons rather than of corporations, firms, or newspapers. "It is not to make a profit, nor to make or declare dividends, and is not to engage in the business of selling intelligence nor traffic in the same." The purpose was specifically limited by precise definition:

> To gather, obtain and procure by its own instrumentalities, by exchange with its members and by other appropriate means, any and all kinds of information and intelligence, telegraphic and otherwise, for the use and benefit of its members, and to furnish and supply the same to its members for publication in the newspapers owned or represented by them under and subject to such regulations, conditions and limitations as may be prescribed by the by-laws; and the mutual coöperation, benefit and protection of its members.

For the most part, the new association paralleled the predecessor in the formulation of its rules and regulations. Although personal, membership inhered in the newspaper represented, ceased with severance from it, and was transferred in that contingency to the succeeding ownership. Likewise, as to the bonds, the holdings that carried not to exceed forty votes, they were conditioned on the right to redeem at face value whenever they might come into the possession of any one not a member of the association. Each certificate of membership was to state the language of publication, the place of publication, whether for a morning or an afternoon paper, whether day or night report was to be furnished, the extent and nature of the protest right, the obligation to furnish the news of a therein described district, and to pay the assessments allotted. There was to be no moving about from one classification to another.

Each member was privileged to cast one vote for directors and such additional votes as his bonds might entitle him, to receive the news report for his paper as specified, to publish it within the stated hours between 11 o'clock of the morning and of the evening, or vice versa, as the case might be, to be protected against publication in his locality of news furnished by him to the association. He was obligated to comply with the by-laws, to pay assessments as fixed, to receive and publish the report regularly in whole or in part, and to furnish the spontaneous news of his district. He was bound to guard the report, not to furnish or permit news received to go to a nonmember in advance of publication, not to furnish or permit news to go to a nonmember "which he is required to supply to this corporation," to print the credits required, not to anticipate publication of any document confided to the association for use on a stipulated date, "however said member may have secured said document." Mostly repetitions, but the dictates of lesson-teaching experience.

The disciplinary powers over a member were in no way weakened. The imposition of fines and penalties by the board, after hearing, was to be final and conclusive, and expulsion might follow any conduct, "on his part, or on the part of any one in his employ or in the employ of or connected with the newspaper," which the corporation "in its absolute discretion shall deem of such a character as to be prejudicial to the interests and welfare of the corporation and its members and to justify such expulsion." By express agreement, neither the corporation nor its officers were to be liable to a member newspaper for loss or damage arising by reason of the publication of any of the news furnished, or by reason of the member's suspension or expulsion, signing the membership roll being a waiver of such claim.

The by-law which drew the most fire, and which was to be repealed eventually in deference to official objection, related again to intercourse with other news sources. The wording had been carefully thought out and phrased:

> Experience having shown that it is very difficult, if not impossible, to avoid or prevent violations of the rules prescribed by the last preceding section, [guarding the news report] or to detect or prove any such violation, if the members are permitted to purchase news from other associations, and that such purchase may be seriously prejudicial to the interest and welfare of this corporation and its members, the Board of Directors may, in their discretion, forbid the members to purchase intelligence from any other such association.
>
> When the Board of Directors, by a vote of two-thirds of all its members, shall decide and notify any member that the purchase or receipt of news from any other person, firm, corporation or association, not a member of this corporation or represented in this corporation by a member, or any other such action by such member, establishes a condition that will be likely to permit the news of the corporation to be disclosed to unauthorized persons, such members shall immediately discontinue purchasing or receiving such news, or such other objectionable action. The decision of the Board, as to the establishment of such condition, shall be final and the fact shall not thereafter be open to question by a member.

The transformation of the Illinois association into the New York association, however, could not pass altogether without challenge. Prospective dissolution of the former was calculated to render futile a compelled admission to its membership, so far as its news service was concerned, but even a belated membership might suffice to qualify for a place on the roll of the new organization without running the gauntlet of a protest right. In the interest of the Hearst nonmember papers, therefore, the application of the New York *Evening Journal* for mandamus under the Illinois adjudication continued to be pressed.[2] Joining both associations as defendants, conspiracy was charged with the deliberate purpose to deprive the Associated Press of Illinois of all its customers and its business in order to circumvent the law and defeat the petitioner's rights. What this might lead to was clearly enough perceived. If forcible entrance could be gained by a Hearst paper in Chicago or New York, it could be repeated for newspapers at any point, and membership privileges would be divested of value. The answer of the Associated Press not only impugned the good faith of the application but, of necessity, maintained the legality of the entire transaction. The controversy grew cold before the courts reached the stage of final judgment, a judgment eventually entered in favor of the Associated Press in an opinion, written by Judge Mack, dealing lucidly with the several points raised:

The first question to determine is whether the transaction by which the property of the Illinois company was transferred to the New York company is a sale or an attempted consolidation. Not the expressions used, but the underlying intention as evidenced by the acts, will determine this.

In this case, while it is possible to find that a consolidation was intended, it is not only equally possible to find that a sale was intended but, on a fair consideration of the facts stated in the petition, the court finds that the parties in fact intended to effect a complete sale.

Whatever may be the right of a stockholder, or possibly of the state, to prevent a corporation engaged in a business impressed with

[2] Associated Press Report, 1901, p. 376; 1907, p. 116.

the public interest from incapacitating itself from further continuing actively in that business, no third person can claim such a right. A corporation to which the state has given special privileges, such as a right of eminent domain or special franchises, may owe some reciprocal duty to continue in the exercise of the part of its business in respect to which it has obtained the special privilege and not to part with so much of its property as is essential to the maintenance of such business; but the mere fact that a business is impressed with a public interest requiring the proprietor, whether an individual or a corporation, to deal with all of the public, imposes upon such proprietor the duty of continuing therein no longer than he desires to do so.

Can the court find anything blameworthy in the corporations defendant? Certain individuals formed an Illinois corporation to do a certain business. They evidently confined that business within certain lines. Because of the nature of the business, their attempt was to confine it, and the Illinois corporation was to deal with all. Rather than do this, the stockholders preferred to give up their business and not act any longer as an entity, as an Illinois corporation. They caused the Illinois corporation to dispose of all of the property upon terms satisfactory to themselves.

No stockholder and no creditor complains. They organize themselves and others into a corporation of a totally different character under the laws of New York, believing that they could lawfully accomplish in this way what could not be lawfully accomplished before, if New York permits this to be done—and on that point I express no opinion.

Shall these individuals be debarred because of that earlier fruitless attempt? Is there any public policy of Illinois which should compel this corporation to continue in the business merely because the business is of a public nature?

Even if the New York corporation is under the same obligations that the Illinois corporation was held to be under, no possible harm results from the transfer; the alleged intended fraud becomes incapable of consummation and the mere intent to do a fraudulent act will not render the transfer void.

But if, on the other hand, the New York corporation is valid, with of all its limitations, and will be so recognized in Illinois,—as to which no opinion is expressed—nevertheless the Illinois corporation was under no obligation to continue its business merely because of its public nature, and its stockholders were under no obligation not to gain the profits that New York, on this assumption, gave them. The Illinois corporation violated no duty in transferring its assets and ceasing business, unless the public had a right to demand that it continue in business indefinitely. Whether the state has this right or not, it can not be claimed for any individual. The assets themselves are not impressed with the public use. I find that the transaction was a sale and not a consolidation.

Taking up the eligibility of the applicant, the court inquired, "Who would say the by-laws could any more clearly express their intention?" With respect to the special proviso, emphasis was laid on the fact that the by-laws contemplate, not "a newspaper entitled to the service of news from the Associated Press of Illinois on September 13, 1900," but "a newspaper entitled to a service of news under an existing contract with the Associated Press of Illinois on September 13, 1900." Assuming the by-laws to be valid, "there can be no doubt that they did mean just what they said." It created a distinct and definite class which did not include the New York *Evening Journal*. The Associated Press, in its new form, could have had no more clear-cut vindication.

CHAPTER XXIII

PROBLEMS OF PROTECTION

Questions of so-called news piracy—Claim of property in news—Finding of the United States Supreme Court—Dissenting views recorded—Safeguards against unauthorized disclosure of news—Safeguards against use outside of the newspaper—Premature publication or breach of confidence—Protecting the prestige and integrity of the association

If it was to cling fast to the protective feature that the new association had been substituted for the old, then, to insure this protection, a reciprocal obligation must rest on the membership. Of what avail would be an Associated Press franchise if publications, which were denied admission, could obtain the same news by roundabout routes without sharing the cost of getting it? Equally important with the renunciation of news alliances with nonmember papers, or opposition news agencies, must be the prevention of news piracy. Unless there were a right to profit from the news scrupulously garnered at joint outlay of the co-operating newspapers, the membership might as well be open to all. Here was the question of the integrity of the news report in its practical aspect, whether the right to print this news belonged to its gatherer, or, like air or sea-water, was free to any one choosing to make use of it. The news is picked up here and there, wherever anything happens. It may be common knowledge at the scene of the event, but it takes time, talent, and money to put it into intelligible form and transmit it to a place of interest in it. That the literary character seldom invested a news report with copyrightable quality was generally admitted; at best, owing to the exigencies of up-to-the-minute publication, copyright could not be a satisfactory reliance.

This volatility of news had been sensed in the early days. Before a parliamentary commission in England, in 1851, Horace Greeley had dismissed the talk of piracy as being indulged "for effect's sake." "On the whole," to quote his words, "I would rather that those who do not take it, should copy than not. All the evening journals copy from us and we rather like it."

"Is there anything entitling you, having incurred the first expense of obtaining that news, to issue it for any period?"

"Not for a moment—anybody may print it—but the public are apt to take the paper which has the first news."[1]

It was Horace Greeley's view that unauthorized copying of news paid a delicate compliment to enterprise. Attempts were made from time to time to stretch the copyright laws to cover the contents of the daily journal. Henry Watterson has recorded memories of a "delightful" winter spent in Washington under commission to secure a congressional enactment on the subject. "A fool's errand," he confessed.[2] "How are you getting along with your bill?" asked Mr. Blaine, sitting next to him at a dinner party. "You won't get a vote in either House," and Blaine proceeded humorously to improvise the average member's argument against it as a dangerous power, a perquisite to the great newspapers, and an imposition on the little ones. Shortly afterwards, "a learned but dissolute old lawyer" assured Watterson that no act of Congress was needed in defense of the news service because it fell within certain decisions

---

[1] Quoted by Hudson, *History of Journalism,* p. 541.
[2] Watterson, *Marse Henry,* II, 104.

of the English courts holding out the protection of the common law. What lawmaker could be expected to favor a monopoly of the news, or the slightest restriction on the privilege of the country weekly to grind out a grist of interesting items from his exchanges? The bill before that Congress was framed cautiously, yes, timidly. It would have given the paper, or association of papers, the sole right to print, issue, and sell its contents only "for the term of eight hours," and "exceeding one hundred words." [3] The disillusioned Colonel Watterson cut short his pleasant sojourn in Washington and was roundly abused for his failure.

In 1899, the Associated Press, blind to the previous object lesson, appointed a special committee to take action looking to the passage by Congress of a news copyright law.[4] No results worth reporting back followed. It's a poor rule, though, that does not work both ways. When, about this time, the Chicago *Tribune* arranged with the London *Times* for exclusive use in this country of its copyrighted Boer War articles, the Associated Press' London correspondent continued to buy the *Times* on the street each morning and to send a compendium of it to the New York office as part of the day's news consignment. The *Tribune's* protest was ignored and its petition for an injunction and damages contested and denied. "As the exclusive right of publication at common law terminates with the publication in London, no protection then exists beyond that expressly given by the statute," said the court which concomitantly held the items of news lifted by the Associated Press among the "selections not predesignate." [5]

Substantially identical issues were to come up in many

---

[3] Quoted by Brandeis, 148 U. S., p. 265.
[4] Associated Press Report, 1900, p. 182.
[5] Tribune Co., *versus* Associated Press, 116 Fed., p. 126.

forms and in many places. The leading, and ground-breaking, case, perhaps, was the so-called "Ticker Case," leading because of a frank allusion in the opinion to its application to news-gathering agencies.[6] Having rented under cover a telegraphic device distributing sporting and financial news, the words and characters on the tape were being copied and passed on at once over a similar set of instruments supplied by a piratical outfit to another group of patrons and at lower rates. It was conceded that the printed strip of paper would not be copyrightable, were the practical difficulties out of the way, its value to the customer consisting almost wholly in the fact that the knowledge conveyed was received earlier in point of time than it reached others not so served. "This is service, not authorship, nor the work of the publisher." The law being inadequate, so the judge observed, "equity should see to it that the one who is served, and the one who serves, each gets what the engagement between them calls for; and that neither, to the injury of the other, shall appropriate more." To rëenforce the argument, the work of the great news-gathering association was graphically described as a pertinent example:

The immediate business brought to our attention in the case under review may not arouse any great solicitude. It relates to the gathering and distributing of news not looked upon, perhaps, in all quarters as essential to the public welfare. But the questions raised are of much wider significance. They involve, among others, that modern enterprise—one of the distinctive achievements of our day—which, combining the genius and the accumulations of men with the forces of electricity, combs the earth's surface each day for what the day has brought forth, that whatever befalls the sons of men shall come, almost instantaneously, into the consciousness of mankind. Thus, a gun thunders in a harbor on the other side of the earth; before its reverberations have ceased, the moral sequence of the event has

---

[6] National Telegraph Company *versus* Western Union, 119 Fed., p. 294.

taken root in every civilized quarter of the earth. Famine arises in India to begin its grim march; it has gotten but little under way until a counter army—the unfailing benevolence of human kind—has been mustered from America to Russia. On an isolated island, and without premonition, a mountain claps its black hands upon the population of a city; almost before a ship in the harbor, with tidings of the catastrophe, could have set sail, relief ships from the harbors of Christendom are under way. By such agencies as these, the world is made to face itself unceasingly in the glass and is put to those tests that bring increasing helpfulness and beauty into the hearts of our race.

Is service like this to be outlawed? Is the enterprise of the great news agencies, or the independent enterprise of the great newspapers, or of the great telegraph and cable lines, to be denied appeal to the courts against the inroads of the parasite for no other reason than that the law, fashioned hitherto to fit the relations of authors and the public, can not be made to fit the relations of the public and this dissimilar class of servants? Are we to fail in our plain duty for mere lack of precedent? We choose rather to make precedent—one from which is eliminated as immaterial the law grown up around authorship—and we see no better way to start this precedent upon a career than by affirming the order appealed from.

Almost coincidentally, but presumably independently, the Supreme Court of Massachusetts rendered a like decision governing the communication of distinctive information to special groups of people.[7] A concern compiling building-trade news sought a remedy against the systematic reprinting and sale, at a lower price, of reports obtained from its clients, even to its patrons. In the view of that tribunal, two questions were propounded: Had the plaintiff any property in the information it got together at great expense for the use of subscribers? Did it lose its property by publication, abandonment, and dedication to the public, when it furnished the data to them under these contracts? Answering, the court said:

---

[7] Dodge *versus* Construction Information Co., 183 Mass., p. 62.

The facts, before it has ascertained them, unless they are held for a special purpose confidentially and as secrets, are not property; but when these have been discovered promptly and by effort and at expense, and have been compiled and put in form, and are of commercial value by reason of the speedy use that can be made of them before they have obtained general publicity, they are property.

It is well established that the private circulation of information or literary composition, in writing or in print, for a restricted purpose, is not a publication which gives the public a right to use it.

Since the information in this case had been communicated for a restricted purpose, it made no difference, legally, whether some was furnished by telegraph or telephone, or orally, or in print, and the business was beyond doubt entitled to legal protection.

Within another year, the same doctrine appeared in a judicial decree forbidding the unauthorized use of market quotations.[8] Brushing aside the taint of gambling possibly involved, the court here declared the real subject matter of the suit to be "the property right in the news, in the reports of prices." "News," it emphasized, "may be the subject of lawful ownership though nine-tenths of the things reported be unlawful. Nor should the property in this case, the news, the continuous quotation of prices, be adjudged contraband because it is susceptible of bad uses as well as good. The news as news is not without the pale of protection and the moral quality is chargeable solely to the user."

Though the preliminary steps had gone this far, further moves to check the common and notorious news theft which was rampant seemed halted. The outcome of the Ticker Case clearly was influenced at least by the newspaper situation, if not by the personal interchange of views between Judge Grosscup and Stone, close friends residing at the time

---

[8] Chicago Board of Trade *versus* Kinsey, 130 Fed., p. 305.

in the same hotel. Of this, there was proof in the text of the opinion. "Meeting Mr. Stone on the train," Judge Grosscup afterward wrote, "I started inquiries respecting his company which resulted in a revelation of the nature and extent of its work, of much of which I had been previously uninformed. I recall his interest, his earnestness, that revealed not only perception by the intellect, but the driving power of feeling. And when the case was decided on principles that have since upheld the right of the Associated Press to protection for its service, I recall his satisfaction and his expression of grim determination to some time bring its principles to the protection of news enterprise." [9]

Despite seeming hesitancy to follow up the opening promptly, it was but a matter of time when the Associated Press must assert its rights and seek to enforce them. For some strange reason, the idea of copyright kept recurring; it was under consideration as late as 1916.[10] Finally, however, on an undeniably flagrant case of piracy proceedings were instituted. Convincing evidence had been collected to show that the International News Service had agents regularly appropriating and systematically rewriting dispatches taken from the early editions of Associated Press papers for dissemination as its own, secretly subsidizing employees of such papers to give access to, or information contained in, Associated Press messages in advance of publication, copying from bulletin boards, etc. Repeated disciplining for breach of the by-law holding members responsible for permitting employees to supply news matter to nonmember journals or news agencies had proved ineffective. Intervention of the federal courts had to be sought

---

[9] *M. E. S.*, p. 70.
[10] *Ibid.*, p. 74.

and carried to conclusion, to the United States Supreme Court, if necessary.[11] In this suit, the bill in equity prayed for an order to restrain the diversion of Associated Press news in three ways:

1. By bribing employes of newspapers published by members to furnish Associated Press news before publication for transmission by telegraph and telephone to International News Service clients for publication by them.
2. By inducing Associated Press members to violate by-laws and thus obtain news before publication.
3. By copying news from bulletin boards and from early editions and selling it, either in the same wording or re-written, to customers.

In the lower court, the Associated Press had made much of the variance of time in transmitting news from ocean to ocean and had insisted that an essential part of its plan required that its reports remain confidential and secret until their publication had been fully accomplished by all of the members, whether on the Atlantic, or the Pacific seaboard, or in between. Its very existence would be imperiled, it asserted, if its news became public property on first printing in San Francisco or New York. As this point failed to move Judge Hand, the judge of first instance, it apparently was not particularly pressed thereafter. The issues treated in the Supreme Court on appeal, therefore, turned on the triple question of whether there was any property in news, whether it survived the instant of its publication in the first newspaper to which it was communicated, whether the conduct complained of constituted unfair competition in trade. The following extracts summarize the majority opinion delivered through Justice Pitney:

No doubt, news articles often possess a literary quality and are the subject of literary property at the common law. But the news

[11] 240 Fed., p. 983; 245 Fed., p. 244; 248 U. S., p. 215.

element—the information respecting current events contained in the literary production—is not the creation of the writer but is a report of matters that are *publici juris;* it is the history of the day. It is not to be supposed that the framers of the constitution, when they empowered congress "to promote the progress of science and useful arts by securing for limited times to authors and inventors the exclusive right to their respective writings and discoveries," intended to confer upon one, who might happen to be the first to report a historic event, the exclusive right for any period to spread the knowledge of it.

We need spend no time, however, upon the general question of property in news matter at common law, or the application of the copyright act, since it seems to us the case must turn upon the question of unfair competition in business. And in our opinion, this does not depend upon any general right of property analogous to the common law right of the proprietor of an unpublished work to prevent its publication without his consent; nor is it foreclosed by showing that the benefits of the copyright act have been waived.

We are dealing here not with restrictions upon publication but with the very facilities and processes of publication. The peculiar value of news is in the spreading of it while it is fresh; and it is evident that a valuable property interest in the news can not be maintained by keeping it secret. Besides, except for matters improperly disclosed or published in breach of trust or confidence or in violation of law, none of which is involved in this branch of the case, the news of current events may be regarded as common property.

What we are concerned with is the business of making it known to the world, in which both parties to the present suit are engaged. That business consists in maintaining a prompt, sure, steady and reliable service designed to place the daily events of the world at the breakfast table of the millions at a price that, while of trifling moment to each reader, is sufficient in the aggregate to afford compensation for the cost of gathering and distributing it, with the added profit so necessary as an incentive to effective action in the commercial world. This service indubitably constitutes a legitimate business.

The question of what is unfair competition, here, is not so much the rights of either party as against the public but their rights as between themselves. Regarding the news as but the material out of which both parties are seeking to make profits at the same time and in the same field, we can hardly fail to recognize that for this purpose, and as between them, it must be regarded as quasi property, irrespective of the rights of either as against the public.

The right of the purchaser of a single newspaper to spread knowledge of its contents gratuitously, for any legitimate purpose not unreasonably interfering with complainant's right to make merchandise of it, may be admitted; but to transmit that news for commercial use, in competition with complainant—which is what defendant has done and seeks to justify—is a very different matter. Stripped of all disguises, the process amounts to an unauthorized interference with the normal operation of complainant's legitimate business precisely at the point where the profit is to be reaped in order to divert a material portion of the profit from those who have earned it to those who have not. A court of equity ought not to hesitate long in characterizing it as unfair competition in business.

The contention that the news is abandoned to the public for all purposes when published in the first newspaper is untenable. Abandonment is a question of intent and the entire organization of The Associated Press negatives such a purpose. The cost of the service would be prohibitive if the reward were to be so limited. Publication by each member must be deemed not by any means an abandonment of the news of the world for any and all purposes, but a publication for limited purposes; for the benefit of the readers of the bulletin, or the newspaper, as such; not for the purpose of making merchandise of it as news, with the result of depriving complainant's other members of their reasonable opportunity to obtain just returns for their expenditures.

The decision was not unanimous. Justice Holmes, with whom Justice McKenna concurred, noted his dissent on the ground that news was not copyrightable and not property, property being the creation of law and not the result of exchangeability. "It is a question," he urged, "of how strong an infusion of fraud is necessary to turn a flavor into a poison. The dose seems to me strong enough here to need a remedy from the law," but, without further legislation, the only correction would be to require crediting the source of the appropriated news, and an injunction might issue for a certain number of hours, "unless defendant gives express credit to the Associated Press."

Likewise dissenting, Justice Brandeis followed more closely the contentions of the defendant's counsel. The Ticker Case, in his judgment, did not apply because it rested on breach of contract or trust. Neither was the right of the producer, despite private exhibition, in point. "An author's theories, suggestions and speculations, or the systems, plans, methods and arrangements of an originator, derive no such protection from the statutory copyright." The theory of limited abandonment by first publication was to be rejected, for "there is no basis for such an implication." As to the charge of unfair competition, "by appropriating without cost to itself of values created by the Associated Press," upon which ground the decision of the court appeared to stand, "to appropriate and use for profit, knowledge and ideas produced by other men, without making compensation or even acknowledgement, may be inconsistent with a finer sense of propriety, but, with the exceptions indicated above, the law has heretofore sanctioned the practice. That competition is not unfair in a legal sense, merely because the profits gained are unearned, even if made at the expense of a rival, is shown by many cases." To use news, gathered at great cost, gainfully in competition with the original collector, was an obvious injustice. "But to give relief against it would involve more than the application of existing rules of law to new facts. It would require the making of a new rule in analogy to existing ones." The legislative body, it was suggested, might act and, in so doing, impose proper restrictions and obligations. "If a legislature concluded (as at least one court has held) that, under certain circumstances, news-gathering is a business affected with a public interest, it might declare that, in such cases, news should be protected against appropriation, only if the gatherer assumed the obligation of supplying it at reasonable rates and without discrimination, to all papers which applied therefor."

The sense of supreme satisfaction over the outcome could not be concealed by the jubilant Associated Press. "Thus the law has been definitely settled by the highest court and piracy of news becomes illegal. It will take time for the full benefits of this decision to reach the members of this organization but the victory which has crowned several years of litigation may well be celebrated."[12] Very soon, warning was promulgated, publication of which, in each issue of every newspaper receiving Associated Press service, was made mandatory:

> The Associated Press is exclusively entitled to the use for republication of all news dispatches credited to it, or not otherwise credited, in this paper, and also the local news published herein. All rights of republication of special dispatches herein are also reserved.

To maintain this claim would call for eternal vigilance and unremitting effort, for outright piracy was not the only vent to which the news was exposed. New rules had to be prescribed, and successive citations go forth, for offenses of omission and commission endangering the integrity of the report. Mere proximity of wires, for example, might enable operators of another news service to listen in, hence this resolution, adopted in 1920:

> Where a member publishing a morning newspaper also publishes in the same office or building an evening newspaper not entitled to the Associated Press service but receiving its news from another news agency, whose operators or wires are maintained in its office, (or vice versa) the E. O. S. [extraordinary occasion service] will

---

12 Associated Press Report, 1919, p. 4.

not be delivered to such member outside the regular hours of publication unless such member shall make arrangements satisfactory to the general manager, or the Board, to protect such service from possible use, by such evening or morning newspaper, or such rival news agency.[13]

The main difficulties seemed still to inhere in the association's relations with the Hearst chain of papers with which the warfare was not abated. Some of these publications were holding Associated Press membership, while others were kept out, all of them linked in with the International News Service which had been organized, as we know, expressly to supply a news report to the debarred journals and others desiring to share it. If the Associated Press were exclusively entitled to all the local news collected by Hearst-owned members, how could the other Hearst papers have joint use of it? Here was a persisting complication responsible for numerous fines for violations of the by-laws, capped finally by this "expression of condemnation" incorporated in the record:

That in the judgment of the Board of Directors, the relations of the newspapers owned by Mr. William R. Hearst represented in membership in The Associated Press with the news services owned by Mr. Hearst, cause an ever-recurring evasion and nullification of the obligations, each to the other, of members of this mutual organization and must be regarded as highly prejudicial to the interests and welfare of The Associated Press and its members, the prime object of the organization being the mutual co-operation, benefit and protection of its members.[14]

Could a resolution so worded be read except as notice that the membership of all Hearst papers in the Associated Press were in jeopardy? When followed by an aggressive effort to admit, over protest, rival papers in Baltimore and

---

[13] *Ibid.*, 1920, p. 89; 1922, p. 58.
[14] *Ibid.*, 1927, p. 67.

Rochester whose applications the directors, though lacking authority to endorse officially, personally recommended and urged, Hearst and his coworkers felt impelled to recognize the distinct hostility of the move and, sensing the dangers of the situation, to consider available means of meeting any ensuing contingency. Expulsion of the Hearst papers from the Associated Press seemed imminent, to be avoided only by withdrawal. Plans, therefore, were prepared at once for expanding the reports of the International News Service to a complete coverage of current events, and lines put out at the same time for closer coöperation and possible merger with the United Press. A vigorous campaign to combat the appeal and protect the threatened Baltimore and Rochester papers proved successful, and the Hearst forces renewed agitation for a "one-newspaper-one-vote" election of Associated Press directors, which some insist was the potent factor in bringing about the later readjustment of the bond-holder vote recounted elsewhere. The idea of alliance with the United Press was set aside, apparently, because of Hearst's indisposition to help build up Scripps journals aiming at the same clientele as his own publications in the same towns and the further recasting of the Hearst organization. The settlement of the Baltimore and Rochester controversies by mutual arrangement, the abandonment by the Universal Service of its full morning report, the presence for the first time of the president of the International at the speakers' table at the annual luncheon of the Associated Press, together with the cessation of the Associated Press cross-fire, may be taken to indicate rapprochement, for the moment at least, with the Associated Press rather than with the United Press.

Since bulletining information exposed it to appropriation by opposition papers or agencies, such use must be subject to definite regulations. Under literal interpretation, Associated Press news was served solely for publication in the member newspaper. Posting was, therefore, a privilege to be closely restricted, at first to a single board located at the office of publication. In time, the display of bulletins at branch offices in the same city was permitted and, later, at branches in other cities where no Associated Press membership existed, or by consent of the Associated Press paper in such city.[15] At moments of tense interest, news of exceptional importance had been occasionally announced from theater stages, or at public meetings, without serious objection, though furnished as part of the report. Similarly, information of special concern had been communicated in reply to telephone inquiries as a favor to a subscriber in advance of printing it. Oral divulgence was not supposed to be capable of extensive use or abuse.

The perfection and projection of the radio suddenly altered the conditions governing dissemination of news outside of the columns of the newspaper. Enterprising journalists were not slow to adventure for themselves with the radio. The broadcasting of news might be regarded as merely reading a succession of bulletins to an invisible audience larger than could congregate in front of the office to scan, or hear megaphoned, what was there placarded. Probably, thoughtless of everything but what would interest the largest number of listeners, newspaper-operated stations began to put on the air, not only the correct time and weather forecasts, but also sport results, election news, and the high spots of the day's events. The thus disregarded rule of the Associated Press would have to be either changed, or enforced by the customary penalties. The first concession was a reluctant official declaration, "*ad interim*," that

---

[15] *Ibid.*, 1922, p. 85.

broadcasting baseball scores would not be considered in violation of by-laws.[16] The question became acute when, in October, 1924, the Chicago *Tribune* advertised its plan to broadcast the news of the approaching presidential election. The publishers were cautioned at once that the rules prohibited such use of bulletins or reports as "incompatible with the interests of the Associated Press." "We think the policy of the Associated Press is lacking in public spirit and foredoomed to failure," was the *Tribune's* comment. "There may be legal obstacles in the way of our giving to the public the full advantage of our news service, but, if so, we intend to test them in court and, if possible, overcome them, as we are confident we can."

The Associated Press board next found itself considering the cases of nearly a dozen important dailies cited for broadcasting returns of the 1924 presidential contest.[17] The Portland *Oregonian* admitted the use of Associated Press bulletins; all the rest denied that the transmitted information was supplied by the press wire and insisted that they had it from other sources. It was notorious that this was nothing but a flimsy subterfuge, that, by a fiction, the local election figures had been gathered and compiled in the name of a City Press Association, which had exchanged with the telegraph companies for outside returns. Action was deferred while the board voted to bide discussion of the subject by the membership already then convened for the annual meeting. As the outcome of the debate, came a resolution recognizing "new problems presented by the tremendous and continuing growth of the radio," and authorizing the board to adopt the necessary regulations, "which shall permit the broadcast of such news of the association as it shall

---

16 *Ibid.*, 1924, p. 17.
17 *Ibid.*, 1925, p. 116.

deem of transcendental national or international importance, and which can not by its very nature be exclusive, provide adequate safeguards, and require that proper credit in each and every instance be accorded the Associated Press."[18] All the citations for broadcasting were thereupon dismissed, save that of the hapless *Oregonian,* which had to pay a fine of $100, and, pending a new rule, the general manager was instructed "to use his own discretion."

The experiment continued with but two protests until the eve of the succeeding membership meeting, when the amended rule relating to radio was formulated. Somewhat cryptic in language, it provided "that the public display of news upon bulletin boards, or the broadcasting of such news as may be authorized in accordance with the resolution adopted by the members at the annual meeting of 1925, does not constitute a violation of the by-laws." But all bulletins must be plainly marked "Associated Press," and a similar ownership clearly announced when news of the Associated Press was broadcast.[19] Disseminating news over the radio was no longer under the ban. With the arrival of the 1928 presidential campaign, the preventive entanglements were completely swept away, the traditions governing release of addresses by the candidates were overturned and, for election night, the dominant broadcasting company was able to effect the unprecedented combination of all three of the big news associations, the Associated Press, the United Press and the International News Service, for pooling the returns and their prompt publication "on the air," anticipating appearance in printed form. Not a few member newspapers also exploited their election news service in the same way for themselves without let or hindrance. The question

---

[18] *Ibid.,* 1926, p. 31.
[19] *Ibid.,* 1927, p. 14.

of chain station broadcasting, as also that of combining Associated Press news with paid advertising programs on the air, remained open and still engulfed in discordant debate.

Keeping the report safe from misappropriation by papers and agencies not entitled to receive it had its counterpart in keeping it safe from misuse by Associated Press members themselves. In the course of practical experience, the danger spots had been uncovered. Morning and evening papers had to be separated by somewhat arbitrary distinctions. The news stream was continuous and unending; it did not divide itself according to definite time schedule. While all members should receive a daily report mirroring the happenings of the entire twenty-four hours, publication hours had to be rigid to avoid conflict—for morning issues between 9 P.M. and 9 A.M., and for evening after 9 A.M. An exception accommodated morning editions "circulated only outside of the city of publication not earlier than the following morning," to permit printing as early as 5 P.M., and for circulation of such papers on Sundays in the home city not earlier than 8 P.M. The afternoon papers, too, might have news service as late as 6 P.M., but during the last two hours only in the form of bulletins. A jealous watch was kept by the journals concerned for delays that would throw important news from one field to the other for first publication. To forestall charges of favoritism, the Board finally authorized the use of Associated Press dispatches, "upon extraordinary occasions," in extra editions, or for bulletin service outside of the regular hours, by both morning and evening papers. When attempts to overstep the bounds had to be checked, admonition issued that every effort to invade by any device the field not covered by a membership certificate not only violated the by-laws regulating the hours of publication, but tended "to bring the Associated Press into discredit by furnishing an inadequate and incomplete report" and would be construed as detrimental to the welfare of the corporation.[20]

Vigilance is ever necessary also in guarding matter supplied in advance, often in utmost confidence, for future release. So strict has been the enforcement of the rule on premature publication that a fine of $100 has come to be imposed automatically, regardless of palliating circumstances or explanation which, at best, could only lessen the amount of the forfeit. Nor could violation of release by one member, even by a competitor in the same local field, warrant another to do the same. But what constituted advance matter subject to release? Under the original rule, a member might anticipate publication of a document with impunity, "unless he shall have received a copy of it from the Associated Press." [21] This, however, had to be qualified by an order that where one of two Associated Press papers, published by the same owners in the same city, refused to accept advance matter subject to release, the same document or speech should not be tendered to the other; that, on such refusal, the source from which the Associated Press was supplied be at once notified; and that no member, after once refusing, should be served with the document until after its release.[22] Again, when a speech or other document, furnished by the Associated Press subject to release, was thereafter amended, any reference in the member's paper to the change, or any publication of the language which had been modified or excised, would constitute a violation "even more flagrant than if the entire speech or document were printed in advance

---

[20] *Ibid.*, 1922, p. 78.
[21] *Ibid.*, 1906, p. 63.
[22] *Ibid.*, 1908, p. 63.

of release."[23] Members have been warned, too, that the practice of preparing plates, and putting them on the press for flash release, with stories attributed to the association but not supplied by it, was unqualifiedly condemned and would be dealt with drastically.[24]

From this viewpoint, it followed logically that members were in duty bound both to uphold the prestige of the Associated Press and to refrain from discrediting it. It devolved upon them to print source acknowledgments as the management might direct, and, *per contra*, to be credited for any exclusive stories supplied to the Associated Press not of spontaneous nature.[25] Publication improperly designated, by commission or omission, as Associated Press matter, "hurtful to the character and repute of the service," would be conduct prejudicial to the interests of the association, warranting discipline.[26] The extent to which the practical application might be carried found illustration in specific examples. In 1919, the Philadelphia *North American*, by its editor, E. A. Van Valkenberg, was cited for printing a dispatch from Washington referring to, and commenting on, a Paris news item, with the remark, "In all probability, it was written in New York or Washington and never was near an ocean cable." Editorial retraction, admitting "its innuendo unfounded," softened the penalty imposed on Van Valkenberg to a fine of $300.[27] At the same session of the Board, the Lancaster *Intelligencer* was permitted to exculpate itself by inserting in its columns an abject apology for having falsely charged the Associated Press with being "scooped" by a rival news

[23] *Ibid.*, p. 32.
[24] *Ibid.*, 1928, p. 78.
[25] *Ibid.*, 1918, p. 49.
[26] *Ibid.*, 1915, p. 46.
[27] *Ibid.*, 1920, p. 20.

agency. On another occasion, James T. Williams, Jr., of the Boston *Transcript*, summoned to explain a statement to Senator Lodge, in private correspondence, that "he could not rely on the Associated Press service," gave assurance that he meant only its inadequate volume.[28] Later, a letter written by S. M. Williams, of the New York *World*, "criticizing a letter of a correspondent of the Associated Press to the Navy Department," was taken under advisement. In 1922, Van Valkenberg was once more "on the carpet" for editorial references to the association in the *North American*. More recently, it would seem as if either the disposition of the members to reflect on their news service were dulled, or the determination to call them to strict account for such breaches held more in obeyance.

---

[28] *Ibid.*, p. 80.

CHAPTER XXIV

QUESTIONS OF MONOPOLY AND CONTROL

The bondholder vote—The protest right—Ruling of the Attorney General—The matter of rotation in office—Revised bond plan—Protest rights accorded to all members

THE accusation most obstinately pursuing the Associated Press had been that it was a gigantic news monopoly, immunizing members against competition even while ruling them with a high hand. "The most powerful and most sinister monopoly in America," so it was called in the overwrought arraignment made by Upton Sinclair.[1] It was on the rock of monopoly that the former association had gone to pieces, a rock which was to be avoided in the new organization, without loss of vantage, by the dual device of bondholder voting and the protest right. True, the multiple voting applied only to the choice of directors, but the directors were to be all-powerful in the conduct of the corporation's affairs and the determination of its policies, the pass-key to admission of applicants for membership, both judge and jury in all questions of discipline, the unappealable arbiters of all controversies. If the bondholding vote regularly determined the personnel of the board, this select coterie of members would be, in fact as well as potentially, in complete control.

About the only business reserved for the annual meeting, the one occasion when the membership convened, was the election of directors and of members blocked by protest.

---

[1] *The Brass Check*, p. 406.

With the bonds originally aggregating $130,000, their holders, representing principally the bigger papers in the larger cities, could cast 5,200 votes, in addition to their own individual votes, out of a possible total approximating 6,000. With the eventual reduction of the outstanding bonds by merger, mishap, or extinction, to $100,000, and the increase of membership to 1,250, the bondholders still might mass more than 4,000 votes and, together, could outweigh all others by 4 to 1. The distribution of voting strength affected none but the members, determining the degree of democracy within the association, but with this notable exception, that it also determined ultimately the attitude to newspapers voluntarily or involuntarily outside the fold. The protest right, on the other hand, more directly concerned the outsiders, placing in those papers possessing it an almost absolute power of exclusion.

The protest right, at the outset, attached primarily to the former members of the old Associated Press of Illinois enjoying "A" contracts and to a very few other journals accepted on the same basis after the break-up of the United Press. In all, there were about 260 protest-right papers, out of 800, the districts in which the privilege could be exercised ranging from 10 to 60 miles in radius, and one, Spokane, controlling an area extending 175 miles.[2] The right of protest was rated a valuable factor, in other words, a membership carrying no such right was less desirable. It has often been asserted by the responsible spokesmen that an Associated Press franchise had no money worth, but the same authorities have also made contradictory statements. While the right of protest was inseparable from personal membership, and membership inseparable

---

2 Stone, Sixty-second Cong., 1st Sess., Sen. Doc. 56, p. 1364.

from a going daily newspaper, vast sums were often paid for properties in which the Associated Press membership was the chief asset and sole inducement for purchase. So too, in the refinancing of newspapers, the press franchise has usually been appraised at a high figure and accepted on the money market as dependable security. Contrariwise, not a few instances might be mentioned of an Associated Press membership being deliberately allowed to lapse where a consolidation sought to clear an overpapered field, or a paper, acquired as a link in a chain, must avoid conflicting obligation to rival news associations.

Doubt as to the legal feasibility of retaining the old-time unconditional veto led to the conception of a protest right which might be overridden by a four-fifths vote of all the members present at the annual meeting. In the twenty-eight years under this provision, only four or five protested members had ever been elected to membership in the Associated Press; of these, one was voted in on the persuasive personal plea of a woman publisher, and most of the other admitted publications were in territory subject to a Hearst-owned daily supposed to be motivated by the interests of the Hearst news service. It would have been strange if this situation, coupled with the embargo on intercourse with *non grata* papers or agencies, did not draw fire on alleged monopolistic practices.

It was 1914, however, before the much talked of move materialized in the filing in the office of the Attorney General at Washington of a presentment, on complaint of the New York *Sun,* charging the Associated Press with operating in violation of the Sherman Anti-Trust Law. Attorney General Gregory, a year later, announced his conclusion, siding with the Associated Press except in one minor particular, and saying:

Assuming that the kind of service in which The Associated Press is engaged is interstate commerce (a question not free from doubt), I am nevertheless of the opinion that it is no violation of the Anti-Trust act for a group of newspapers to form an association to collect and distribute news for their common benefit, and, to that end, to agree to furnish the news collected by them only to each other, or to the association; provided, that no attempt is made to prevent the members from purchasing or otherwise obtaining news from rival agencies. And if that is true, the corollary must be true, namely, that newspapers desiring to form and maintain such an organization may determine who shall be, and who shall not be, their associates.

This, of course, is not to say that such an association might not develop into an unlawful monopoly. The facts adduced, however, in my opinion, do not show that that has happened in the case of The Associated Press.

As regards the first ground of complaint, assuming as I do that the collection and distribution of news amongst the several states is interstate trade or commerce, any by-laws, or other regulation adopted by The Associated Press, which would have the effect of preventing, or seriously hindering, its members from purchasing or otherwise obtaining news from a rival agency, would be, I think, a restraint upon interstate trade or commerce and an attempt to monopolize. The contention that The Associated Press has imposed such a regulation upon its membership, or at least has the power to do so, has a foundation in the by-laws. The president of The Associated Press states that the power reserved in this by-law has not been exercised. As I understand it, the complainant disputes that assertion. It is not necessary, however, for me to determine that issue of fact, since my conclusion is that this by-law, whether it has been enforced or not, should be abrogated. I am advised by the president of The Associated Press that this will be promptly done.[3]

With the legitimacy of its activities thus officially certified, the soundness of the structure and policies of the Associated Press seemed to be established more firmly than before. It was complying with the law to the satisfaction of the Attorney General. It was now exempt from

[3] Associated Press Report, 1915, p. 119.

assault by foes crying monopoly. But the unequal voting power and protest privileges remained, and still chafed, and internal unrest manifested itself in various ways.

Appreciating the standing invitation to adverse criticism, the directors themselves initiated a policy aiming to restrict the exercise of protest. No new protest right was to be granted, "unless there are special and peculiar reasons." [4] The precedent had been laid down early, that papers wishing to maintain exclusive service in their protest territory would be charged on the population of the entire area.[5] By a campaign of persuasion and pressure and extension of the practice of imposing this surcharge, not on the city, but on the particular publisher declining to execute a requested waiver, more than 100 members, who had protest privileges covering more or less extended territory beyond the point of publication, were induced to forego their rights in order to facilitate admission of a very considerable number of new members. "A very limited number have shown an unwillingness to make any such surrender." [6] For justification of the procedure, members were reminded that exclusion of otherwise eligible applicants deprived the association of revenue and correspondingly tended to increase the assessments which the rest must pay. The interesting question as to whether one newspaper standing on its rights might properly be subjected to a discriminating assessment in excess of that levied on a competitor receiving the same report, in the same city, but possessing no protest right, was not brought in issue. With all members on a par in this respect, as they have since become, the point might yet be of consequence, should one Associated Press paper

---

[4] *Ibid.*, 1902, p. 33.
[5] *Ibid.*, 1903, p. 80; 1916, p. 90.
[6] *Ibid.*, 1917, p. 3.

refuse to grant a waiver conceded by the others sharing its right to protest. Renewal of the plea to members, in 1921, "for the best interests of the organization," not to use a right of protest beyond ten miles from the boundaries of their cities of publication, apparently fixed that area as the territorial unit of exclusive service.

The overshadowing bondholding vote, moreover, had never been relished by the rank and file of the membership. The original directors were the self-named incorporators; they represented the bondholding strength of the reformed association. As their terms expired, they were almost invariably reëlected over and over, and the same persons and interests were perpetuated in office. The influential big city morning papers predominated in the board. Some readjustments were made to balance better the evening publications and the different sections of the country when directors were dropped out by death, or by resignation upon ineligibility due to disposing of their newspaper properties, or, at rare intervals, by voluntary retirement. But because of the preponderant voice of the bondholders and their unified interests, the feeling prevailed among those with but a single vote that, once in, a director could not be dislodged, that a coöperative association should have more rotation in office, and this in spite of reiterated assurances that the elections were not predetermined by the bondholding vote and that, in scarcely an instance, would the choice have been different if only the membership votes had been counted.

A special committee, reporting in 1908, submitted a proposal that, of the places to be filled, whether full term or vacancies, not more than two of the outgoing directors might be reëlected, the two to be those among them receiving the largest number of votes, eliminating the votes cast for all other candidates from the immediately preceding board. This form of rotation was urged as the best way to gain advantage of new men in the board and, at the same time, retain experienced members.[7] The idea, however, ran afoul of a legal opinion; it impaired vested rights of members; first, the right to offer themselves as candidates for election at any time; and, second, the right to nominate and vote for such candidates as they deemed best; while inclined to believe a reasonable by-law prescribing the eligibility of members to be directors would be sustained, the question was not free from doubt. As viewed by the corporation's counsel, the proposal was "unreasonable, uncertain and impracticable." For was it not possible that all of the outgoing members might receive precisely the same number of votes for reëlection, and it then be impossible to ascertain which two had been reëlected? Furthermore, "I doubt whether it would be held proper to make their eligibility for reëlection dependent upon the number of votes which they might receive."[8] On the strength of these objections, the board declined even to submit the proposed by-law to the membership. The latter, nevertheless, in quest of a remedy, adopted a resolution on the subject declaring it to be the sense of their meeting:

> That, in additon to the nominations presented from the floor at annual meetings, there shall be selected each year a nominating committee to present a ticket for the consideration of the membership.
>
> That this nominating committee shall consist of eight members, two from each division, to be elected by the members of the respective divisions at their meetings.
>
> That it shall be the duty of this nominating committee to present for the consideration of the members at each annual meeting a ticket of not less than ten members as candidates for directors.

[7] *Ibid.*, 1909, p. 47.

[8] *Ibid.*, p. 4.

The nominating committees began to function by offering lists of names at successive annual meetings, but without appreciably influencing the procedure. The "new-material" candidate, regularly, either withdrew in favor of the incumbent, or was defeated when both names went to a vote. Only where outsiders were pitted against one another did the new material score. In 1919, the committee purposely refrained from renominating two outgoing directors, but they were nominated from the floor and reëlected.[9]

The next year, the nominating committee submitted the names of only those whose terms were expiring.[10] "After careful consideration of the subject, while under a vote of the membership the committee's duty is to make two nominations for each vacancy, it is not a practical measure, after having renominated all of the retiring directors, to present other nominees." Because of what had happened the preceding year, the committee had found it impossible to prevail on members, other than the outgoing directors, to permit the use of their names. "Being unable to do anything to secure a reasonable amount of rotation," it recommended "that, each year, one or two of the directors whose terms expire shall retire by mutual arrangement, so that new material may be selected. Only by some such arrangement can the continuance of the nominating committee be justified." In the lively discussion, the committee was roundly excoriated for not presenting a full slate, its proposal to ask members of the board to decide which should retire was characterized as "an impropriety," the outgoing directors declined to accept a nomination "in the terms that it was tendered to us," but, at the same time, were renominated and reëlected.

---

[9] *Ibid.*, 1920, p. 54.
[10] *Ibid.*, 1921, p. 47.

The matter was ostensibly settled for all time. Yet only ostensibly. The multiple bond votes continued to blight every election of directors and to center potential control. At length, the problem was tackled once more, and a comprehensive report was submitted by a committee specially appointed to discover the solution.[11] The total of outstanding bonds had come down by this time, it was stated, to $100,575, but no legal authority existed to call or enforce redemption. No redeemed bonds had ever been resold, though the board had been empowered to resell them. "Not thinking it appropriate to take any action affecting the election of the board itself, although no member of the board as constituted owes his election to the bond vote, and also believing that in taking any such action, it would be impossible to avoid the appearance of favoritism." Resale, at all events, was not advisable unless the mandate came from the membership. It was advisable, nevertheless, if possible, to broaden the list of bondholders by issuing bonds to members not then holding them, "in proportion to the regular assessments which they paid." This would be in recognition of the fact that the general newspaper alignment has changed greatly since the original issue of bonds, and that many members do not have a voice in the election of directors proportionate to their contribution to the organization.

The data which must serve as the foundation for every such plan was compiled. Weekly assessments, paid by 1,222 members, were totaling $161,348, subdivided as follows:

357 paying less than $50 each............	$9,457
406 paying between $50 and $100........	31,037
459 paying over $100....................	120,852

[11] *Ibid.*, 1928, p. 18.

So 37 per cent of the membership, paying over $100 a week, were contributing three-fourths of all the revenue; the sixty-one paying more than $500 a week apiece were providing $46,211, while sixty-one paying less than $15 a week were providing $768. To correlate the voting power more equitably, the recommendation called for a resolution of the members commanding redistribution along these lines. Brought before the annual meeting, the committee's suggestion met with favor but did not go far enough to suit the preponderating sentiment. A substitute resolution, as adopted, devolved upon a committee of six, including the president, the duty to report both a definite bond plan and also an adjustment of protest rights.

The work of this new committee reached the members at their 1928 meeting. It had been found once more that, though the existence of the outstanding bonds assured certain rights, vested in the owners, which could not be disturbed, the association could be strengthened materially by expanding its financial resources in the form of liquid balances. By authorizing an additional bond issue, then, both purposes might be subserved if the new bonds were imbued with the same voting rights as the old and allotted to subscribing members in the ratio of their weekly assessments.[12] Each $25 bond would entitle to one vote, but every member, regardless of the amount of his assessment, should have the right to subscribe for four bonds and pro rata additions above $50 a week.

As to protest rights, a recasting of the by-laws was urged at the same time to this effect, that, "without the consent in writing of each member representing a newspaper printed in the English language, which has been represented in membership for more than five years, in continental United

[12] *Ibid.*, 1929, p. 26.

States, and published not less than six days a week, the Board may not elect a new member in the same city of publication, the same field (morning or evening) and to be published on the days on which the existing member regularly publishes, except that consent to the election of a morning paper need not be obtained from an evening member, the membership of which includes the right to a Sunday morning edition. Provided, that this shall not affect the status of members who have protest rights as of the date of the adoption of this amendment, and it shall not have the effect of either enlarging or decreasing the right of such members as defined in their certificates of membership with such waivers as have subsequently been given." A rather intricate statement—but it was dealing with a complex proposition. The sum and substance of the changes would be that, when and where the limitations on the powers of the Board were effective and not waived, "new members could be elected only by a vote of four-fifths of those present, in person or by proxy, at an annual meeting, or at a special meeting called for that purpose."

Unanimous approval followed, and appropriate resolutions incorporated the suggested action in the fundamental structure of the association. It was really a strange dénouement, that objection to a privileged class of bondholding members in position to monopolize the voting power, and demand for revocation of these special prerogatives, should have led the members into voting themselves as a whole the same privileges. From this time on, all so desiring were to have votes for directors in proportion to contributions gauged by the weekly assessment roll, not an absolutely exact proportion, to be sure, for the overweight of the original bondholders was not reduced, though offset, in a way, by conferring an excess influence on the member with minimum payments. Assuming that all the new bonds authorized by the revised plan should be subscribed, and the last report showed, in round figures, $150,000—$50,000 of them conversion of old issue to new—to have been taken, the total number of votes should approximate 9,500. With this rebalance of power, though the relative interests of large and small papers, of one section as against another, of evening as against morning publications, remained unaltered, Associated Press elections should accord with the membership preferences, and the retention, or rotation, of directors be quite within the determination of a voting majority. The first trial of the new arrangement took place in 1929, but all the outgoing directors were rechosen, as usual.

What had been done in regard to protest rights savored similarly of anticlimax. The outside criticism to be disarmed had been directed at the possession and exercise of the right to exclude competitors in local territory. Within the association, a deaf ear had been consistently turned to all appeals for new protest rights, and steady pressure had been applied to curtail the areas over which the existing privilege extended in the several cities. Protest rights, generally speaking, were regarded with disfavor and discountenanced, and their number, never more than a third of the membership, had been shrinking absolutely, as well as relatively, in total membership. This policy was here completely reversed—instead of being enjoyed by a limited few, protest rights were to belong to one and all—instead of making it easier to gain admission, it was to be more difficult—instead of leaving the directors free to act on many cases, no application whatsoever could be granted, without waiver of protest, except by the next to impossible overriding four-fifths vote of the members. The trend in the arena of American journalism has been to consolidation and extermination, and to a diminishing number of dailies, a trend whose continuance this tighter shutting of the door to Associated Press service must further and stimulate.

CHAPTER XXV

THE ASSOCIATED PRESS—ADMINISTRATION

Wire tolls and cable rates—Relations with the telegraph operators—Equalizing assessments—Use of latest mechanical devices—Enlargement of foreign news service—Changing methods of handling the report—Addition of feature services—Rearrangement of circuits—Recasting the personnel

How to check growing expenditures seems to have been an ever present problem. The biggest single outlay was for wire transmission. Efforts began as early as 1899 for more liberal terms of rental on leased wires.[1] The Associated Press complained that, although it was the largest buyer of leased wire service, it was being charged more than brokers and individual newspapers. The rates paid to the big telegraph companies were uniformly $24 a year per mile for daytime hours and $12 for night use. Some smaller contracts with railway systems provided for lump sum rentals which, computed on a mileage basis, figured about $13 a mile per year for day wires and about $6.50 for night wires. The cable rates from London and Paris were ten cents a word, from Berlin fourteen cents a word. These were the only three European points from which any considerable amount of news was being received. No news was coming direct from South Africa, then the scene of the Boer troubles, dependence being placed on the European news agencies and the specials to the London dailies. The cable tolls from Manila to New York were ordinarily 85 cents a word, while, to expedite very im-

1 Associated Press Report, 1900, p. 171.

portant news, the night and day rates ran up to $2.37 and $6.37 a word respectively. The cable tolls from Havana were five cents a word; from Santiago, Cuba, eighteen cents a word; from Bermuda, fifteen cents a word; from Porto Rico, twenty cents a word.[2]

To the request for a reduction, the Postal Telegraph Company expressed a willingness to concede $20 and $10 per mile per year, "if the Western Union Telegraph Company will agree to do the same." For the latter company, President Eckert, however, accompanied his refusal with a lengthy statement of reasons:

> It is evident that the telegraph companies, by leasing wires to the press associations, practically create a private telegraphic system for the service and benefit of the entire press of the country. By means of that system, the press associations interchange and distribute all the principal news dispatches of the day or night, without any regard to the number of newspapers served by them in any one city. Such a complete service must necessarily affect the revenues which would otherwise come to the telegraph companies from the transmission of special or combination dispatches to newspapers. These conditions were carefully reviewed when the rates of $24 day and $12 night were made for press association wires. If there is any change in the conditions to-day, it is only that the establishment of more newspapers in the larger cities that are served by the Associated Press without any increase in the cost of wire service emphasizes the cheapness of the rentals charged by the telegraph companies, as the advantage lies entirely with the Associated Press.[3]

President Eckert went on to remind the papers of the further gain to them in the special service rendered for wire trouble and the substitution of wires to keep lines open at all times. The committee vigorously repudiated the claim that transmission of the press report over leased wires reduced the income of the companies from news-

[2] Diehl, private letter, July 11, 1900.
[3] Associated Press Report, 1900, p. 173.

papers, insisting that it really developed special telegraphic correspondence and increased the employment of the telegraph by the individual journals. The Western Union Telegraph Company "proceeds on the theory that it is entitled to charge all the traffic will bear," instead of "a fair and just rate." But nothing more tangible resulted than indulging a regret that the relations between the telegraphs would prevent the Postal company from acceding on its own part and putting into effect the reduction of rates "which it recognizes as fair and just."

Strange to relate, the failure to win the desired favor was not without its compensating feature. It buttressed the denial, under attack, that there was discrimination in telegraph rates for or against the Associated Press. "We lease wires precisely as other agencies do, and precisely as a great many stockbrokers do," was the testimony of Stone, "at a higher rate in fact," because of the "drops," the report being delivered simultaneously at all the cities and towns on the circuit.

Commercial telegraph and cable tolls were reduced from time to time, but not until a lapse of fifteen years, with periodic and urgent pleas, was a readjustment of the leased wire tariff obtained which permitted of a substantial annual saving.[4]

The lengthening tentacles of the leased wire system, gradually reaching out to nearly every journal printing daily telegraphic news forced a corresponding enlargement of the corps of operators sending and receiving the report. The men engaged in this part of the press service regarded their work as unusually exacting. It indisputably called for superior skill and ability relative to that ordinarily required in the craft. That only expert telegraphers could

---

[4] *Ibid.*, 1917, p. 3.

JOSEPH MEDILL

WILLIAM PENN NIXON

RICHARD SMITH

WILLIAM HENRY SMITH

man the press wires satisfactorily was conceded by all. By the spring of 1903, 374 operators were attached to the Associated Press service, making the most numerous group of employees, and a group of no little solidarity, who through representatives voicing common grievances, asked for a 20 per cent increase in their salaries.[5] "For the past ten years, there has been a steady increase in the demands of our work upon our nervous energies, for which there has been no recompense. It has reached a point where the limit of physical endurance is demanded of us, 365 nights in the year, or in the case of day workers, 312 days, with a sufficient number of hours added to compensate for the Sunday holiday. Our maximum earning capacity having now been reached, we are powerless to meet the increased price of rent, fuel, and the necessities and comforts of life unless our employers grant us a sufficiently increased wage to offset these increased expenses."

While admitting the substantial allegations in respect to the higher cost of living to be true, Stone insisted that some other facts were worthy of equal consideration. These he enumerated in submitting the matter to the board. When the leased wire system was inaugurated, the salaries of the Associated Press operators had been fixed in uniformity with what was paid by the telegraph companies, then $17 a week days, and $19 a week nights, and these figures had been raised without solicitation up to the prevailing level of $25 days, and $29 nights on trunk lines, though no advance had been made in the interval by the telegraph companies. Of the 40,000 telegraph operators in the United States, the Associated Press was employing less than one per cent at fully 25 per cent higher salaries than were paid for like service by either of the telegraph companies or any

[5] *Ibid.*, 1903, p. 87.

of the railways. During the preceding two years, the salaries of a number of Associated Press operators had been increased, in several cases by more than 20 per cent. "For these reasons," Stone declined to recommend a horizontal raise "in advance of any like action by telegraph and railway companies," but asked authority to give each operator of one year's standing a two weeks' vacation with pay, to buy and maintain for the operator the typewriting machine used in the Associated Press service, to relieve the operator of the necessity of paying a substitute more than his own wage, and to adjust any inequalities in the payroll which might be disclosed. Approval and execution of these recommendations reëstablished an era of good feeling, but abuses of the vacation privilege led, before long, to rescission and instructions to limit the grants "to such operators as by exceptional loyalty and zeal prove themselves deserving of it."[6]

Though the wheels were running smoothly, restlessness was not entirely allayed. Certain operators, evidently interpreting the concessions as a sign of weakness or fear, began propaganda to induce the men to join the Commercial Telegraphers' Union as part of its program to unionize all the wires in the country. As a result, a fresh demand, in September, 1905, summoned the Associated Press to enter into a written contract with the Commercial Telegraphers' Union. "Not only was the scale of wages very greatly increased, but a set of rules of the most arbitrary character and of an intolerable nature was to be kept in force. The salaries of many operators would have been more than doubled, and even the appointment of operators to positions would have been placed in the hands of the

---

[6] *Ibid.*, 1906, p. 54.

men themselves."[7] The board, of course, refused to accede.

A year later, the Commercial Telegraphers' Union issued a circular, dated October 3, 1906, proclaiming a boycott of the Associated Press, announcing it to be the policy of the Union that operators reject employment with that organization, and requesting telegraphers employed by it to seek other positions. This attempt to interfere with the work of the Associated Press proved wholly unsuccessful and at no time was it found difficult to secure an adequate number of capable men to transmit the report to every newspaper entitled to receive it.

But in July, 1907, a series of strikes against the Western Union and Postal Telegraph Companies was precipitated in various parts of the country. That these outbreaks were inspired or inaugurated by the Union was denied by its national officers who, nevertheless, finally gave the strike official approval. No formal or general request had been made upon the association by its own employees up to that time. When the excitement over the strike against the telegraph companies became tense, a number of operators took possession of the press wires during the hours when news should have been transmitted and asked authority of their fellow workers to sign their names to a petition formulating their demands. This occurred on Sunday night, August 11, 1907, and the document required the reply by 7:30 o'clock the next evening. The answer for the Associated Press asserted that the proposal of the men, if agreed to, would add more than $200,000 a year to its annual outlay and would have first to be presented to and considered by the board, "something impossible within the time stated." Whereupon, "without further conference or

---

[7] *Ibid.*, 1907, p. 120.

parley," a considerable body of the men abandoned their keys and quit work.

The strike ran along in a desultory manner, more or less annoying in certain localities and sections, but on the whole ineffectively. Some public sympathy for the strikers was elicited by the charge that the Associated Press, alone of all the news agencies using leased wires, was holding out, both the Hearst service and the United Press having met the Union's demands. The only offset to this lay in disseminating the information that the total number of operators employed for the Hearst lines was extremely limited and exclusively in the larger cities where the cost of living was admittedly high and where the Associated Press itself had always paid exceptionally high salaries; that, although the United Press had signed the agreement with the Union, it had done so with the distinct understanding that its scale should not equal what was demanded for Associated Press operators who, in the meantime, were receiving at every point larger salaries than were paid to United Press operators; that the Laffan Bureau had refused to subscribe to an agreement with the Commercial Telegraphers' Union. So far as unionizing the wires of the Associated Press was concerned, the strike failed completely but it won for the men a substantial increase in the wage schedule, and an adjustment of inequalities dated back to the first of March, in the aggregate amounting to ten per cent of the total operating expenses.[8]

In 1913, the payments to operators went up once more by additions approximating $82,000 a year.[9] On the heels of another huge expansion of leased wire mileage in 1918, the number of operators employed by the Associated Press

[8] *Ibid.*, p. 2.

[9] *Ibid.*, 1913, p. 83.

reached 660.[10] "The body of operators who copy the report in every state of the union with a single exception," it was stated, "is greater than the combined operating force of all the other press associations in the world." By 1920, the corps of wire experts numbered 785. The World War, of course, cut in on the already diminishing supply of competent operators and brought the craft its proportionate share of the resulting salary increases.

The equitable distribution of expenditures on joint account by a method satisfactory to the participating papers is always of vital concern. The original practice made delivery of the report to each city the unit of computation. From the early days of the harbor boats, the assessments were imposed on Boston, or Philadelphia, or New York, and the amount divided equally among the journals receiving the service at each place. An indictment of this system, or rather lack of system, charged that it, "like Topsy jes' growed up," was thoroughly arbitrary and unscientific, limited either by what the papers could stand or by what could be collected from them.

As far back as 1894, the Associated Press board was recorded in favor of "a fair and reasonable adjustment" based on "due consideration" of (*a*) reading population, (*b*) proximity to news centers, (*c*) cost of collection and transmission, (*d*) such other elements as might properly enter into the cost of the report and its value in the respective cities of publication, but treating each locality and each newspaper on the same principle.[11] Seeing nothing eventuating, yet many growing restive under delay, James E. Scripps, of the Detroit *News*, took it upon himself to improvise a scheme which would have some uniformity

---

[10] *Ibid.*, 1918, p. 6.
[11] *Ibid.*, 1894, p. 90.

without changing substantially the existing results. Convinced that neither population nor wire mileage would do, he hit upon a plan of separating the cities into classes and establishing a rate per thousand population for each class, first grouping them into one wherever two or more municipalities immediately adjoined. His proposed assessments were to be primarily by cities, levied on the assumption that there was but a single news service delivered, with suitable allowance "where in any city opposition associations temporarily divide the field," distribution of the assessment between the papers within the city being left to the local board. This plan would embrace three grand territorial divisions, with the cities in the eastern division listed in five classes, those in the western division in four classes, those in the southern division in three classes, paying assessments ranging respectively from $1.00 to $3.00 per thousand of population, from $3.50 to $9.00 per thousand, and from $2.50 to $5.00 per thousand. The equitable basis thus adopted would be horizontally increased or diminished from time to time as the requirements of the association might demand or permit.[12]

Shortly afterward, but producing no more visible result, data was requested bearing on assessment revision as follows: (*a*) census population of cities being served; (*b*) allotment of territory to each; (*c*) white population in such territory; (*d*) ratio to population of the country; (*e*) ratio of population to whole population served by the Associated Press; (*f*) proportion of cost of Associated Press operations to be assessed each city on this basis.[13] Still a year later, a report by Stone, obviously utilizing the Scripps's memorandum for a guide, recommended this plan

---

[12] Private circular, to fellow members, Dec. 1, 1894.

[13] Associated Press Report, 1895, p. 180.

of apportionment as "the nearest approach to an ideal system":

1. Decennial readjustment on census returns.
2. Grouping of immediately adjacent cities into one assessment district.
3. Four grand divisions—Eastern, Central, Western, Southern.
4. The city, so construed, to be the unit of assessment in each case.
5. Base rate to be graded by districts and by population within the unit:

Population	Rate per 1,000 of population		
	East & Central	Western	Southern
over 1,000,000	$1.50		
over 200,000	2.00	$3.50	
over 100,000		5.50	2.50
over 75,000	2.50		
under 75,000	3.00		
over 50,000		7.50	3.50
under 50,000		9.00	4.50

6. Cities transferrable from one class to another in discretion of the directors.
7. Arbitrary rates to be fixed by directors for "peculiar circumstances."
8. These assessments to serve merely as a guide for modifications of existing rates until the board deems it wise to carry them out in entirety.

Though some of the rough spots were occasionally ironed down, the assessment schedule was never thoroughly overhauled during the life of the Illinois corporation. As it stood at the end of that régime, the list disclosed glaring discrepancies and inequalities. It showed that an evening paper in Denver was paying the highest assessment in the country, more than 60 per cent above the next highest evening paper assessment and more than 50 per cent above that of any Denver morning paper. It showed two New Orleans papers each paying 25 per cent more than the corresponding New York publications. It showed San Francisco morning dailies on a par with those in New York and 50 per cent higher than those in Chicago. It showed a Baltimore evening paper paying more than any Baltimore morning paper and a like condition in Cleveland, Cincinnati, St. Louis, Kansas City, Minneapolis, and St. Paul, while in Indianapolis the evening paper was rated 30 per cent above either morning publication. It showed as flagrant disproportion in many other places.

Taking over the old association with a definite assurance of unchanged rights and privileges, the Associated Press, starting for the most part with a clean slate, was subrogated to this ancient assessment incubus in a seemingly insoluble tangle. It necessarily engaged immediate attention as the subject of a report by President Noyes, reviewing the situation and exposing its embarrassing features.[14]

"Present assessments," so members were told, "have been made almost solely by rule of thumb and are the concrete results of the rate wars involved in the past press association rivalries. The general theory on which the leased wire assessments have been figured is that a paper should pay a certain percentage to the general fund over and above the expense of laying down the leased wire report in the city affected. When increased revenue has been required, as in the case of the Spanish War and from then to the present time on account of the large increase of the cable service from South Africa, the Philippines, China, and

---

[14] *Ibid.*, 1901, p. 82.

Cuba, it has been secured by levying an additional assessment of an equal percentage on existing assessments. The fatal defect of this system is that it penalizes those who, by reason of their remoteness from distributing points, are justly charged high initial rates by making those high rates the bases on which their proportions of the necessary increased revenues are figured." Citing for illustration a California paper assessed regularly at $300 a week as against one in New York at $100 a week, and therefore compelled to bear three times the latter's burden involved in an extra assessment, Noyes proposed acceptance of three bases for rate-making, namely: (1) The local operating expenses of the leased wire system; (2) the proportion of the rental of the sectional leased wire; (3) the proportion of the contribution to general expense. The last item alone would be variable in uniform percentage to varying requirements.

But that it was not particularly a condition arising out of extra levies was brought home in its treatment by a special committee to which the subject was referred. The report, submitted in 1902, contained new assessment tables, again worked out by Noyes, to accord with the principles which the Board had recommended.[15] In order to place all the cities upon as nearly equal a basis of population as possible, a radius of ten miles from the center of each city was adopted. The total assessment against each city was then made up under four headings: (1) Weekly dues, being an assessment of $10 a week for each daily paper served. (2) Local costs, being the salaries of receiving operators and messengers employed in each city. (3) Wire charges, being the total rental of wires on any given circuit, computed on a weekly basis, together with the salaries of the sending operators, apportioned among the cities on the

[15] *Ibid.*, 1902, p. 78

circuit according to population. (4) General costs, being a charge against all the cities, based on population, to provide the fund needed to pay all the expenses of the association apart from the delivery of the report. In preparing the tables, it was found that a weekly charge of 55 cents for each 1,000 of population would meet general expenses of the association, including expenses incurred in collecting the foreign and domestic news, office rentals, executive and editorial salaries, and all incidental expenses. In cities where only one field was occupied, either morning or evening, the population charge was fixed at two-thirds of the total charge where both fields were occupied. A minimum of 20,000 population was set for all places having less than that number of inhabitants for figuring under that heading. In dividing the total assessments of each city between the afternoon and the morning papers, moreover, consideration was given to the relative cost and use of wires and to all elements of expense in which discrimination between the two classes of papers was possible. Here was a plan that denoted progress in the right direction, at least a plan shorn of haphazard makeshift, and it was promptly accepted. Orders were issued to employ the accompanying schedule of rates.

As conditions were constantly changing, so must assessment schemes change, if the equities were to be observed. In 1915, another special committee, grappling with the problem, worked out a modification of the preceding formula along slightly different lines, which may be summarized:

1. An application generally of the already established principle of a specific charge against members exercising protest rights beyond their immediate home territory.

2. Individual dues to be charged as heretofore.

3. The country to be divided into homogeneous areas.

4. General expense to be allotted to these homogeneous divisions in proportion to their literate population, population employed in gainful pursuits, value of products, and commercial-financial resources.

5. The proportion of each division to be divided among the cities in that division receiving a leased wire report in proportion to population and resources.

6. The uniform population basis for defining what populations are chargeable as "immediate home territory" to rest on United States census practice.

7. Wire charges (single wire) to be made against circuits, and divided among cities on circuits, according to population as at present, save where they can be charged against divisions and divided as divisional charges without revolutionary changes.

8. Actual cost of second and third paralleling wires should be made individual charges against members participating in their use.

9. Local expenses to be assessed against the cities where actually incurred and divided between morning and evening fields according to service rendered in each field.

10. General expense to be divided between the morning and evening fields in proportion to the delivery of the report, measured by days of service to each: seven days to morning papers and six days to evening papers.

11. Wire charges between morning and evening issues to be divided by the hours: morning papers from 3 P.M. to 3:30 A.M. and evening papers from 8 A.M. to 3 P.M. The hours between 3:30 A.M. and 8 A.M. on trunk circuits to be charged to general expense. Where there is no 24-hour wire, the wire charge and also the charge for operators to be according to the actual use of the wire.

12. Net pony revenues to be credited to the divisions in which the pony members are located and to the morning and evening fields respectively as an offset to the general expense charge of the division.[16]

When the 1920 census provided fresh data for another revision, the goal was redefined as a plan of assessment "which will most nearly approximate the equitable amount each member shall contribute toward the expense of the

[16] *Ibid.*, 1916, p. 90.

organization in accordance with the opportunity in the field in which his membership exists." Again, the population area of each city and surroundings within a 10-mile radius was to be deemed the home territory, and the three elements of wire charge, local charge, and general charge regarded as basic.[17]

According to information vouchsafed in explanation, if the member was receiving an additional wire service, a state mail service, or special service of any kind, his contribution for that service was to be added as an individual charge. While every city must have at least one wire to bring to it and carry from it the news of the world, for efficiency, circuits had to be arranged, and taking each state as a unit, it was possible to operate a state circuit connecting the various cities therein; but to furnish a comprehensive news service, trunk circuits were also necessary to link together the various state circuits. So the plan assessed, as a wire charge to each state, the proportion of the cost of the trunk circuit serving it and the entire cost of the state circuit. If the membership within a state did not justify a circuit of its own, regional circuits embracing two or more states were established and similarly treated. The state wire charge was to be distributed according to population so that each city within the state would pay the same wire rate per thousand of population. As the leasing rate for day wires exceeded that for night wires, the wire charge was to be divided proportionally between morning and evening fields on a ratio of the rental exacted by the telegraph companies for the hours of service utilized by each field. The evening proportion, as worked out, was 57 per cent and the morning and Sunday 43 per cent. The

---

[17] *Ibid.*, 1923, p. 6

wire charge included the salaries also of sending operators and filing editors.

In the local charge was comprised the salaries of the receiving operators and messengers, as well as five per cent of the total salaries paid, to provide for vacations and emergencies, the amount divided according to actual hours of service in morning or evening field.

The expenses of the organization not specifically covered went into a general charge allotted to, and assessed against, each state according to the percentage of literate population by an intricate apportionment. "As the afternoon papers are served only six days a week, while service is available to morning papers seven days or nights, the afternoon field is charged with six-thirteenths, or 46 per cent of the state allotment, and the morning field with seven-thirteenths, or 54 per cent." Before redistribution of the state allotment within the state by city population, each field was credited with the amount of the net revenue from the pony circuits respectively and, as in the wire charge, each city in a state paid the same general rate per thousand of population. Assessments conforming to this revised scale were gradually put into effect, payable weekly in advance as always.

Privately conducted, profit-making, news-gathering agencies were never circumscribed by any "rule of thumb" in fixing the terms for their services. They have usually gauged their rates, it is true, to the city as the basic unit, but because seldom enlisting more than one customer in the evening or the morning field in the same city. Their contract stipulations, therefore, would deal principally with the character and volume of the news to be supplied, and nothing would prevent fitting the charges to the different degrees of benefit to accrue to different papers even in the same city. Nothing would prevent, either, offering inducements to obtain new customers. Special rates or temporary concessions might be well worth while with a view to building up a paying future business, or contributing toward the overhead already incurred for regular service. This would apply regardless of competitive conditions prompting such a move in order to deprive a rival of revenue, or of a foothold in a strategic territory. The later inclusion of supplemental and optional services gave additional opportunity to bargain in the negotiation of the contract, the more so in collective dealings with groups or chains of newspapers. Protest is not uncommon to the effect that accepted methods of figuring charges for news service favor the big-city journals and in each multi-paper city, favor the larger and stronger publications. The outlay for the news report, however, has come to be so inconsequential in the budget of the average daily paper that a disparity in assessments, which formerly would cause complaint, could now hardly be seriously disturbing.

The milestones of progress for the Associated Press, since its transplanting to New York, are to be counted in steady expansion of membership and constant development in organization, equipment, and efficiency. It could not stand still while all the newspapers were going forward. It necessarily had to keep in step with the innovations and speeding-up distinguishing coeval journalistic enterprise. The tremendous widening of the circle of newspaper readers, and the corresponding spread of popular interest to events in every quarter of the globe, no matter how remote, sufficed to account for the notable increase in variety, coverage, and volume of news service. Successive strides in mechanical invention were indispensable to make all this possible. The long-relied-on telegraph was supplemented by the introduction of the telephone and by its multiplied use converting it into a system of universal intercommunication. The wireless telegraph arrived, and was followed by wireless telephony and by radio broadcasting, and every means of transmission was quickly bent to the purpose of converging and conveying the news of the world for further dissemination in the printed page. The leased-wire network of the Associated Press has grown till it measures in round numbers 150,000 miles, linking together every city sharing the full report: at first, with operators manifolding the copy for distribution by messenger; the operators' location sometimes alternating from one newspaper office to another, sometimes in independent quarters, to insure each equally prompt deliveries; later, separate receiving operators for each member; still later, the automatic printing telegraph unrolling the typed report in each office. When the printing telegraph attains a speed producing an economy of time and outlay for all classes of messages, or photo-transmission reaches the point which renders it advantageous to transmit in facsimile the typed report, sheet by sheet, the army of telegraph operators manning the press wires must begin to be demobilized, and be reduced, inevitably, to smaller and smaller numbers. In the meantime, the once bitter controversies as to which paper was entitled to the local Associated Press offices, or as to whether the latter were near or far from the publications served, have had nothing left for them to feed upon.

It used to be assumed that the press association must be lodged in close proximity to Newspaper Row and also be inseparable from the telegraph companies. For years, the Associated Press occupied a floor in the Western Union Building for housing its general staff. In 1914, it removed to an office building on Chambers Street, a few squares distant, "splendidly lighted and admirably suited for the work of the organization." After another ten years, it betook itself uptown to a location at Madison Avenue and 46th Street, several miles from the main offices of the telegraph companies and well separated from most of the newspaper plants.

In the beginning, the accepted and unquestioned source of foreign news rested in the confederated group of European news agencies with which reciprocal arrangements were maintained. The tide-turning contract, negotiated with Reuter's at a crucial moment, will be recalled. Similar exchange alliances with the neighboring Canadian Press, and with agencies on other continents entered into from time to time, provided for interchange of intelligence. The Associated Press, in 1900, had four forwarding stations in Europe, in which its special representatives made up the cable dispatches of the entire alien world from reports supplied by the several European news agencies. By 1910, the number of such offices had increased to sixteen.[18] The growth of foreign representation, thus evidenced, was the result of a tactful campaign to secure an open door for press dispatches out of censor-ridden old-world capitals. As narrated by Stone, the story of his parleys, preliminary to procuring a lifting of bans and the issue of orders for prompt transmission of press messages, reads like a fascinating romance.[19] After being received by kings and dined by emperors, conferring with prime ministers and attending a private audience with the Pope, a measure of freedom for filing dispatches addressed to the Associated Press, and their expedition on the wires, was brought about in France, Germany, Italy, and even Russia, through this unofficial ambassador. The Associated Press gave assurance of its readiness to com-

---

[18] *Ibid.*, 1911, p. 3.

[19] Stone, *Fifty Years*, p. 243.

mission its own competent men in each of those countries, if conditions enabling them to render satisfactory service were established. "I told them our people must be absolutely free, that there must be no attempt to influence them. While in order to be useful the representative of the Associated Press accredited to any capital must be on friendly terms with the government at that capital, he must not be a servile agent of that government. We could not deny ourselves the right of free statement, and anything we might do must be done with the distinct understanding that the government would not influence the character of the service as to its impartiality."

The mission proved eminently successful and the new order of affairs abroad began January 1, 1904. The British fount of world news, suspected always of presenting only British viewpoints, was no longer to be our sole reliance. Strictly American interpretation of old-world doings was to prevail at all times. The way was paved, at any rate, for brilliant reporting of fast on-rushing big events—the death of Pope Leo XIII, the Russo-Japanese War, the controversy over the discovery of the North Pole, the diplomatic moves on the European chessboard, the assassinations at Serajevo, up to the eruption of the World War. Then, over night as it were, the news stream welled up to flood heights, and at the same moment all the old blockades to untrammeled expression and free transmission were reërected. Censors, clothed with the ancient vestments of infallibility, took command everywhere in the warring countries. All telegraph and telephone wires became at once part of the fighting equipment. Radio masts and submarine cables, if not cut to destroy their use altogether, were operated by the military or naval establishments. Throughout Europe, propaganda was substituted for truthful information and news-suppression crowded out the function of news-dissemination.[20] Judged by mere volume of matter passed along, however, the censors were not to be censured, for our foreign news inflow was up to 50,000 words a day ere many moons had turned. The regular staffs of the Associated Press at London and at Paris had been doubled within a fortnight, and men moved to all the stragetic stations that could be occupied. The same was true, for that matter, of the other news agencies and of the great metropolitan journals maintaining their own corps of overseas correspondents. According to one reasonably authoritative guess, ventured as not far from correct, 500 American newspaper workers were doing assignments in Europe at the close of 1914, which number must have multiplied tremendously afterwards. And we are told that, nothwithstanding the fact that relatively few of our war correspondents got anything like a smell of gunpowder, the army of the press managed to "shoot the stuff over" to the papers on this side of the Atlantic at the rate of about a word a second.[21]

What was to go on the wires to the individual papers was, after all, the really important factor. In a twentieth-century era, the mere sifting and selection of news collected and printed by member publications with first thought for themselves could not fully answer requirements. In 1908, a committee, specially charged to study the service and suggest improvements in it, submitted a number of pertinent recommendations. Among the items, it favored: better writing and editing, and closer condensation; systematic inspection of all reports as served on side circuits, or sent and received at relay points; employment of a general sports editor;

[20] *Ibid.*, p. 317.

[21] Crane, "Mobilizing the News," *Scientific American,* Feb. 6, 1915, p. 134.

livelier treatment, abridgement of the routine, more careful scrutiny of Washington service; lighter and more interesting handling of cabled news, and a supplemental foreign mail service; more frequent and systematic adjustment of the market reports on all circuits; exchange of filing editors on the main leased-wire lines; more attention to advance matter and its preparation, with an abstract and brief introduction, where possible, so that it might be used without waiting for the telegraphic lead; the supply of certain local needs, such as state news, on circuits serving papers with uniform demands; experimental testing of a system of scheduling (afterwards known as the budget system) so that members might know ahead of time what was coming in the report each day; appointment of a night service superintendent to keep in closer touch on the night side; improvement in the editing of the so-called pony reports.[22] Many of these suggestions were accepted and, before long, a plan was also adopted to cover the more important domestic occurrences by Associated Press staff men rather than through local correspondents, compensating for the greater cost by the better and altogether quicker reporting of events wanted by the press in all parts of the country.[23] To this end, a complement of highly trained newspaper men was recruited to the ranks to head the various bureaus and for the staffs at the principal news centers.[24]

As an outgrowth of the custom of sending speeches and documents to the papers by post, subject to release later by wire, a mail service was added to carry reading matter of a news character not rated of that degree of urgency demanding immediate transmission and publication. The com-

[22] Associated Press Report, 1909, p. 33.
[23] *Ibid.*, 1910, p. 3.
[24] *Ibid.*, 1911, p. 6.

mencement of this went back to 1913,[25] giving the opening, eventually, for "features," for informational and "human interest" stories, for other side-lines. One valuable function of this mail service consisted of advance obituaries. "When a prominent man gets to be 50," to quote the general manager, "we prepare his obituary and send it out to all our papers. At 60, if he is still in the public eye, we rewrite it in greater detail. And as for old men like the Pope, or John D. Rockefeller, or Chauncey Depew, their life stories are brought to date yearly. Within a few seconds after such a man closes his eyes for the last time, every important newspaper in America can begin to issue his story." [26]

Under recent régime the mail service has lost its strangle-hold on the lighter-vein articles. The report as a whole has been "brightened up," men encouraged to put their personality into their writing, and the authorship occasionally hall-marked by attaching signatures. The Associated Press has gone so far, even, as to provide political surveys and forecasts in serial letters written and signed by staff correspondents touring the debatable states during a presidential campaign. This, of course, constituted a long jump from the days of the announcement that "its men are nameless," that "no matter how skilled as a writer, how ingenious as a news-getter, or how well informed as an investigator, an Associated Press man may be, his personality is never allowed to intrude into the news," and that "By the Associated Press," was "the sole guerdon" of identity. "To develop interesting matter," not necessarily spontaneous happenings, "without encroaching on the more important general news," was to be the new news policy, which, in 1926,

---

[25] *Ibid.*, 1914, p. 60.

[26] Barton, "How Did That Get In the Paper?" *American Magazine*, Aug., 1926.

claimed credit for eight notable interviews, "the biggest news of the day," signed in each instance by the correspondents who procured and wrote them. The feature service thereupon was pronounced "settled in a niche seemingly awaiting it," covering in addition to the flow of supplementary news the fields of business, science, labor, agriculture, fashions, politics, aviation, radio, moving pictures, art, drama, music, sports, and virtually every news sidelight in modern newspaper-making.[27] A still later departure was the installation of a news picture service, soon said to be responding finely to the demand for a larger transmission of current event illustrations, some of them coming by telephoto process. Though voted down by the Board more than once, the inclusion of comic strips in the general feature service was already in sight.[28]

The broad territorial divisions for working purposes, Eastern, Central, Southern, Southwestern, and Western, funneling into New York, Chicago, Atlanta, Kansas City, and San Francisco, respectively, long remained unchanged except for the segregation of Washington and the establishment of subdivisions by states centered in the state capitals. But in 1928, a departmentalized organization was substituted for the divisional plan, so that an executive staff headed the now distinctly differentiated departments, and bureau correspondents at thirty-eight "strategic centers" became directly responsible to the general manager for the discharge of the duties previously devolving on four superintendents, financial disbursements and accounting being centralized at the executive headquarters. For the new arrangement, specific advantages were claimed; namely, quicker action on administrative problems; closer contact

---

27 Associated Press Report, 1928, p. 6.

28 *Ibid.*, 1928, p. 71; 1929, pp. 14, 66.

between members and the general manager and, through the general manager, with the Board of Directors; more prompt collection and distribution of the news; broader opportunities for a larger number of members of the staff; and an inspiration for better work—all without any counteracting disadvantages.[29]

The movement of telegraphic dispatches in and out of the strategic centers constitutes a practically never-ending stream. Applying a different metaphor, the arterial trunk-lines have been aptly termed "the Appian Ways of the news routes." The big Washington wire travels through storm-proof conduits between the nation's metropolis and its capital; the New England line links New York and Boston; four trunk lines go out of Chicago to the Northwest, Southwest, Pacific and the Old South, the last zigzagging to Atlanta and back to Washington; the Pacific-Coastal wire ties Spokane and San Diego through San Francisco. General news is carried into and out of trunk-line terminals and on to main headquarters, while localized news plies the circuits serving the publications particularly interested. The cable messages for the most part enter by the New York and San Francisco gateways. The amount of foreign news handled has greatly increased, being in far wider demand than formerly and no longer limited by meager mechanical facilities. The Dawes plan agreement came to the Associated Press direct, 50,000 words, "the largest cable message ever transmitted." The service was extended in 1918 to some of the more prominent papers of South America and, after a full year, the Board voiced its conviction that the admission of these forty-one Latin-American journals was "one of the most progressive steps we have taken."[30] "Our member-

[29] *Ibid.*, 1929, p. 6.

[30] *Ibid.*, 1920, p. 4.

ship spreads from Alaska to Argentina, and, as we have started a modest service to the Philippines by wireless, it reaches also from Manila to Havana." News bureaus operate in Havana, Panama, Mexico City, and Buenos Aires; likewise at Honolulu and Manila; staff correspondents are stationed at Pekin, Shanghai, and Tokio. Domestic bureaus, regularly manned, are found in 61 of the principal cities of the United States, and an exchange with the Canadian Press Association supplies Canadian news. The Washington establishment, day by day, is the most prolific producer of copy. The seat of government is the point of concentration of those nation-wide activities which most acutely interest the entire reading public, and the biggest single force of news-gatherers and writers is maintained there. Exemplifying the diversity of their news transmission, members were not long ago reminded that they were being served in the continental United States over 59 leased wire circuits, 118 telephone circuits, and 42 telegraph circuits.[31] The full coverage of world happenings on a 24-hour basis leaves no gaps in the unwinding news reel. Associated Press receipts and expenditures have come to exceed $8,000,000 a year and the employees to count up some 2,000.

These various developments were accompanied by, and oftentimes the result of, changes in the administrative personnel. At the head, Frank B. Noyes has remained as the president, retained by unanimous consent and approval year after year, but Stone, heeding advancing age, in 1920 took an indefinite leave of absence and, a year later, retired from the position of general manager, being continued as "counselor," until his death shortly after the turn of the year 1929. On occasion of Stone's completion of twenty-five years of directing Associated Press activities, the annual

[31] *Ibid.*, 1919, p. 5.

meeting assumed the form of a testimonial to his achievements in the association's behalf. The foremost journalists in the country paid tribute to his character and work, a souvenir volume, *M. E. S.*, containing his addresses and writings prefaced by a biographical memoir, was published in limited edition for the contributing admirers, and a special presentation copy, interleaved with twenty-five $1,000 Liberty bonds presented as a token of the esteem and appreciation of the members of the association. Stone had set the record for length of continuous active service in his position in the world of news-gathering.

After functioning as substitute for his chief, Frederick Roy Martin, assistant general manager since 1912, was commissioned his successor. Martin had been born in 1871 in North Stratford, New Hampshire, had graduated from Harvard, had gone on the staff of the Boston *Journal* for five years, then, in 1898, to the Providence *Journal*, of which he subsequently became the editor. He was a director of the Associated Press when he resigned to assist Stone. He continued with the Associated Press now for another five years, at the expiration of which time he resigned to enter private business.

The general managership, thereupon, passed to Kent Cooper, to whom it came also by way of promotion. A native of the little town of Columbus, Indiana, Cooper, at this time just turning forty-five, typified a distinctly younger generation of journalism than his predecessors, and was akin to a career man in news-gathering work. He had attended the University of Indiana, and had had a taste of newspaper reporting and copy editing on Indianapolis dailies, but, joining the Associated Press in 1910 as traveling inspector, he had gone the route of chief of the traffic department and assistant general manager in training for the higher level. This he reached in April, 1925. It was Cooper who had installed the machinery for extending the service to South America and had accelerated the distribution of the report on the various circuits which he helped rearrange on state lines. Coming into supreme charge, free from traditional incumbrances, and disregardful of the conventions of ultra-conservatism, he was ready to try out new methods and start new departures which previously had encountered dubious shaking of heads. Cooper, too, has devoted much attention to the sources of foreign news, representing the Associated Press at the different international assemblies considering such questions.

CHAPTER XXVI

THE UNITED PRESS ASSOCIATIONS

The Scripps-McRae Press Association—The Scripps News Association—The Publishers' Press Association—The triple merger—Organization, management, expansion—Retrospect of the founder—Refinancing

ALMOST paradoxically, it was to be again a United Press that was to dispute the field of news-gathering in the United States with the Associated Press. Reviving the name, more precisely the United Press Associations, we see here once more the unification into a compact system of several independent projects to provide opposition journals with news fitted to their needs. A Scripps enterprise, pivoted on the Scripps chain of papers, it was a union of constituent elements, or "presses," three in number, devoted territorially to publications of the eastern, central, and Pacific coast states, respectively, which had been operating in close alliance since the extinction of the old United Press.

First of these was the Scripps-McRae Press Association, dating as such from January, 1897, a few months antecedent to the finish of the big news fight. The four links in the Scripps chain, forged by Edward W. Scripps and located at Cleveland, Cincinnati, St. Louis, and Kansas City, had been affiliated with the United Press and should be kept distinct from the Detroit *News,* owned by his brother, James E. Scripps, continuously a member of the Associated Press. As one of the inducements to cement their support, General Manager Phillips had placed the United Press leased wires at their disposal for a nominal per-word filing fee to transmit special dispatches to all four chain papers. The cheapness of this extra news—it cost each only one-sixteenth of a cent a word, which was less than the mere operators' expense—led to its amplification and to regularity of use until it had become a supplemental service which took on the name of the Adscititious Report. By way of further concession, the Scripps papers were permitted to merchandise this news among clients of their own so that, balancing income and outgo, the United Press report was costing them not more than $20 a week apiece. It was to put this part of the business in more satisfactory shape that the Scripps-McRae Press Association was projected to handle the Adscititious Report. Other reasons, no doubt, also entered into the plan, probably adopted in prevision of what was impending in the press association conflict and out of a sense of precaution against the necessity of looking out for themselves in the news quest, if not for vantage in trading with the Associated Press for admission into its ranks. The active spirits behind the move were Edward W. Scripps and Milton A. McRae, whose names conjoined in that of the corporation, for which Ralph F. Paine was the first general manager.

The Scripps News Association was the organization functioning similarly for the Scripps Coast League. It had been known previously as the Scripps-Blades Report, a special service carried on by Blades, who now dropped out. This chain had been developed by Edward W. Scripps, beginning with the San Diego *Sun*, acquired by him in 1891 and integrated for news supply with his later purchases of coast dailies, the Seattle *Star*, the Tacoma *Times*, the Spokane *Press*, the San Francisco *News*, the Los Angeles *Record*, none of which was eligible to Associated Press membership without consent of a competitor. The headquarters were in San Francisco, and the managerial head at first Hamilton B. Clark and then Clayton D. Lee.

The Publishers' Press Association was incorporated in New York in March, 1898, although it had been organized the previous year on the eve of the break-up of the old United Press. Seeing the gathering clouds, a meeting of publishers depending on that source of news was called in New York City. The papers represented, if not ineligible to membership in the Associated Press under the rule excepting from consents, either regarded the Associated Press assessments as too high or viewed the Associated Press report as in excess of their requirements, among them being the Pittsburgh *Press,* the Brooklyn *Citizen,* the Washington *Times,* the Springfield (Mass.) *News,* the New York *Evening Journal,* the New York *News,* the Buffalo *Enquirer,* the Erie *Herald,* the Columbus *Citizen,* the McKeesport *News.* A temporary organization was effected, with these officers: Pierce Stephens, of the Columbus *Citizen,* president; James B. Shale, of the McKeesport *News,* secretary; Colonel William Brown, of the New York *News,* treasurer. With the bulk of the United Press working force taken on, service began April 8, 1897, the very next day following the demise of the United Press report. The service was to be exclusively for afternoon papers, and a close contact was maintained with the *Sun* and the Laffan Bureau. A few months later, the organization was perfected, with Shale as president and general manager, T. J. Kennan of the Pittsburgh *Press,* secretary, and Pierce Stephens, treasurer. The plan contemplated stockholding memberships, carrying an allotment of twelve shares each, akin, in their participation, to previous press associations. A Saturday night report was soon added and, in 1901, a morning report. The Publishers' Press even went so far as to challenge the proscription of its telegraph operators from the offices of Associated Press members in a petition to the Attorney General of the state to take suitable action in its behalf, on which that officer declined to move.[1] Deciding now to install a European service for themselves and associates, John Vandercook was commissioned to go to London to establish and take charge of the foreign news. The association was growing apace but evidently was spreading over too much ground and unduly weighting its expense of doing business, despite the sale of exclusive franchises for lump sum revenue. It was claiming at the time of its culmination nearly 500 clients, probably including those served through the coöperating agencies, many of them on leased wire circuits.

All three of these associations observed consistently a mutual accord for division of territory and exchange of their news. The question of combined effort had been raised at the outset. Scripps had tried to effect a union with Laffan, but the latter had determined to keep up his own report. He endeavored, too, to persuade the Publishers' Press to go out of the arena and turn its clients over to him. He succeeded only to the extent of reaching a definite agreement for coöperation, that the Publishers' Press have the Atlantic states for its activities, that the Scripps-McRae Press Association have all the territory between the west line of the Atlantic states and the east line of the Pacific states, that the Scripps News Association carry the Pacific coast states, and that the three associations jointly buy their foreign news from the Laffan Bureau by payment of $200 a week for its cables. All three maintained New York quarters in near proximity.

---

[1] Associated Press Report, 1903, p. 199.

In 1904, the Scripps interests quietly possessed themselves of the Publishers' Press, installing as its manager John Vandercook, who had been abroad for several years engaged in the European news service. The negotiations were carried on by Shale and T. J. Kennan, who together practically owned the Publishers' Press, and Mr. Vandercook as agent for Mr. Scripps. The price of $300,000 to $400,000 fell to $150,000 when that sum was offered with the alternative prospect that its rejection would terminate the existing arrangement and the suggestion that, if coöperation ceased the Publishers' Press would have to gather its own news all over the country and pay the entire bill for its cables. At that, it was said to have taken forty hours to force the issue and get the names "on the dotted line." [2] What the Scripps people feared was that other parties, perhaps Hearst, might seize upon the remnants if the Publishers' Press fell apart. Vandercook was at once placed in active charge.

While ultimate consolidation was contemplated all the time, no changes of striking importance were visible for a year or two. But in 1907, a complete merger and reorganization brought about the birth of the United Press Associations, incorporated by Clayton D. Lee, John H. B. Clark, and John Vandercook, the first-mentioned becoming the president. Little or no actual money was involved. The three associations were separately appraised and the valuation covered by an issue of preferred stock allotted pro rata to the owners of the absorbed institutions. The common stock went to the promoters and active administrative officers, safe majority control resting in Scripps hands. Nothing restricted stockholdings to concurrent newspaper ownership but some of the minority shares were made available to the

---

[2] McRae, *Forty Years in Newspaperdom*, p. 121.

newspapers subscribing for the report so far as they desired such an investment, subject to conditions governing transfer and resale.

On the death of Vandercook the next year, Roy W. Howard, once a newsboy in Indianapolis with subsequent training in journalism in the Scripps school in Cincinnati, was made general manager. Howard, born in Gano, Ohio, January 1, 1883, knew the needs of newspapers from the variety of the work he had performed for them as reporter on the Indianapolis *News,* sports editor on the Indianapolis *Star,* assistant telegraph editor on the St. Louis *Post-Dispatch,* news editor on the Cincinnati *Post.* He had been in New York City already two years as correspondent for the Scripps-McRae Association and as chief aid to his predecessor in the Publishers' Press. He was ready to do things on his own initiative.

At this formative period, the United Press staff consisted of twelve persons, "including the office-boy," though its clientele counted up to nearly 300, and it was a red letter day when 500 words of news were cabled from abroad.[3] The paucity of its foreign intelligence stressed the urgency of reorganizing its European news sources, a task begun in earnest in 1909.[4] Because of their exclusive exchange contracts with the Associated Press, it would be useless were it desirable, to approach the big foreign news agencies, those which over many years had established such confidential connections that their news bore the stamp of governmental approval and stood as "either semi-official in character or directly under the control of and subsidized by their individual governments." No other news was coming across the Atlantic except through the correspond-

[3] Bent, *Ballyhoo,* p. 269.

[4] Howard, "United Press," *Publishers' Guide,* XXI, 31.

ence of three or four large New York and Chicago papers. Seeking to develop along the lines pursued by the special correspondents, the United Press erected its own bureaus in London, Paris, Berlin, and Rome, placing each under a home-trained man, with a similar staff under him. Each of these bureaus was to evolve its own corps of private correspondents in its territory and supplement with the service of a native news-gathering agency wherever such an organization existed without being subsidized by, or subject to, any branch of the government. Such connections were made with the Exchange Telegraph Company in London, the Hirsch Bureau in Berlin, and the Fornier Agence in Paris. Exchange arrangements were set up with important papers in the great European cities. An alliance followed also in the Orient with the Nippon Dempo Tsushin Sha, and with the Independent Cable Association of Australasia, an independent agency active in the Antipodes.

A stiffening of the domestic service likewise was soon under way. At the start, the United Press had its own representatives in only half a dozen cities. Gradually the list of these bases of operation where the leased wire report was edited and relayed, as well as condensed for the smaller papers, embraced Boston, Albany, New York, Philadelphia, Washington, Raleigh, Pittsburgh, Cleveland, Columbus, Detroit, Indianapolis, Chicago, Milwaukee, St. Paul, Springfield, Ill., St. Louis, Memphis, Des Moines, Oklahoma City, Houston, Lincoln, Denver, San Francisco, Portland, Ore., Los Angeles.

With Howard in the forefront, a vigorously aggressive policy spurred the organization's growth. "It held to the popular point of view."[5] A distinctive news report was the aim. Conceding the importance of a certain amount of

---

[5] Irwin, "United Press," *Harper's Weekly*, April 25, 1914, p. 6.

commercial news and of covering that field adequately, it professed a determination, not to subordinate everything else to commercialism, but to humanize the commercial news topics by throwing light on the persons and personalities figuring in it. Events classed as news, which were transpiring year in and year out in the same manner, in the same fields, and concerning the same groups of people, were to be ruthlessly eliminated and lines of activity tapped that had never been considered within press association purview. Interviews and features were to be played up in preference to mere routine. Signed articles, written by, and from the angle of, the men and women making the news, were introduced as a regular part of the day's report. At the same time, its absolute divorce from partisanship was stressed by soliciting and disseminating statements of both sides to controversies of wide interest, without injecting the opinions of its own agents. Launched as an exclusively afternoon service and having no morning clientele, the United Press boasted, too, that it had no incentive to dismiss big afternoon occurrences with mere bulletins and to hold the details for the morning journals. The morning field, however, could not be wholly eschewed. A morning paper service was inaugurated under the name of the United News.

By 1914, the United Press report was traveling over 15,000 miles of leased wires to more than 200 papers getting the full daily service, and over about 30,000 additional miles of telegraph and telephone wires operated by the various communication companies to serve 300 other papers with abbreviated reports ranging from 500 to 3,500 words a day.

In 1920, Howard was transferred to a different executive position, and Karl August Bickel was elevated to be president and general manager. This promotion was the fruition of a long service with the Scripps interests. Bickel was only 38 years of age; his birthplace was Geneseo, Illinois; he had been educated in the California schools and in Stanford University; his induction into newspaper work had been on the *News* and *Examiner* in San Francisco in 1906 and 1907. Bickel went to the United Press in 1907 in the capacity of news editor in the San Francisco office, whence two years' work procured for him the position of local manager for the association at Portland, Oregon. After another two years, he became publisher of the *Daily News* at Grand Junction, Colorado. Returning to the news-gathering service, he began another continuous advancement, giving him experience in all the various phases of the work, not only in this country, but also abroad and encircling the globe. As representative of his organization, he had a prominent place in the World Press conferences at Geneva. It was largely his personal pioneering that pushed the outposts of the United Press to the far-flung foreign lands which they have come to occupy.

By the close of 1928, the United Press reported a newspaper membership in the United States and Canada of 952, and a total, including other countries, of about 1,150. Of these, 118 were morning service clients. Consequent upon an unexampled expansion of its world service, the association had become international in scope. It was particularly strong in the Far East and asserted a claim to dominance in South America. It was supplying news to papers printed in 19 languages scattered through 40 countries. Its cable messages, received every day, were running in excess of 10,000 words average, it had 28 foreign bureaus, 51 bureaus in the United States, correspondents at all other important news centers, and was leasing more than 105,000 miles of wires for the transmission of its telegraphic dispatches.

The Scripps chain, latterly the Scripps-Howard Papers, grown to 26 in number, continued the mainstay in this country, professing a belief in its sufficiency and superiority by a policy placing sole reliance for its news service upon the United Press. In several instances, most conspicuously in the purchases of the New York *Telegram*, the Memphis *Press-Scimitar*, and the Denver *News*, indubitably valuable Associated Press memberships, which might have commanded substantial prices, were "scrapped" rather than risk being enmeshed in irreconcilable dual obligations. Retention of an Associated Press service for a later acquired Denver paper, however, would seem to indicate a change of this basic "policy."

No small number of "firsts" were inscribed on the United Press escutcheon. According to its sales-talk, it first projected the interview and the human interest story into the regular press association service. It first completed the sports program of the day for the same day's issue. It first utilized the facilities of the long-distance telephone wires for telegraphic news transmission. It first engaged the use of the telephone as a means of distributing pony reports, unfettered from the limits of word measurement. It first took up extensively the printing telegraph machine for regular delivery of complete service to clients beyond the borders of a single city, its circuit embracing Greater New York, Newark, and Jersey City, dating from 1915. It first reached out to the radio as an ally rather than a potential competitor, its national "hook-up" for the 1924 election proving a powerful assisting lever in raising the embargo on radio news broadcasting. Some of these claims, of course, are vigorously disputed.

The United Press has frankly admitted the charge that it was both a commercial undertaking and a gain-getting institution. "The United Press is organized, as is every great and enduring privately owned American newspaper, to render a service and make a profit and I know of no properly operated newspaper in America to date that has found anything objectionable in a proper profit," says Bickel.[6] "The press association business is purely a business, just as the newspaper business is a business, and there is no more reason to believe that a socialistic experiment in the press association field is the one and only method of attaining efficiency—experience having demonstrated to the contrary—than there is to believe that such an economic adventure is essential to make newspapers sound and prosperous."

Reviewing the extraordinary rise of the new United Press, certain salient factors stand out. Necessity at the outset enforced virtues from which benefits accrued as a natural consequence. The only newspapers which a minor news service might possibly enlist lay outside the fold of the Associated Press, and a free-lance news agency must appeal to the free-lance newspaper. The path must be kept open to convey the report to all qualified applicants according to their demands and ability to pay and regardless of the aid or consent of any other patrons in the vicinity. No franchises, no exclusive rights not terminable within proximate time. Its cue was to decry news monopoly and to uphold that profession by example. Since duplication of its news to more than one client in a locality would be a rarity, the overlapping of competing papers in the same territory presented no grave problem. Knowing that the entrenched Associated Press had hard and fast working arrangements with the big telegraph companies, better

---

[6] Bickel, "The First Twenty Years," *Editor and Publisher,* April 30, 1927, p. 11.

terms or other compensating advantages might be secured for the opposition news service only by dealing with smaller or independent companies with extra wire capacity which was going unused. Its leased wire service was limited, in the nature of things, to cities and towns on main trunk lines; for customers off the chief arteries of communication, abbreviated reports must be delivered by telephone or as special dispatches at press rates. As the organization and its operations expanded, the big telegraph and cable companies had to be employed and differentials relinquished but, by this time, loss of small favors was of no great moment.

A not-yet-arrived agency, such as the United Press, could be, furthermore, an innovator in many respects: it was compelled by circumstances to experiment; it had nothing to lose and everything to gain from giving its clients stories which the staid Associated Press papers did not print, by endeavoring to treat news in unique manner, above all by straining to score beats on the most thrilling happenings for which superiority might be vaunted. A United Press "flash" heralded the success of the Wrights, so pregnant for the future, in lifting their airplane by its own power. Overzeal gave the United Press the unrelished rôle of sponsoring and disseminating that greatest of false news items, the spurious premature report of World War truce. So, too, the routine matter could not well be neglected altogether, but it was willfully minimized and made secondary to headline material. No obstructive neutral policy stood in the way. The United Press was working in intimate cooperation with Scripps services supplying features to the same journals; it took the lead in graphic news-feature stories, in news photography, in special signed correspondence, in covering distinct fields such as sports or politics, or particular assignments, by special writers. Hindered by no inelastic rules, the service could be accommodated to the exigencies of the events reported rather than to the dead-lines of publication hours allotted to different classes of papers. "To-day's news to-day," became its slogan.

To retain as customers publications which had no other common interests than to print news sure to hold their readers devolved upon the United Press management unmistakable obligations. Catering to the sharply competitive evening field, news had to be provided up-to-the-minute and reliable, and also written in the breezy style adapted to papers conducted along Scripps lines of policy, and still avoid color or bias which might render it distasteful to newspaper patrons differing in political or social outlook. True, the United Press members, publishing in competitive areas in which they were shut out of the Associated Press, had, as a rule, no other place to go for their news, but, on the other hand, at least a few, which were in position to make a choice, preferred the United Press, presumably because of the variety and liveliness of its report, to say nothing of inducements in the form of lower charges. With a good degree of justification, the United Press has insisted that the development of the afternoon newspaper and its advancement in power and prestige, as compared with the morning press, may be traced directly to the projection of this agency concentrating upon news especially for the afternoon field.

In what degree has the United Press vitalized the aims and ideals of its far-seeing founder? That Edward W. Scripps must have had an inspiring vision and a definite goal when he formulated the program and mapped the course goes without saying. The impelling motives and the object in view, as stated in his own language, therefore furnish, not only the key to its origin and development, but also a most illuminating retrospect:

For nearly a quarter of a century, I had had personal experience with various press associations. I had been convinced of the correctness of the proverb that what is everybody's business is nobody's business when applied to a purely mutual press association, considering the membership as a whole. Clique rule is an inevitable outcome of all mutual institutions, I believe. The inner circle gets in its work in the way of graft as well as in the way of improper influences, control, and use.

My experience with the United Press also had taught me that there was little to choose between an ordinary stock company of this kind and a mutual association, so far as proper and honest conduct was concerned. But there was an additional danger in a stock company association in that contending parties must form, to be followed by strife for stock control. I had known many newspapers to fail because of quarrels amongst stockholders and the constant shifting of balance of power. The United Press suffered more from internal strife amongst the stockholders than from any other cause.

I believe in one man control—in other words, the 51 percent rule —just as firmly as I believe in the distribution, or sharing, of profits amongst all the important and capable administrators of a business. I proposed to avoid the dangers of a mutual concern as well as the dangers of shifting balances of power of the company of stock-holding ownership.

The United Press, as it now exists, would never have existed, had identically the same stockholders held all the stock, had not one man had the power to decide any important question. It is almost impossible to find two men that will always agree, and it is absolutely impossible to find four or five. It is possible to find one man who can control weaker men who are his fellow stockholders, or enough of them to keep control. But in such an organization as ours, it is desirable to have all the men strong and capable.

But I had not only a selfish, but also an altruistic motive in founding the new association. I do not believe in monopolies. I believe that monopolists suffer more than their victims in the long run. I do not believe it would be good for journalism in this country that there should be one big news trust such as the founders of the Associated Press fully expected to build up.

I not only wanted to start a new paper if I chose, but I wanted to make it possible for any other man to found a newspaper in any city in the Union. The men who hold controlling interest in the present Assocated Press and Mr. Hearst would inevitably combine into a trust were it not for us.

Perhaps my greatest reason, however, for objecting to becoming an integral part of the Press Association in the crisis was that I knew that at least 90 percent of my fellows in American journalism were capitalistic and conservative. I knew that, at that time at least, unless I came into the field with a new service, it would be impossible for the people of the United States to get correct news through the medium of the Associated Press. I determined to be as free in the matter of gathering telegraph news and printing what I wanted to print as I was in gathering local news and printing what I wanted to print. In those my youthful days of pride, I swelled up with vanity at the thought that I was to be the savior of the free press in America. Of course, I have learned now that it requires more than one man to guarantee such freedom.

However, I confess that even now I feel no small sense of satisfaction on account of the results of my effort.

I believe, too, that I have done more good indirectly with the United Press than I have done with it directly, since I have made it impossible for the men who control the Associated Press to suppress the truth, or successfully to disseminate falsehood. The mere fact that the United Press can be depended upon to disseminate news that is of value to the public, and that is against the interests of the plutocrat band, makes it not only worth while, but positively dangerous for the Associated Press to withhold any information from the public. If a United Press paper in Cleveland gets a piece of news that the Associated Press client there doesn't get, there is a kick from the Associated Press paper to the management. If the Associated Press should attempt to give only real news to its client papers in towns where there were United Press papers, then other Associated Press papers in other towns would kick because they didn't get as full service as did those Associated Press papers in United Press towns.

I am convinced that no such political situation as exists in this country to-day, [1912] would have existed had it not been for the direct and indirect results of the United Press work.

To meet requirements of enlarged business, a refinancing of the United Press took place in 1928, whereby the 1,000 shares of common stock were replaced by 2,500 shares of no par common stock carrying exclusive voting power, 7,500 shares of no par Class "A" stock, and 70,000 shares of no par preference stock entitled to a $6.00 annual dividend after the 6 per cent dividend on the old 3,000 shares of preferred stock in which no change was made. All the new stock was exchanged for the previous common, or sold to executives and department managers of the association.

CHAPTER XXVII

THE INTERNATIONAL NEWS SERVICE

The American News Service—Dual International and Universal Services—Wartime difficulties—Organization and management

Part and parcel of the Hearst newspaper program and definitely under Hearst control and management, the International News Service was projected to function at once as a joint bureau of the enchained journals and also as a mechanism for general news collection and distribution. As already seen, one result of the great news war was the acquisition of an Associated Press membership for the New York *Journal* by the almost forced purchase of another New York paper, presumably the only way open to get around the exclusive prerogative of the *World*. The *Evening Journal,* whose publication was begun the following year, found itself likewise outside the Associated Press fold and was compelled to procure its reports of current events through different channels. The Hearst papers in New York and San Francisco were the two ends of a special leased wire for joint service. The addition of a morning and an evening daily in Chicago in 1900 and 1902, respectively, laid a further load upon this wire which, in 1904, was extended again to Boston upon the appearance of Hearst in that field. The dispatches handled included the essential spot news and the news feature stories of the staffs at these points and at the national capital. Here was a foundation ready-built for a more far-reaching service which might be shared with other papers. What had been conducted previously as units or adjuncts to the several Hearst organizations assumed separate entity in May, 1909, denominated the American News Service, and designed to provide a general news report which would be suitable to any newspaper.

After only a few months' operation, two new organizations replaced it, the International News Service furnishing a night report seven days a week for morning issues, and the National Press Association furnishing a six-day report for afternoon papers. A merger and reorganization in 1911 produced the International News Service, supplying both morning and afternoon papers, until changing conditions in the two fields led, in 1917, to a separation once more that shifted the morning patrons to the Universal Service, each thenceforth operated independently as to management and clientele. The last-named, however, announced, in 1928, that its efforts would be restricted to a supplemental and special news service.

Recital anew of the friction and clashes between the International News Service and the Associated Press would be repetition. Suffice to observe that characteristic Hearst aggressiveness was calculated to beget troubles for the news service in counterpart to the antagonism engendered in various quarters to the Hearst papers as a type. The position of the International News Service, for this reason, became especially uncomfortable during the World War, in which the sympathy and support of these journals had been bestowed on the German cause up to the time the United States was definitely ranged with the Allies. Everywhere abroad, officialdom came down heavy on displeasing dispatches. The extremity of retaliation on the Hearst exploits was the closing of the mails and cables and the expulsion of the correspondents. The first message announcing such action was received by Hearst in October,

1916, while chatting at his home with one of his executives. His London representative informed him that the prohibition would be effective at once, "unless Hearst would give his personal assurance that all despatches would be printed exactly as received after passage through the British censorship."[1] Hearst, it was said, flushed and trembled with anger. He handed the message to his companion, who in years of association had never before witnessed "the faintest flutter in his uncanny calm." "What are you going to do about it?" asked the employee. "Do?" exploded Hearst. "I am going to tell them to go to hell!" His demeanor speeded the British to make good their threat; the reason, as given, was "the continued garbling of messages and breach of faith on the part of the International News Service." Hearst replied, "The exclusion of the International News Service is not due to any delinquency on its part or on the part of Hearst papers, but is due to the independent and wholly truthful attitude of the Hearst papers in their news and editorial columns." French, Portuguese, and Japanese governments followed suit in succession, and an order was promulgated barring Hearst papers from Canada. The necessity of securing, at all hazards, the denied war news for newspaper clients which had not offended was the excuse offered for the "piracy" complained of by the Associated Press and finally stopped by court decree.

Functioning as the news-marketing and distributing arm of the Hearst combination, the International News Service controlled more or less the disposition of Hearst features in general, furnished in various forms such as news matrices, photographs, photo matrices, printed supplements,

---

[1] Winkler, *Hearst,* p. 264.

and all sorts of mailed material.[2] The news report proper was relayed out of central points for condensed pony service by telegraph or telephone. Staff offices were maintained at the prime news centers of the United States and the capitals of the chief foreign countries, and special correspondents at other places of importance. According to its latest proclamation, its news-gathering "blankets the world."

The policy determining plan and scope of report was formulated early. "The International News Service always makes most careful preparations, well in advance, to cover all big forecasted news events through experts most familiar with the subjects handled," citing wire reports of world's series baseball and notable football games, etc. Stories of important happenings scheduled ahead and written in anticipation, forwarded to clients by mail, to be released subsequently by wire, became an auxiliary, labeled "Advance News Service." Special postal delivery, later air mail, furnished prints of news photographs of events in all quarters of the globe. Patron papers were also assured of readiness to act as their special correspondents and to execute special assignments for them.

Distribution of the telegraphic report was expedited over a wide network of leased wires wholly controlled and operated by the International News Service. Trunk lines radiating from New York, Chicago, Boston, Washington, Atlanta, Pittsburgh, Columbus, Kansas City, San Francisco, feed other circuits that penetrate to the smaller cities and towns. With printer transmission in the main, from 20,000 to 30,000 words are delivered daily over an eight-hour period. Certain papers get a condensed report by prepaid mes-

[2] McKean, "How a Modern News Service Operates," *Publishers' Guide*, January, 1914.

sages, and still others by "Public News Telephone," which means that, at stated hours each day, the vital news happening up to that time is read to clients over telephone circuits. Additional wire services supply specialized requirements: the race news service conveys complete reports from all the tracks; special financial wires provide such papers as order them with market quotations and information of stocks dealt in on the various exchanges; in season, special wires cover in detail baseball and football games, commanding public attention throughout the country, coincident with the play. The feature side of the news is strongly pressed, all news stories to be written in bright and entertaining fashion.

In 1917, the International News Service and adjuncts were credited with about 400 newspaper patrons and an outlay of $2,000,000 annually. Last reports raised these figures to approximately 600 newspapers in all parts of the United States and a total expenditure of $2,500,000 a year. Of the papers, 29 located in 18 different cities were included in the Hearst chain. Journals in 17 foreign countries, distributed in Europe, South America, and the Orient, were receiving International News Service reports. The organization, though incorporated, remained a proprietary institution. It was headed in its incipiency by C. J. Marr, who was succeeded by R. A. Farrelly in 1909, and he, in turn, by Fred Wilson in 1916. In 1918, M. Koenigsberg, long connected in important capacities with the Hearst newspapers, as well as with the development and commercialization of their feature services, took charge as president and became responsible, for the next ten years, for its executive direction and policies. In 1928, the positions of president and general manager were combined and entrusted to Frank Mason, who had previously represented the service abroad. Under him, in the new régime, were the divisional and department chiefs, a business manager handling all business affairs, a general news manager concerned with gathering and distributing the report, a superintendent overseeing Morse and printer operators, a sales director captaining the selling staff, a traffic manager for the multiplicity of detail in the complicated wire system, regional directors, superintendents, and news managers dealing with activities in their respective areas. Relations between International News Service and its clients are substantially those of news-vender and news-purchaser, the specific terms of mutual obligation in each case defined in the contract.

CHAPTER XXVIII

THE SUPPLEMENTAL SERVICES

The Consolidated Press Association—The Federated Press Association—The Central News of America—The Jewish Telegraphic Agency—Plate and ready-print services—The Canadian Press

CAST on somewhat different lines, the Consolidated Press Association was formed to provide a supplementary service to papers already receiving the general news of the day from some other source. The originating spark was struck by David Lawrence, prominent among the corps of Washington newspaper correspondents, and fanned to flame by his many years' experience on the staff of the Associated Press reporters at the national capital and as Washington representative of the New York *Evening Post*. Lawrence had just passed thirty when his new idea took tangible shape. Born in Philadelphia in 1888, his initial essay in journalism came in working his way through the high school in Buffalo. His first big newspaper scoop was a flash on the death of Grover Cleveland in the summer of 1908, scored while still a student at Princeton. Joining the Associated Press forces afterwards, he drew significant outside assignments: to Mexico, in 1911, to cover the Madero revolution; in 1912, to write of the Orazco uprising; in 1912, to the McNamara trial in Los Angeles; then to accompany Woodrow Wilson through his presidential campaign. Lawrence was the White House man for the Associated Press for two years, leading up to full charge of the news of foreign affairs sent out from Washington. With the close of 1915, he became affiliated with the New York *Evening Post* and achieved a reputation as a political writer by his swing around the circle for the second Wilson campaign, when his diagnosis proved exceptionally accurate. He reported the Peace Conference in Paris, and traveled with President Wilson in Italy and Great Britain. From time to time, he was contributing to various magazines and periodicals.

This biographical record was the key to the plan of the Consolidated Press Association, which aimed essentially to capitalize his personal journalistic work and, in the same way, that of those to be associated with him. For, leaving the *Post* in 1919, he had undertaken to syndicate his telegraphic Washington correspondence as David Lawrence, Inc., reorganized and enlarged the following year under the new name. What had been accomplished in the arena of politics with the Lawrence letter was to be repeated in certain other chosen fields consolidated into a daily wire service of current topics, each treated by expert authorities. No thought, evidently, of supplying "all the news," or of accepting every applicant. It was to be a service for evening papers and their Sunday morning issues only, for not more than one patron in a city or town, to be used to supplement or substitute for parts of the regular news report which each subscribing journal was assumed to be enjoying. By combination with the Chicago *Daily News*, the distribution of the latter's extensive foreign intelligence, coming from twenty special correspondents at widely scattered points abroad, was brought in. The service promised the flavor of exclusiveness, in fact might be printed and advertised as its own by each participating publication. The value of such news stories obviously lay largely in the identity of the writers, who must contribute over their signatures. So the proclaimed object was to give "the news behind the news," to furnish "a national perspective to the day's developments in sports, business, politics and economics," with interpretations by specialists founded on personal contacts. Subsequent spread marked the addition of fashion news, radio activities, "big events" covered by specially assigned staff men.

In its distribution mechanism, the Consolidated Press kept to established methods of regional assembling and leased wire transmission. Headquarters at Washington were balanced by offices at New York, Chicago, and San Francisco, all linked together by trunk lines. Adjustment to the practical needs of afternoon papers, as distinguished from morning papers, was stressed. Relieved of the pressure of general news reports and free from the interference of unexpected spot news, the traffic department was charged with arranging the movement of the dispatches on a time schedule that would put each section of the service on the desk of the receiving editor with regularity at the same time each day, facilitating composition and make-up, accommodating successive editions, avoiding replacement of earlier stories. Fast Morse operators and one-way transmission were relied upon for extra speed. For papers not on the leased wire circuit, the live news would be relayed in the form of press messages while matter without vital time element would be posted from the nearest center. At last account, the daily report averaged in excess of 15,000 words, the newspapers in the combination numbered 57, the auxiliary current news feature service separately incorporated.

Still another aspect of news-gathering has been manifested in the formation of the Federated Press and its exploitation as a movement to counteract alleged unfairness and unreliability, and more especially the capitalistic

CHARLES A. DANA

EDWARD W. SCRIPPS

MELVILLE E. STONE

VICTOR F. LAWSON

character of the big news agencies. Protesting inability to obtain unbiased news from the existing press associations, thirty-two editors, representing the Socialist and Farmer-Labor parties, the Non-Partisan League, and certain foreign language and labor groups, met in Chicago in November, 1919, to arrange for a news service of their own.[1] It was to be non-profit-making and coöperative on lines of the Associated Press, "to furnish straight uncolored news of all sorts," with emphasis on world happenings suppressed or ignored by other associations. In brief, it was to be a clearing house of news of radicals, by radicals, and for radicals. This program was, however, not adhered to strictly; several papers in the original list either disappeared before long or turned to paths which led to the previously denounced conservative news sources, and the new organization became, avowedly, "Labor's News Service," aiming "to gather news of and for labor," regardless of factional influence and without favoring or antagonizing any one wing. "The general tone is pro-labor," it was said, "as the board and staff do not think there is such a thing as neutral news outside market reports and baseball box scores, if there." It went without saying that the news furnished members by other agencies was neither to be duplicated nor paralleled.

The plan of the Federated Press looked to holding the group together by setting up full membership rule. Members were placed on a plane of absolute equality, each accorded one vote in the annual meeting which determined policy and elected the excutive board of nine for overlapping three-year terms. The board, in the intervals, wielded supreme power; it also chose the managing editor on a

[1] Long, "The Federated Press," *Survey,* Oct. 23, 1920.

three-year tenure, though, of course, removable for cause. By way of further safeguard, referendum measures were provided to facilitate control and accountability. Through accretions, the membership has expanded variably to about sixty, twelve dailies, mostly foreign language, and the rest weeklies and monthlies, the largest bloc belonging to or holding endorsement of American Federation of Labor unions. At the beginning, E. J. Costello, once employed by the Associated Press as one of its district staff, was put in charge, succeeded in 1922 by Carl Haessler.

A news-gathering association, so constituted, had to confine its operations, in the nature of things, within narrow limits of expenditure and could scarcely be self-supporting on the adopted scale of assessments rising from $1.50 a week for the smallest weeklies to a maximum of $15 a week from the largest dailies. Were it not for outside help, in the main a subvention from the American Fund for Public Service, the budget, averaging a modest $25,000 a year, could not escape a chronic deficit. The resources have sufficed, nevertheless, to sustain three bureaus, located in Washington, Chicago, and New York, to collect news and give it the desired form. The inexpensive mails, rather than costly leased wires, had to be the medium of transmission. The service went each day from each bureau to all daily paper members and other special subscribers. All publications enrolled received the day's mimeograph release once a week and all received copies also of the weekly printed labor letter, with a monthly service of longer articles for feature uses. To this material, in addition to the bureau corps, quite a number of correspondents in cities here and abroad contributed. The foreign territory embraced chiefly England, Germany, Russia, and Australia. One distinctive department has been developed to supply an economic service, under an experienced research director, which interprets industrial and financial trends, explains corporation exhibits, government reports, wage findings of Federal authorities, and similar data. On occasions, correspondents were sent afield, and the organization of the Federated Press has made a special service of reporting conventions of the American Federation of Labor and some other labor assemblages.

The Central News of America, an agency supplying newspapers, along with commercial clients, with a daily telegraphic financial news service, was incorporated in 1914, although it had been operating some little time before that date. Its program called for the collection of financial quotations and market news and their dissemination over a system of leased wires by printer telegraph, giving up-to-the-minute information. Particular stress was laid on the matter of accuracy and reliability in the tables recording the sales, as well as in the so-called gossip, of the street, and opinions and forecasts of the captains of industry. More lately, however, daily tables of exchange transactions, because available through other sources, were discontinued in order to leave the wire free for more exclusive features. The Central News of America was intimately allied, from the outset, with the *Wall Street News,* especially for its news of the Wall Street district. It maintains its own staff in Washington, with representation in the press galleries of Congress and a widely scattered corps of correspondents in different parts of the country. Its reports have been going to twenty-seven cities, in quite a few of them to newspapers in supplement to their regular wire services. Except for sports bulletins, nothing but financial news and views is furnished to subscribers. On the other hand, the Central News of America functions also as the

American agency of the Central News, Limited, of London, to which it cables accounts of daily happenings of all kinds on this side of the Atlantic in exchange for the foreign financial news of the day. The main offices are in New York City, the executive management being vested in Milton J. Woodworth as president of the corporation.

Devoting itself to chronicling news coming within a particular classification and of primary interest to one racial group, the Jewish Telegraphic Agency has been made, in a comparatively short period, a service of broad geographical extent. It describes itself as "a universal Jewish news-gathering and distributing enterprise." Established in the year 1919 by a company headed by Jacob Landau as managing director, it began with two offices and seven correspondents. Its operations steadily broadened so that, before the decade had passed, offices were being maintained in New York, London, Paris, Berlin, Warsaw, and Jerusalem, along with 146 correspondents supplying the more important Jewish newspapers throughout the world and thus reaching, so it was asserted, 20,000,000 readers representing two-thirds of the Jewish population in all lands. The activities of the Agency were to be consistent with the basic idea implied by the name. The plan was to present, with strict impartiality, the actual conditions of Jewish life everywhere, and especially the progress of social, civic, and religious movements in a way that would win general appreciation regardless of Zionist or non-Zionist, Orthodox or Reform, Liberal or Conservative, tendencies. The search was to be made for news items, not only springing out of Jewish life internally, but also occurring outside that immediate sphere, such as events which affected directly or indirectly the economic, political, cultural and religious situation of the Jewish population.

Because of the absorbing interest in the rebuilding of the home land, an associated company was organized in 1925 under the title, the Palestine Telegraphic Agency, for the purpose of transmitting the news of Palestine to the outside countries and bringing the news of the outside to Palestine, in other words, as a general news agency for a special territory. Incidentally, the service was to interpret current events in mediation between the East and the West and thus to help shape the relations between the Jews and the peoples among whom they live.

Besides its usual outlets, such of the dispatches handled by the Agency as met the tests of general news value were offered to all possibly interested papers, and occasionally carried by other associations in their regular reports, with the customary credit to the source. The material also reached an additional group through a daily publication, *The Jewish Daily Bulletin,* issued to a selected list of subscribers, and for which a classified index was prepared annually to facilitate its use for information and reference purposes. While giving emphatic assurance that it was in no sense a propaganda institution, the appeals for support nevertheless urged the protective value of the service in raising danger signals against every recurrent menace to the status of the Jewish inhabitants of different localities and in stimulating an alert interest in Jewish causes. In the practical operation of the Jewish Telegraphic Agency, the foreign news was first assembled in the London bureau, whence it was cabled to other offices. After its receipt in New York, the service to papers in this country went as press messages by the commercial lines, the mails transmitting less urgent matter.

During this entire period, various other agencies were providing limited news service to combinations of journals, but designed chiefly to share between them the expense of special representation in Washington or New York or abroad. In years past, the *Herald* and the *Sun* set the example, followed now by leading papers in many large cities. In stricter sense, such activities constitute the sale or pooling of the news collected primarily for the paper taking the lead in the enterprise and may be as properly ranged with the feature syndicates. To be noted, because of the unique mechanism employed, is the somewhat similar service rendered by the ready-print and plate establishments organized more for production economies than for news collection. The former, sponsored by a number of centralized printing plants eventually absorbed by the Western Newspaper Union, sold to smaller publications, issuing as a rule only weekly or semi-weekly, sheets printed on one side to be completed by covering the reverse with local news or other local matter. The ready-printed part included a résumé of current events as a leavening for items of general information, popular fiction, etc. The plate service, on the other hand, catered to the minor dailies, to which stereotyped castings of news stories were expedited by express from the central office in each district and used, as desired, concurrently with the home print. The American Press Association, which developed the plate business farthest, maintained a source of news supply by contracting with the different press associations to deliver copies of the daily reports as received, thus making it often possible to send out the same news in stereotyped form as soon, or sooner, than it could go in editions of the member newspapers. Objection to this practice as a sort of competition with themselves led to a decision on the part of the Associated Press not to renew the arrangement upon its expiration. The plates have continued to flourish in a way as a supplemental service, even along with the wider spread of the telegraph and telephone circuits.

Although it does not supply news directly to papers published in the United States, the Canadian Press, serving Canadian journals, operates in intimate reciprocal alliance with the Associated Press, after which it was closely modeled. It also maintains its own independent news agents in New York and Seattle, the points of exchange, and in Washington and London. Canadian newspapers continued for many years to rely on their rather meager individual news-gathering facilities, supplemented by special services based largely on the telegraphic reports published in the United States, or supplied by the Canadian telegraph companies. The paucity of strong journals—except in the Provincial capitals—the scattered settlements, and intervening expanses of sparsely populated regions, the consequent slower development of wire communication, and the high cost of transmission have been recognized as the chief obstructing factors. Probably more for the purpose of building up the country than of looking to a lucrative traffic, the Canadian Pacific Railway and the Great North-Western Telegraph Company undertook to provide the general news service necessary to the publication of a creditable journal in Canada. The former arranged to secure, at Buffalo, the news assembled by the United States press associations and to compile and distribute a regular report to all Canadian papers able and willing to pay the moderate charges exacted. The Great North-Western provided at similarly low rates a compendium of domestic Canadian news put together by various district agents. Only the financially entrenched dailies, principally those in Montreal and Toronto, amplified this extremely restricted news menu with contributions from their own correspondents and by sharing such special services of New York or Chicago publishers as were at their command.

"Poor but cheap," seemed to be the most that was claimed for this régime which labored also under the more serious indictment of being a news service produced not by the newspapers vitally concerned, but by a private corporation engaged in a totally different business. The possibility of abuse to promote selfish interests, especially since the same telegraph companies had many other irons in the fire, the absence of competing agencies, and the natural desire of the press to have some effective way of shaping the character of the news received, together with the examples of successful coöperative service across their southern border, stimulated the hope of a Canadian news association controlled by its own membership. Failure of this hope to find fulfillment time and again forced the conclusion that the goal was not to be achieved in a single move. No country-wide effort forthcoming, the newspapers in Winnipeg, in 1907, took the lead in forming the Western Associated Press which, for several years, sustained a vigorous fight against the Canadian Pacific in what are known as the Prairie Provinces. Strengthened finally by accession of the important dailies at Vancouver and Victoria, the association managed to maintain itself. Its success led to the organization, in 1910, likewise on the coöperative plan, of the Eastern Press Association, and was followed soon by a favoring decision on its protest to the Railway Commission against the excessive rates for its press messages compared with the low charges on the company's own news service over the same wires. The official proclamation of telegraph charges, uniform for like service, brought from the company an offer to retire from the field in favor of a mutual association accepting responsibility for providing a satisfactory supply of news for all Canadian dailies desiring to join in and for the return service of Canadian news, which was the condition of the exchange agreement with the Associated Press.

Incorporation of the Canadian Press, Limited, in 1911, signalized the outcome of a meeting of the newspaper publishers who had gathered in Ottawa for the Railway Commission's hearings. This association admittedly functioned only as a holding company for the rights accruing from the contract with the Associated Press, every existing daily in Canada being offered membership on equal terms. The cost of bridging the long, unproductive spaces, still blocking a complete leased wire system national in scope, loomed as an insuperable obstacle to any coast-to-coast service. The Western Associated Press retained exclusive jurisdiction over western Canada, the Eastern Press Association over the Maritime Provinces, and the morning and the evening newspapers in Ontario and Quebec, in separate groups, before long formed two additional self-serving unions. There were thus four independent news sections exchanging certain news of their own areas, combined only by common membership in the Canadian Press, Limited.

The World War unexpectedly produced the solution of the, until then, baffling problem of Canadian news service. Realizing the value and the imperative necessity of unifying all parts of the Dominion behind the national policy, the war-time premier, Sir Robert Borden, proposed an annual subvention of $50,000 toward closing the three gaps in the required leased wire network between Montreal and St. John, Ottawa and Winnipeg, and Calgary and Vancouver. The welding of the sectional news associations proceeded at once and played its part in the prosecution of the war. Establishment of peace could only foreshadow the eventual termination of the grant to the press. On its withdrawal, the item, burdensome though it must be, was absorbed into the budget devolving on the papers —not wholly a calamity, for there were significant signs that interested politicians saw in the subsidy an opportunity to influence the news transmission. "This considerable sum," so it was authoritatively stated, "is felt to be not too great for the daily press of Canada to pay for freedom, not indeed from Government control which never existed, but from even the suspicion of Government control."

At the outset an incorporated stock company, The Canadian Press, later prevailed on the Parliament to enact a special charter permitting it to become a membership association and to eliminate the word *Limited* from the title. The organizers had followed closely the Associated Press in the matter of structure, disciplinary features, administrative machinery, and content and character of news report. In several respects, however, they made noticeable deviations, particularly in emphasizing the principle of equality. Each participating publisher was accorded one vote, each possessed the same protest right that made necessary a two-thirds majority of the board members present, and a majority of the full board, to approve an application for a new membership in his allotted territory, and each was entitled to the complete report served to others within its classification. But for new members, where there was an existing membership, an "entrance fee" was to be required. The fee is computed in an amount equal to three times the annual assessment items for "national cost" and the district fixed charges, a minimum of $5,000 for leased wire service, and $2,500 for pony reports, and becomes the absolute property of the association to be invested in bonds and held in a reserve fund. In considering applications, the board is committed to open the door to the widest extent compatible with sound business and the public service; yet, in determining the feasibility of profitable operation, to give due weight to the conditions of competition in the district and the experience of newspapers similarly situated and, lacking the essentials to commercial success, "without which no real, adequate, permanent and satisfactory service can be rendered the public," to reject the applicant.

The Canadian Press proclaims itself "mutual, coöperative and non-profit-making." Its stated purposes and powers embrace the collection and distribution of news not only for publication in daily papers, but also for a service to associate members consisting of less frequently issued journals such as weeklies, semiweeklies and triweeklies, and a limited service to commercial companies "not in conflict with the rights and interests of any member"; and further to purchase, lease, own, and operate "means for the transmission of news, including telephones, telegraph instruments, wireless instruments, and other apparatus for long distance communication." All the daily newspapers in Canada, with negligible exceptions, have been enlisted in the enterprise. Head offices are located in Toronto. According to the roster, E. Norman Smith, of the Ottawa *Journal*, is honorary president, John Scott, managing director of the Toronto *Mail and Empire*, is president, and J. F. B. Livesay, an experienced newspaper man, is secretary and general manager. The board is made up of fifteen members, geographically apportioned.

The leased wire system connects all the important cities of the Dominion, and pony reports go from radial centers by telephone or telegraph. A large part of the delivery has been printerized with Creed instruments, which are being installed throughout the service. The basic news supplied covers all events of moment everywhere and, in greater detail, the domestic intelligence of Canada, financial, sporting, political, and especially the proceedings of Parliament at Ottawa and the various provincial legislatures. The original dependence on the Associated Press alone for cable messages led to a questioning of their sufficiency for the Canadian public, particularly as relating to the news of the British Empire. By the long established arrangement, the news in question was, in the main, the Reuter service, a British service, but sent to Canada by way of New York after it was subjected in London to selection, condensation, and rewriting for the newspapers of the United States. British news through an American filter tended to provoke Canadian criticism. To disarm adverse comment, a first action placed an agent of the Canadian Press in the New York office of the Associated Press to reëdit "any too obvious Americanisms" out of the cable news destined for Dominion consumption. The next step was to set up a Canadian representative in London, with immediate access to the Reuter and other news collections, entrusted with selecting the news of special interest to Canada not handled, or differently handled, by the Associated Press. Extension of staff reporting to the European continent for big events in which Canada (and not the United States) was party followed naturally in keeping with the avowed ambition to make the Canadian Press "a truly national news service."

The Canadian scheme of assessing service costs presents certain distinctive features. Population, as usual, is the variable factor as between different cities, and equal division is retained in places where there is more than one publication receiving the same report, morning or evening.

But all are called on for a fixed initial charge per week, namely, for leased wire points, ranging from $10 to $20 between populations from 15,000 to over 30,000 and from $5 to $10 for pony report papers. Otherwise the expenditures are grouped under three headings: (a) the national cost, or overhead and general outlays, the benefits of which are shared by all members; (b) the inter-divisional cost; and (c) the circuit costs, the latter two chargeable against the papers served. Abatements may be allowed in the discretion of the board to the publisher of a French-language journal up to one-third of the national cost factor, "towards his cost of translation." The last reported financial audit showed that expenditures had reached the aggregate of $569,000 during the fiscal year 1929. Of this total, about 10 per cent went for cable news cost, $17,000 as cash differential to the Associated Press, and $10,000 for Washington representation. The sum of $10,000 was kept available in a contingency fund. The Canadian Press at this time counted 83 member papers receiving leased wire service, 18 member papers receiving pony reports, and one associate member paper.

CHAPTER XXIX

TENDENCIES FOR THE FUTURE

PASSING in review the successive advances from rowboat to radio, no one can fail to realize what a tremendous leap has been taken in the realm of news-gathering. How little of the future may be foreseen at any moment is well illustrated by the fact that in his history of the telegraph, Dr. Alexander Jones, the first general agent of the first Associated Press, insisted that the only hope of carrying foreign news across the ocean by electric current rested in the construction of a transcontinental line that would cross Bering Straits and enter the Siberian back door. And this Alaskan telegraph was being actively promoted up to the very instant of final success with the Atlantic cable. No less wide of the mark was the expressed conviction of Frederic Hudson, twenty-five years after he had helped to form the Associated Press, that that organization would be scrapped as soon as the telegraphic facilities proved adequate to convey the messages required by the big papers in the more important centers. To-day, the people of the United States look for their news of current happenings to nearly 2,000 daily journals, which, in turn, excepting for local events, rely on the telegraphic reports served to them by the several general news associations. To a considerable extent, these agencies duplicate one another's efforts, sending simultaneously, over huge stretches of leased wires running side by side, identical messages for delivery to member or client papers, with no possibility of advantage beyond a few minutes' time. Complete merger seems hardly practicable, were it desirable, which is not conceded, but it is not difficult to believe that the movement to eliminate waste in newspaper-making will effectuate, eventually, a much closer union of the news-gathering alliances. With an earnest purpose, coupled with a discontinuance of mutual suspicion, a working accord would materialize. Whether this be proximate or remote, the service grows more and more essential to the modern daily newspaper, its scope more and more varied, its tendency toward standardization more pronounced, its force for informing and thus directing public opinion more potent.

APPENDIX I

REGULATIONS OF THE GENERAL NEWS ASSOCIATION OF THE CITY OF NEW YORK, 1856

It is mutually agreed between HALE, HALLOCK AND HALLOCK, of the *Journal of Commerce,* J. & E. BROOKS, of the *Express,* J. G. BENNETT, of the *Herald,* MOSES S. BEACH, of the *Sun,* GREELEY & McELRATH, of the *Tribune,* J. W. WEBB, of the *Courier and Enquirer,* and RAYMOND, WESLEY & CO., of the *Times,* to associate for the purpose of collecting and receiving Telegraphic and other Intelligence, under the following regulations:

I

This Association shall be deemed to be a consolidation of the Harbor News Association, formed January 11th, 1849, with the subsequent Telegraphic and General News Associations, entered into since that time, between the parties hereto or their predecessors; all property in boats, furniture, or other articles belonging to either of the other associations, being hereby transferred and conveyed to this Association, and all rules and regulations of the former associations being annulled.

II

The officers of this Association shall be elected by, and serve during the pleasure of a majority of its members. They shall consist of a President, Secretary, and Executive Committee; the incumbents of those offices in the former associations, to wit: Gerard Hallock, President; Moses S. Beach, Secretary; George H. Andrews and Frederic Hudson, Executive Committee; continuing as such in this until other action is taken.

III

The President shall preside at all meetings of the Association, and the Secretary shall keep a record of all proceedings thereat, in a book provided for that purpose. He shall also call meetings of the Association, at the request of any other officer, or of any two members thereof. The Executive Committee shall perform such duties as are herein prescribed, or may be entrusted to them.

IV

No new member shall be admitted to this Association, without the unanimous consent of all the parties hereto; but the news obtained may be sold to other parties, for the general benefit of the Association, on the vote of six-sevenths of its members.

V

All expense occasioned by or growing out of the arrangements of this Association, shall be borne, in equal proportions, by its members, except in cases hereinafter provided for; but all bills before being assessed, shall be audited by the Executive Committee or other proper officer of the Association.

VI

If any bill, after being duly audited and presented for payment to the party by whom the same is due, shall remain unpaid for more than one week after presentation, the Executive Committee shall have the power to withhold further news from such party or parties, until payment is made; but the party or parties so neglecting payment, shall, notwithstanding, be held liable for their proportion of current expenses, the same as when receiving the news. And if such payment be neglected or refused for a period of thirty days from the time when the bill is first presented, then the defaulting party or parties shall forfeit all rights pertaining to this Association.

VII

A person, chosen by the Association, and known as the Agent of the Association, shall be appointed, who shall receive a stipulated sum per week for his services. His duty shall be to receive all Telegraphic communications for the Association, and to transmit them immediately, by manifold copies, to each of the parties who may be entitled to receive the same. He shall collect the weekly bills of tolls and other expenses—after having submitted them to such auditor or committee as may be appointed for the purpose by the Association—and when collected, shall attend to the payment of all bills and accounts after they shall have been approved. It shall also be the duty of the Agent to provide for the reception and immediate delivery, to each paper, of all Telegraphic despatches arriving at any hour of the day or night; to keep a regular account of his outlays and incomes for the inspection of the members of the Association, and perform such other duties connected with the Telegraphic business of the Association as the Executive Committee may direct.

VIII

Agents or correspondents shall be appointed at Washington and at Albany, to furnish, by telegraph or otherwise, the Congressional and Legislative proceedings. Correspondents shall also be appointed at such other places as may be designated by the Executive Committee of the Association, and they shall transmit their despatches to the Agent in this city, who shall distribute them as above directed.

IX

All news received by Telegraph shall be sent to the offices of publication without unnecessary delay; but its delivery or publication may be withheld until a specified hour, by direction of the Executive Committee, through the Agent of the Association.

X

The supervision of the arrangements to be made by the Agent of the Association, shall be entrusted to the Executive Committee, who shall make all necessary regulations for the reception of news, and whose contracts shall be binding on the Association. They shall designate the time of the publication of the foreign and other Telegraphic news, and the terms of sale of news to parties out of the city.

XI

All European and California news, and all election returns received by special express or Telegraph, obtained by any member of the Association, shall be the common property of all the members who may desire to make use of it, and the expense assessed upon the members who so use it, in equal proportions; and all such news, together with all other news, except as specified in the XIIIth, XIVth and XVth sections, shall be immediately handed over to the Agent of the Association, to be copied and delivered to the several papers of the Association, in the same manner as other Telegraphic news is delivered.

XII

No party receiving news from this Association shall enter into any arrangement with rival Telegraphic news agents in this or any other city, or with any person in their employ, nor shall they receive from them any Telegraphic news, from Washington, Albany, or any other part of the country, nor shall such parties, nor any persons not connected with this Association, be permitted to avail themselves of the facilities of the Association, for the reception of California or European newspapers, circulars, or other intelligence arriving at this or any other port.

XIII

No member of the Association, and no party receiving news from the Association, will be permitted to receive regular Telegraphic despatches from his own private correspondents, nor can he make arrangements to receive any special news by telegraph, without first informing the members of the Association, and tendering a participancy in it to them. From this restriction are excepted reports of conventions, political meetings, trials, executions, public dinners, sporting intelligence and the legislative proceedings of other States. Any member can order, through the Agent of the Association, special items, or Telegraphic reports; but these items or reports so ordered must be tendered to each party to this arrangement, and paid for by the parties accepting the same, or any portion thereof.

XIV

Despatches received from a resident editor, or resident reporter, of any one particular paper connected with or supplied by the Association, can be used by that paper for its own sole use and benefit; but news thus received, it is understood, must not be contracted for by any previous arrangement.

XV

It is agreed that news originating in Washington City and Albany, shall be excepted from all the foregoing rules, and each paper is at liberty to receive telegraphic despatches from its own correspondents there, and publish the same for its own use and benefit.

XVI

Parties to this arrangement have the option of declining such news as they may think proper, and are released from their share of expense of such declined news. This is not to be considered as applying to immaterial items, but to apply to the daily receipts of any one particular matter. If declined, no report of any one day, or any important point of the matter declined, can be taken to the exclusion of immaterial points.

XVII

Such papers as are published on Sunday, shall have the privilege of publishing all Telegraphic Despatches belonging to the Association that are received too late to be of service to the other papers on Saturday, by paying the charges for tolls on the same. They shall also have the privilege of publishing the leading points of the foreign news, not exceeding one quarter of a column, received over the wires for the Association, by paying one-fourth of the share of the expense allotted to this Association. The remaining three-fourths to be paid equally by the seven papers.

XVIII

Such Paper or papers as may publish Foreign News in Extras on Sunday, shall pay full tolls for the same, together with all other necessary incidental expenses, provided said news is received by Telegraph or Express.

XIX

A person shall be appointed by the Association, and known as the Marine News Collector of the Associated Press, who shall receive a stipulated sum per week for his services. His duty, under the direction of the Association, or of the Executive Committee, shall be to collect all marine and other news, which may transpire at the port of New York, and transmit the same by manifold copies, to each of the parties to this agreement. He shall make out, weekly, a correct statement of all expenses incident to the duties assigned him, which statement shall be submitted to an auditor or committee appointed for the purpose by the Association, and if found correct, the amount shall be assessed, pro rata, upon the several parties interested, and collected by him. It shall also be the duty of the News Collector to make efficient arrangements for the prompt delivery of all packages of newspapers or other news, which may arrive at this port addressed to any members of the Association, and he shall perform such other duties connected with the collection and delivery of the Marine and other harbor news of the port as the Association or the Executive Committee may from time to time direct.

XX

Ship news, or other news obtained by the collector or any of his assistants, shall be deemed the common property of the members of the Association, and shall be served to them without favoritism and with the least practicable delay; and in all cases where full files of papers for all the members of the Association cannot be procured by the News Collector, he shall deliver whatever number he may obtain, at the earliest practicable moment, to the General News Agent of the Association, who shall without delay proceed to extract such interesting news as the said papers may contain, and shall, without loss of time, furnish a copy of said news, simultaneously as near as possible, to all the members of the Association; and in all such cases, it shall be the duty of the News Collector to notify each member of the Association of the title and date of the paper or papers delivered to the General News Agent.

XXI

If ship news or other news from vessels arriving at this port, should be received by either of the associated establishments from any outside source, such news shall be deemed the common property of the Association, and shall be imparted to each member without unnecessary delay; and each paper shall be bound to pay his proportion of the cost. This article applies as well to news received from pilots, either directly or indirectly, as from other extraneous sources; but it does not apply to the private correspondence of any paper—to sealed packages of papers or letters, or both, made up for any paper and directed to it in any other port—nor to private letters nor verbal information that may be obtained by any paper from captains, consignees, or passengers when ashore; provided such verbal information is elicited by direct application on the part of an employee of such paper.

XXII

No member of the Association shall disclose any portion of the news received by the same, until the time designated by the Executive Committee, except in posting the arrival of a vessel on a bulletin; and any person in the employ of any office who shall be detected in improperly using the news received for the Association, shall be reprimanded or discharged; and on the second offence, shall be immediately discharged, and shall not be employed in the office of any member of the Association, except by unanimous consent.

XXIII

Any member of this Association may withdraw from the same, by giving six months previous notice, in writing, and paying up his proportion of any expenses and debts owing by the Association up to the day of his withdrawal.

XXIV

No member of this Association shall, without the unanimous and written consent of the other members, sell his interest in the small boats or other property, or any part of his interest therein—whether relating to the boats themselves, or to his right of receiving news by them—to any other person or persons than the other members, in equal proportions. Should any member signify a wish to dispose of his interest in the concern, it shall be the duty of the other members to purchase the same at two-thirds of its value, at the time of such overture, as estimated by three appraisers, selected in the usual way. In making said appraisal, only the visible property of the share sold shall be included—small boats, &c.—but not any supposed value in the share itself, over and above the value of said visible property.

XXV

If any member shall deliberately violate the rules of this Association, or any of them, and shall continue to do so after being remonstrated with by a committee appointed by this Association for that purpose, or a majority of the members, the other associates shall have the right to exclude him from the Association, and take possession of his interest in the property of the Association agreeably to the terms of the preceding section; i.e., at two-thirds of the then appraised value. This provision shall not apply to an honest difference of opinion as to the meaning of any rule or article; but in case of such honest difference of opinion, a majority of votes shall decide what the meaning is; which being done, the member or members in the minority shall acquiesce, and govern themselves accordingly.

Moses S. Beach, *Secretary* Gerard Hallock, *President*

George H. Andrews,
Frederic Hudson, } *Executive Committee*

Adopted, New York, Oct. 21, 1856

APPENDIX II

BY-LAWS OF THE ASSOCIATED PRESS OF NEW YORK

ARTICLE I

OBJECTS

The incorporators of this Association are certain persons, who, owning or representing newspapers, unite in a mutual and co-operative organization for the collection and interchange, with greater economy and efficiency, of intelligence for publication in the newspapers owned or represented by them. Other owners or representatives of newspapers, from time to time, may be elected to membership in the manner and upon and subject to the conditions, regulations and limitations prescribed by these By-Laws, and no persons not so elected shall have any right or interest in the Corporation or enjoy any of the privileges or benefits thereof.

The objects and purposes for which the Corporation is formed are to gather, obtain and procure by its own instrumentalities, by exchange with its members, and by any other appropriate means, any and all kinds of information and intelligence, telegraphic and otherwise, for the use and benefit of its members, and to furnish and supply the same to its members for publication in the newspapers owned or represented by them, under and subject to such regulations, conditions and limitations as may be prescribed by the By-Laws; and the mutual co-operation, benefit and protection of its members. In furtherance of its said objects and purposes it shall have power to purchase and acquire in the State of New York and elsewhere such real and personal estate and property as may be necessary or proper, and to mortgage the same to secure the payment of any bonds which may be issued by the Corporation, and generally to do any and all things which may be necessary or proper in connection with its objects and purposes, which may not be contrary to law.

The Corporation is not to make a profit, nor to make or declare dividends, and is not to engage in the business of selling intelligence nor traffic in the same.

ARTICLE II

MEMBERSHIP

Who Are Eligible

SECTION 1. The sole or part owner of a newspaper, or an executive officer of a corporation, limited liability company, or joint stock or other association which is the owner of a newspaper, shall be eligible to election as a member of this Corporation, in the way and upon and subject to the conditions and limitations hereinafter specified, provided that not more than one person at a time shall be eligible by reason of connection with any one newspaper. No other person shall be eligible.

Proof of Ownership or Representation to be Filed

SEC. 2. Every applicant for membership in this Corporation shall file with the Secretary of the Corporation such proof as may be required by its Board of Directors of his ownership or part ownership, or of the ownership by a corporation, limited liability company, or joint stock or other association of which he is an executive officer, of a specified newspaper. In case he shall be only a part owner, he shall file also the consent of his co-owners to his election. In case he shall be an executive officer of a corporation, limited liability company, or joint stock or other association, he shall file also a certificate to that effect under its seal in such form as may be required by the Board of Directors.

Change of Ownership

SEC. 3. In case any member shall cease to be the owner, or part owner, of the newspaper specified in his certificate of membership; or shall cease to be an executive officer of a corporation, limited liability company, or joint stock or other association which is the owner of the newspaper specified in his certificate of membership, he shall *ipso facto*, and without action by this Corporation, cease to be a member, and he shall no longer enjoy any of the privileges of the Corporation. He may, however, in that case (provided that he is not then under process of discipline for violation of any By-Law, rule or regulation of the Corporation) assign his certificate of membership to any other owner or part owner or executive officer of the Corporation, limited liability company or joint stock or other association which is the owner of such newspaper, who shall thereupon become a member upon signing the roll of members, and assenting to the By-Laws, and, even without such assignment, such other executive officer, owner or part owner, thereupon shall become entitled to membership, and upon filing the certificate or satisfactory proof that he is such officer, owner or part owner, hereinbefore mentioned, and upon signing the roll of members, and assenting to the By-Laws, he shall at once become and be a member with all the privileges and subject to all the duties of membership, provided, however, that his predecessor was not, at the time when he ceased to be a member, under any process of discipline for violation of any By-Law, rule or regulation of this Corporation. In case of the death of any member who is the sole owner of the newspaper specified in his certificate of membership his legal representatives may assign his certificate of membership to his successor in the ownership of said newspaper who shall thereupon become a member upon signing the roll of members and assenting to the By-Laws. In case of the death of any member who is the part owner of the newspaper specified in his certificate of membership a co-owner of said newspaper shall be entitled to succeed to his membership upon signing the roll of members and assenting to the By-Laws.

Transfer of Certificate with Sale of Paper

SEC. 4. When a change shall be made in the ownership of any newspaper for which a member of this Corporation is entitled to receive a news service, the member may transfer his certificate of membership with his newspaper, and the new owner shall be constituted a member by virtue of such assignment upon complying with the requirements prescribed by the next succeeding article of these By-Laws.

Change of Name

SEC. 5. Whenever the name of any newspaper mentioned in any membership certificate shall be changed in any respect, the member holding such certificate shall thereupon give written notice of the change to the Secretary and shall return his certificate of membership to be cancelled, whereupon a new certificate in like terms shall be issued, designating the newspaper by its new name.

Termination of Membership

SEC. 6. All rights and interest of any member in the property and privileges of the Corporation shall cease with the termination of his membership.

Relation of Members to Newspapers

SEC. 7. Every member shall be eligible to election and to enjoy the privileges of membership, solely by virtue of his relation to the newspaper named in his certificate of membership, and shall be held responsible for any violation of the By-Laws by himself or by any other person connected with such newspaper to the same extent that he would have been responsible had the violation been committed by him personally.

ARTICLE III

ADMISSION OF MEMBERS

Election by the Corporation

SECTION 1. Members may be elected by the affirmative vote of not less than four-fifths of all the members of the Corporation at any regular meeting of the members of the Corporation or at a special meeting called for that purpose. Such votes may be cast in person or by proxy. No vote shall be taken at any regular or special meeting of the members of the Corporation upon any application for membership unless the same shall have been filed with the secretary at least sixty days prior to such meeting, and it shall be the duty of the secretary to give notice by mail to each member of the Corporation at least thirty days prior to such regular or special meeting of any and all applications for membership which are to be voted on thereat.

Election by Directors

SEC. 2. Members may also be elected by the Board of Directors, when no meeting of members of the Corporation is in session, provided that whenever any member of the Corporation is entitled as hereinafter specified to protest against election of any new member by the Board of Directors, the Board shall have no power to elect such new member unless it shall have received a waiver in writing of such right of protest from all members entitled thereto, but no right of protest shall be held to prevent the Board of Directors from electing to membership the owner, part owner or executive officer of any corporation, limited liability company, joint stock or other association, which is the owner of any newspaper which was entitled to a service of news under an existing contract with The Associated Press (of Illinois), on the 13th day of September, 1900.

Admission of Successor

SEC. 3. When any person shall have ceased to be a member and his successor shall have become entitled to membership as provided in the last preceding article, such successor, upon filing with the Secretary proper proof that he is entitled to membership, and signing the roll of members and in writing assenting to the By-Laws, shall forthwith become and be a member, and be entitled to all the privileges and subject to all the duties and obligations of membership, and the Board of Directors at the next meeting held thereafter shall formally elect such successor and ratify his admission as a member.

Written Assent to By-Laws Essential to Admission to Membership

SEC. 4. A person elected or entitled to become a member in any of the ways hereinbefore provided, shall not be admitted to membership, nor shall he be a member, nor shall he be entitled to any of the rights or privileges of membership until, either in person or by proxy duly constituted in writing, he shall have signed the roll of members and in writing shall have assented to the By-Laws and agreed to be bound thereby and by any amendments thereto, which may be thereafter regularly adopted.

Form of Certificate

SEC. 5. To each member there shall be issued a certificate of membership signed by the President and by the Secretary of this Corporation, and bearing its seal. The certificate shall designate the newspaper for which the member shall be entitled to receive the news report of this Corporation, until he shall cease to be a member or until his right shall be suspended or terminated under the By-Laws; it shall specify the language in which the newspaper is to be printed; whether it is a morning or an afternoon newspaper, and the place of its publication; it shall state whether the member is to receive a day or a night report; it shall state the extent and nature of the member's right of protest, if such right shall have been accorded to him under the By-Laws as hereinafter set forth; it shall state the obligation of the member to furnish news of a prescribed district, and to pay the regular weekly dues and other assessments as they may be, from time to time, fixed by the Board of Directors; it shall state that the holder thereof has assented to and is in all respects subject to and bound by the By-Laws; in other respects it shall be in such form and shall contain such provisions as shall be prescribed by the Board of Directors; it shall not be transferable except to the extent and in the way hereinbefore provided.

Right of Protest

SEC. 6. Each member of this Corporation representing a newspaper printed in the English language, which has been represented in membership for more than five years in continental United States and entitled under such membership to receive a news service six or seven days a week, and upon whom no right of protest had been conferred in the year 1900, shall have the right of protest as defined herein against the election of new members by the Board of Directors. Such right of protest shall, except as provided in Section 2 of this Article, empower the member holding it to demand a vote of the members of the Corporation on all applications for the admission of new members on behalf of newspapers published in the same field (morning or afternoon), on the same days and in the same city wherein any newspaper represented by membership entitled to such right of protest herein conferred is regularly published, provided, however, that a member representing an evening newspaper, the membership of which includes the right to a news service for a Sunday morning edition, shall not be entitled to protest against the election of a member representing a morning newspaper.

No applicant for admission to membership in a field where a protest right granted under the terms of this Section is not waived shall be admitted as a member except in accordance with Section 1 of this Article. Members upon whom rights of protest were conferred in the year 1900 shall continue to enjoy such rights of protest only as are defined in their certificates of membership, with such waivers as may have been subsequently given.

Waiver of Right of Protest

Sec. 7. If a member having a right of protest makes a waiver, subject to specified conditions, such waiver shall be effective only as stated therein.

ARTICLE IV

MEETING OF MEMBERS

Annual Meetings

Section 1. The annual meeting of the members of The Associated Press shall be held in the City of New York, at eleven o'clock A. M. on the Monday preceding the fourth Thursday in April of each year, for the election of Directors and such other business as may be presented.

Special Meetings

Sec. 2. Special meetings of the members shall be called by the President and Secretary upon the order of the Board of Directors or the Executive Committee, or whenever a request in writing therefor shall be received by the Secretary bearing the signatures of fifty of the members of the Corporation. No business shall be transacted at a special meeting except such as may be embraced in the call therefor.

Notice of Meetings

Sec. 3. The Secretary shall give notice of all meetings of the members by mailing to each member at his given address a written or printed notice stating the time and place of meeting, and the business to be considered, if a special meeting. Such notices shall be mailed thirty days before the annual meeting, and fifteen days before special meetings. Special meetings may, however, be held for any purpose, without notice, at any time when all the members are present or duly represented by proxy.

Proxies

Sec. 4. A member may be represented at any meeting by a properly authorized proxy who shall file a lawful power of attorney with the Secretary. No salaried officer or employee of the Corporation shall hold a proxy or vote upon the same.

Quorum

Sec. 5. To constitute a quorum for the transaction of business, at least a majority of the members must be present either in person or by proxy, except as otherwise provided by Section 25 of the General Corporations Law of the State of New York in the case of special elections of Directors. A minority may adjourn from time to time until a quorum shall be present.

ARTICLE V

BOARD OF DIRECTORS

Number of Directors

Section 1. The affairs of the Corporation shall be managed by fifteen Directors, at least one of whom shall be a resident of the State of New York.

Who May Be Directors

Sec. 2. Each Director shall be a member of this Corporation, and any Director who shall cease to be so qualified shall thereby cease to be a Director.

Three Classes

Sec. 3. The six Directors to hold office until the first annual meeting of the members of this Corporation shall be those named in the Certificate of Incorporation. The Directors elected at such first annual meeting shall forthwith divide themselves by lot into three classes of equal number. The Directors of the first class shall hold office until the first annual meeting after their election. The Directors of the second class shall hold office until the second annual meeting after their election, and those of the third class shall hold office until the third annual meeting after their election.

Election of Directors

Sec. 4. At each annual meeting the members and those entitled to vote upon bonds, as hereinafter provided, shall elect Directors to succeed those whose terms expire at such meeting, and also to fill any vacancies in the Board of Directors which may have occurred since their last annual meeting. At each annual meeting after the first, the Directors elected to fill the places of those whose terms have expired, shall be elected for a term of three years, and Directors shall in all cases continue in office until their successors are elected.

Powers of Board

Sec. 5. The Board of Directors shall, in addition to the powers elsewhere granted by the By-Laws, or otherwise conferred by law, have power to make contracts; to fill vacancies in their own number until the next annual meeting; to elect and remove officers and agents; to engage and discharge employees; to fix the compensation of officers, agents and employees; to borrow money; to issue bonds; to authorize a mortgage or mortgages; to expend the money of the Corporation for its lawful purposes, and to do all acts, not inconsistent with the Certificate of Incorporation, or the By-Laws, which it may deem for the best interests of the Corporation, and in general shall have the control and management of all the affairs of the Corporation, except as otherwise provided in the By-Laws. The votes of a majority of all the Directors shall be required to elect or remove an officer.

Executive Committee

Sec. 6. The Board of Directors shall annually appoint an Executive Committee of not less than five of its own number, who shall hold office for one year or during the pleasure of the Board and shall have the same powers as the Board except the powers in respect to the election and discipline of members as specified in Articles III and X of these By-Laws. The Executive Committee shall keep a full record of its acts and proceedings, and report all action taken by it to the next meeting of the Board. Vacancies therein shall be filed by the Board of Directors.

Auditing Committee

Sec. 7. The Board of Directors shall annually appoint an auditing committee of not less than two persons, not of its own number, to examine the accounts of the Corporation.

Other Committees

Sec. 8. The Board of Directors from time to time may, by resolution, appoint other committees for special purposes designating their duties and powers.

Reports

SEC. 9. The Board of Directors shall make a report of all its doings and of the affairs of the Corporation for each fiscal year, a copy of which shall be sent to each member at least twenty days prior to each annual meeting. Such fiscal year shall end on December 31st in each year. The Board of Directors shall also cause to be mailed to each member a report of the proceedings of each meeting of the Corporation and of the Board of Directors as soon after the holding of such meeting as practicable.

Seal

SEC. 10. The Board of Directors shall have power to adopt a corporate seal and alter the same at its pleasure.

Meetings

SEC. 11. The Board of Directors shall hold, at the City of New York, a meeting on the Friday preceding the annual meeting of the members, and also another meeting for the election of officers and for other purposes, immediately after adjournment of the annual meeting of the members. It shall fix, by resolution from time to time, the dates of the other regular meetings of the Board, of which there shall be not less than two, in every year, in addition to the two herein provided for. Special meetings of the Board may be called by the President or any three Directors. Notice of all meetings shall be given by telegraphing or by mailing a notice thereof to each Director at least five days before the date of the meeting, which notice shall be sent either by the Secretary, the President or the Directors calling the meeting. A majority of the Board shall constitute a quorum, but in case a quorum shall not be present a minority may adjourn from time to time until a quorum shall be obtained. The meetings of the Board of Directors—except as hereinbefore provided—shall be held either in the City of New York, or elsewhere, as may be specified in the resolutions of the Board fixing the dates of regular meetings, and in the notices calling special meetings.

General Authority

SEC. 12. The Board of Directors, from time to time, by resolution may provide for all matters in respect to which no provision is made by these By-Laws.

ARTICLE VI

OFFICERS

Election

Section 1. The officers of the Corporation shall be a President, a First Vice-President, a Second Vice-President, a Secretary, an Assistant Secretary, and a Treasurer, who shall be elected annually by ballot by the Board of Directors at its first meeting after the annual meeting of members. The President shall be selected from among the Directors; the Vice-Presidents shall be selected from the membership of the Corporation; the other officers need not be members of the Corporation.

Term of Office

Sec. 2. All officers shall hold their respective offices for one year after their election and until their successors are elected and qualified, unless removed by the Board of Directors.

Duties of President

Sec. 3. The President shall preside over all meetings of the members and Board of Directors at which he may be present, and shall exercise general supervision and control over the affairs of the Corporation, subject to the direction of the Board.

Duties of Vice-Presidents

Sec. 4. It shall be the duty of the First Vice-President, in case of the absence of the President, or his inability to act, to exercise all his powers and discharge all his duties; in case of the absence or disability of both the President and First Vice-President, it shall be the duty of the Second Vice-President to exercise all the powers and discharge all the duties of the President; and in case of the absence or disability of the President, the First Vice-President, and the Second Vice-President, a President *pro tempore* shall be chosen by the Board.

Duties of Secretary

Sec. 5. The Secretary shall attend all meetings of members, of the Board of Directors and of the Executive Committee, and shall keep a true record of the proceedings thereof; he shall cause to be kept in the office of the Corporation all contracts, leases, assignments, other instruments in writing, and documents not properly belonging to the office of Treasurer; he shall execute all certificates of membership, bonds, contracts and other instruments authorized to be made or executed by or on behalf of the Corporation; *provided,* that all instruments requiring the corporate seal shall also be executed by the President or a Vice-President. He shall also perform such other duties as may be assigned to him by the Board of Directors.

Duties of Assistant Secretary

SEC. 6. It shall be the duty of the Assistant Secretary, in case of the absence of the Secretary, or his inability to act, to exercise all his powers and discharge all his duties.

Duties of Treasurer

SEC. 7. The Treasurer shall receive all moneys of the Corporation, safely keep the same, and pay out such sums as may be authorized by the Board of Directors. He shall give a bond in such amount as the Board may require.

Compensation of Officers

SEC. 8. The officers may receive such compensation as may from time to time be prescribed by the Board of Directors.

ARTICLE VII

RIGHTS AND PRIVILEGES OF MEMBERS

Right to Vote

SECTION 1. At all meetings of the members of the Corporation, each member may cast one vote by virtue of his membership, and such additional votes as he may be entitled to cast as the holder of bonds issued by the Corporation.

Receipt of News Service

SEC. 2. Each member shall be entitled, upon compliance with the provisions of the By-Laws to receive a service of news for the purpose of publication in the newspaper specified in his certificate of membership and for that purpose only. The nature and extent of the news service to be so received by the member shall be determined by the Board of Directors, upon his admission, and the initial dues or assessment shall be fixed at the same time and by the same authority, subject, however, to change as hereinafter provided in Article IX.

Change of News Service

SEC. 3. The nature and extent of the news service to any member may be changed from time to time by the Board of Directors; *provided* that this section must not be construed to give the Board of Directors authority to grant a news service in violation of the right of protest as hereinbefore specified, or to omit the news service to any member except for cause as provided in these By-Laws.

To Whom News May Be Furnished

SEC. 4. The news service of this Corporation shall be furnished only to the members thereof, or to the newspapers represented by them and specified in their certificates of membership.

Use of News

SEC. 5. A member shall publish the news of The Associated Press only in the newspaper, the language, and the place specified in his certificate of membership and he shall not permit any other use to be made of the news furnished by the Corporation to him or to the newspaper which he represents. Only the place specified in the certificate of membership shall appear in the title, name or heading of the newspaper wherein the news of The Associated Press is published.

Hours of Publication

SEC. 6. The time limits for the receipt and publication of news by members shall be (standard time in all cases at the place of publication) as follows: Morning papers to receive not later than 9 A. M. and to publish not earlier than 9 P. M., except that for editions to be circulated only outside of the city of publication not earlier than the following morning, morning papers may publish not earlier than 5 P.M. and that Sunday editions so published may be circulated in the city of publication after 8 P. M. Saturday; afternoon papers to receive not later than 6 P. M. and to publish not earlier than 9 A. M., the service to afternoon papers between 4 P. M. and 6 P. M. to be of bulletin character; *provided,* that the Board of Directors may authorize that upon extraordinary occasions The Associated Press dispatches may be used in extra editions or for bulletins outside of the hours named.

Method of Withdrawal

SEC. 7. By the vote of a majority of the Board of Directors, a member may be permitted to withdraw upon payment of all dues, assessments and other obligations, and upon the surrender and cancellation of his certificate of membership and upon such other terms as the Board of Directors may fix. If any member shall apply to the Board of Directors for permission to withdraw, and the same shall be refused, he may nevertheless give written notice to the Secretary of his intention to withdraw, and two years after such notice shall have been received, he may terminate his membership upon payment of all dues, assessments and other obligations to the date of his final withdrawal.

Association to Protect News

SEC. 8. No news furnished to the Corporation by a member shall be supplied by the Corporation to any other member publishing a newspaper within the district which the Board of Directors shall have described in defining the obligations of such member to furnish news to the Corporation.

ARTICLE VIII

DUTIES AND OBLIGATIONS OF MEMBERS

General Obligations

SECTION 1. Each member shall comply with all the provisions of the By-Laws and such amendments as may be adopted from time to time.

To Pay Assessments and Other Obligations

SEC. 2. During the term of his membership or until his right to the receipt of the news report of this Corporation shall be terminated in the manner hereinafter provided for, each member shall pay all dues, assessments and other obligations as the same may be fixed and apportioned by the Board of Directors.

To Receive and Furnish News

SEC. 3. Each member shall take the news service of the Corporation and publish the news regularly in whole or in part in the newspaper named in his Certificate of Membership. He shall also furnish to the Corporation, all the news of his district, the area of which shall be determined by the Board of Directors.

How News Shall Be Furnished

SEC. 4. In places where the Corporation has a correspondent, the members shall afford to such correspondent convenient access at all times to the news in their possession, which they are required to furnish as aforesaid, and in places where the Corporation has no correspondent the members shall supply the news required to be furnished by them in such a manner as may be required by the Board of Directors.

What News to be Furnished

SEC. 5. The news which a member shall furnish as herein required shall be all such news as is spontaneous in its origin, but shall not include any news that is not spontaneous in its origin, or which has originated through deliberate and individual enterprise on the part of such member or of the newspaper specified in his certificate of membership.

To Guard News Report

SEC. 6. No member shall furnish, or permit any one in his employ or connected with the newspaper specified in his certificate of membership to furnish, to any person who is not a member, the news of the Corporation in advance of publication, or to another member any news received from the Corporation which the Corporation is itself debarred from furnishing to such member, nor conduct his business in such a manner that the news furnished by the Corporation may be communicated to any person, firm, corporation, or association not entitled to receive the same.

Sale of News by Members

SEC. 7. No member shall furnish, or permit any one to furnish, to any one not a member of this Corporation, the news which he is required by the By-Laws to supply to this Corporation.

To Print Credits

SEC. 8. Members shall print in their newspapers such credit to the Corporation, or to any paper or other source from which news may be obtained, as shall be required, from time to time, by the Board of Directors.

Public Documents

SEC. 9. No member shall anticipate the publication of any document of public concern, confided to this Corporation for use on a stipulated date, however said member may have secured said document.

ARTICLE IX

APPORTIONMENT OF EXPENSES

How Apportioned

SECTION 1. The cost of collecting, exchanging and transmitting the news service, as well as all other expenses of the Corporation, shall be apportioned among the members by the Board of Directors, in such manner as it may deem equitable, and the Board shall levy assessments upon the members therefor. The Board of Directors may change such apportionment and assessment, from time to time and may also levy assessments upon the members in order to accumulate a surplus fund for emergency purposes, provided that any increase of assessment exceeding 50 per cent. shall require the affirmative vote of two-thirds of all the Directors. There shall be no right to question the action of the Board of Directors in respect to such apportionment or assessments, either by appeal to a meeting of members, or otherwise, but the action of the Directors, when taken, shall be final and conclusive.

Payable Weekly in Advance

SEC. 2. All regular assessments levied against members shall be payable weekly in advance, and the Treasurer or other authorized agent of the Corporation shall draw on each member therefor. Such assessments shall be paid promptly, and, if any assessment draft shall be unpaid at the end of three days after presentation, a penalty of 10 per cent. thereon shall be added thereto, and it shall be the duty of the Secretary thereupon to notify the member in default that the news service will be discontinued at the expiration of two weeks from the date of the notice, unless all overdue assessments and penalties shall have been paid to the Treasurer of the Corporation before that date, and, if the same are not so paid, such news service shall thereupon be discontinued.

ARTICLE X

FINES, SUSPENSIONS, ETC.

Powers of Board to Fine, Suspend or Present for Expulsion

SECTION 1. When the Board of Directors shall decide that a member has violated any of the provisions of the By-Laws, it may, by a two-thirds vote of all the Directors, impose upon such member a fine not exceeding one thousand dollars, or suspend his privileges of membership or present him for expulsion as hereinafter provided, or it may both suspend his privileges and present him for expulsion. Before any such action shall be taken, however, it shall give to the member affected an opportunity to be heard in his own defense upon ten days' notice in writing of the time and place at which he will be so heard.

Effect of Suspension

SEC. 2. When the privileges of a member are suspended, his news service shall be discontinued, and notice of the suspension shall be sent at once, by the Secretary to all the members. Any order of suspension may be repealed by the affirmative vote of a majority of the whole Board of Directors, and notice thereof shall be sent at once by the Secretary to all the members.

Term of Suspension

SEC. 3. The term for which a member may be suspended by the Board of Directors shall not extend beyond the next annual meeting of the members.

Right of Suspended Member

SEC. 4. Any member so suspended may, at his option, retain his membership, and, at the expiration of the period for which he shall have been suspended, or upon the repeal of the suspension as hereinbefore provided for, he shall again become entitled to receive the news service as called for in his certificate of membership, or such member may withdraw from the Corporation upon paying all dues, assessments and other obligations then due or incurred and unpaid.

Action Conclusive

SEC. 5. The action of the Board of Directors on any of the foregoing matters mentioned in this article shall be final and conclusive. No member shall have any right to question the same.

ARTICLE XI

EXPULSION OF MEMBERS

Right to Expel

SECTION 1. The members of the Corporation, at any regular meeting, or at a special meeting called for that purpose, shall have the right to expel a member for any violation of these By-Laws, or for any conduct on his part, or on the part of any one in his employ or in the employ of or connected with the newspaper designated in his certificate of membership, which in its absolute discretion it shall deem of such a character as to be prejudicial to the interests and welfare of the Corporation and its members, or to justify such expulsion. The action of the members of the Corporation in such regard shall be final and there shall be no right of appeal against or review of such action.

Formal Presentation

SEC. 2. Before the Corporation may entertain a motion to expel a member there shall be a formal presentation of such member either by the order of the Board of Directors after a hearing as hereinbefore provided, or through a written notification signed by five members. The member affected shall have a right to be heard in his own behalf before the motion to expel is put to a vote.

Notice to the Member to be Presented

SEC. 3. If a member is to be presented for expulsion without previous hearing by the Board of Directors the notice of presentation shall be filed with the Secretary of the Corporation at least three weeks prior to the meeting of the members at which action is to be taken, and the Secretary shall forward a certified copy to the member affected within three days after receiving such notice.

Vote Required to Expel

SEC. 4. When a member shall be presented by the order of the Board of Directors he may be expelled by the affirmative vote of a majority of all the votes cast on the question. When a member shall be presented through a notification signed by five members and without the order of the Board of Directors, he may be expelled only by the affirmative vote of four-fifths of all the members.

Readmission

SEC. 5. A member who has been expelled shall be eligible for readmission only upon the terms and conditions applicable to new members.

ARTICLE XII

BONDS

Right to Issue Bonds

SECTION 1. This Corporation shall have power to borrow money, and to make and issue bonds, as evidence of indebtedness therefor, and to secure the same by mortgage upon its property; provided that such bonds shall not be issued to an amount exceeding the aggregate sum of $500,000.

How Issued

SEC. 2. The Board of Directors, at any regular meeting or at any special meeting called for that purpose, may authorize the execution and issue of such bonds in such amounts not exceeding the aggregate principal sum of $500,000, to such persons including themselves, payable at such times and with such rate of interest and in such form as it may deem advisable, *provided,* that every bond, so issued, shall contain a provision that the Corporation shall have the right to redeem the same at its face value, with the interest due or accrued thereon, whenever it shall come into the possession of any one not a member of this Corporation. And it shall be the duty of the Board of Directors, whenever bonds are presented for registration in the name of any one not a member of this Corporation, to exercise the right of redemption herein provided for and pay for such bonds out of any funds in the Treasury available for the purpose or out of an assessment to be levied upon members in proportion to the weekly assessment paid by them. The Board of Directors may make such provision for the registration of such bonds it may deem best. The Board of Directors may also authorize the execution of a mortgage upon the property of the Corporation to secure the payment of such bonds.

Voting Power of Bonds

SEC. 3. The registered owner and holder of any such bonds may file with the Secretary a waiver of any claim to interest on the bonds held by him, and he shall thereupon become entitled at any meeting of the members of this Corporation for the election of Directors to cast one vote, either in person or by proxy, for Directors upon each $25 of such bonds registered in his name for not less than twenty days prior to such meeting, provided that no bondholder shall have the right to vote upon more than $1,000 of said bonds, and shall not have the right to vote on any bond that shall have been called for redemption at any time before such election.

ARTICLE XIII

PUBLICATION

What Constitutes

SECTION 1. The publication required to be made by every member shall be that of a *bona fide* newspaper, continuously issued, as specified in the membership certificate, to a list of genuine paid subscribers. A publication conducted for the purpose of preserving a membership, and not for public sale and distribution, shall not be or be regarded as a sufficient compliance with the By-Laws. The irregular publication of his newspaper shall be sufficient ground for suspension of a member, in the discretion of the Board of Directors.

Six or Seven-Day Publication Optional

SEC. 2. A Membership Certificate which authorizes publication on seven days in a week shall be held to be fully complied with by publication on six days, and such cessation of publication on one day shall not affect the member's right to receive and publish the news service on seven days whenever he may elect to do so.

ARTICLE XIV

DISCLAIMER OF LIABILITY

No Right for Damages

SECTION I. Neither the Corporation nor its Officers nor Directors nor any of them shall in any event be liable to a member for any loss or damage arising by reason of the publication of any of the news received by him from the Corporation, or by reason of his suspension or expulsion, and his signature to the roll of members and assent to the By-Laws shall constitute a waiver of any such claim.

ARTICLE XV

AMENDMENTS TO BY-LAWS

How Amended

SECTION I. These By-Laws may be amended only by the Board of Directors at any regular meeting of said Board by an affirmative vote of two-thirds of all the Directors of the Corporation, but no amendment shall become operative or take effect until the same shall have been recommended or ratified by a vote of four-fifths of all the members of the Corporation at a meeting, regularly convened.

APPENDIX III

BIBLIOGRAPHY

ADAMS, F. C.—"The Two Smiths" (pamphlet, 1880).
American Newspaper Reporter, July 3, 1871.
American Telegraph Magazine, October, 1852.
APLIN, William.—"At the Associated Press Office," *Putnam's Magazine,* July, 1870.
Appleton's Cyclopedia of American Biography (1888).
Appleton Dictionary of New York (1887).
Associated Press (of Illinois).—Reports (1894 to 1901).
Associated Press (of New York).—Reports (from 1900 on).
"Atlantic Cable Mismanagement, Correspondence between James W. Simonton and Cyrus W. Field and Others" (pamphlet, 1871).
BANCROFT, Hubert Howe.—*Chronicles of the Builders* (Vol. V, 1890).
BARTON, Bruce.—"How Did That Get in the Paper?" *American Magazine,* August, 1926.
BENT, Silas.—*Ballyhoo* (1927).
BICKEL, Karl August.—"The First Twenty Years" (pamphlet, 1927).
BLEYER, Willard Grosvenor.—*The Profession of Journalism* (1918).
———*Main Currents in the History of American Journalism* (1927).
BOLTON, Edith Stanwood.—"Memoir of Samuel Topliff," in *Topliff's Travels* (1906).
BOWEN, Abel.—*Picture of Boston* (1838).
BROWNE, Junius Henry.—*The Great Metropolis* (1869).
BUCKINGHAM, Joseph T.—*Specimens of Newspaper Literature* (1852).
———*Personal Memories and Recollections of Editorial Life* (1852).
CAMP, Eugene.—"What's the News?," *Century Magazine,* June, 1890.
Canadian Press.—Reports.
CHISHOLM, Hugh.—"Newspapers," *Encyclopedia Britannica* (11th edition, 1911).

CLARKE, Joseph I. C.—*Memories* (1925).

CLEMENS, Samuel L.—*Roughing It* (1871).

CLENDENIN, Henry W.—*Autobiography* (1926).

COLLINS, H. M.—*From Pigeon Post to Wireless* (1925).

COLTON, Calvin.—*The Last Seven Years of the Life of Henry Clay* (1856).

Congressional Globe, 1857, 1865, 1866, 1868.

CONNERY, Thomas B.—"The Collection of News," *Cosmopolitan Magazine*, May, 1897.

CORNYN, J. H.—"Press Associations," *Encyclopedia Americana*, (1919).

Correspondence in Relation to the Cable News Company (published by the Chicago *Tribune*, 1891).

CRAIG, Daniel H.—"A Review of 'An Exposition of the Differences between Different Presses and Different Lines of Telegraph respecting the Transmission of Foreign News,'" (1850).

——— "Answer of Daniel H. Craig to the Interrogatories of the United States Senate Committee on Education and Labor" (pamphlet, 1883).

——— "Annual Report of the General Agent to F. Hudson and H. J. Raymond, Executive Committee, Associated Press" (1863).

CRANE, Charles E.—"Mobilizing the News," *Scientific American*, February 6, 1915.

CRAWFORD, M. C.—*Old Boston* (1909).

CUCHEVAL-CLARIGNY, M.—*Histoire de la Presse* (1857).

DAVIS, Elmer, *History of The New York Times* (1921).

Diary of James K. Polk (edited by Milo Milton Quaife, 1910).

Diary of Philip Hone (edited by Allan Nevine, 1927).

DIEHL, Charles S.—Letter dated July 11, 1900; also Letter, April 9, 1928.

DURANT, William, *Fifty Years of Service, 1834-1884* (1884).

FIELD, Cyrus W., *Cyrus W. Field, His Life and Work* (edited by Isabella Field Judson, 1896).

FLETCHER, Henry H.—Letter to author, July 15, 1927.

FOWLER, N. C.—*The Handbook of Journalism* (1913).

FRANCIS, John W.—*Old New York* (1858).

FREIDLY, E. T.—"Newspapers in the United States," *Wetherill's Directory of Newspapers* (1870).

General News Association.—*Rules* (1874).

GEORGE, Henry, Jr.—*Life of Henry George* (1900).

GOBRIGHT, Lawrence A.—*Recollections of Men and Things* (1869).

HALLOCK, William H.—*Life of Gerard Hallock* (1869).

HAPGOOD, Hutchins, and MAURICE, Arthur Bartlett.—"The Great Newspapers of the United States," *Bookman* (Vol. XV, 1902).

HASWELL, Charles H.—*Reminiscences of New York* (1896).

HAWLEY, W. C.—"Development of the American Newspaper," *Popular Science Monthly* (December, 1899).

Hearing on Competing Telegraphs, Forty-fifth Congress, 3rd Session, Senate Report 805.

HILL, A. F.—*Secrets of the Sanctum* (1875).

HOMANS, I. S.—*History of Boston* (1856).

HOWARD, Roy W.—"The United Press," *Publishers' Guide*, June, 1913.

HUDSON, Frederic.—*Journalism in the United States from 1690 to 1872* (1873).

HYDE, William.—"Newspapers and Newspaper People of Three Decades," Missouri Historical Society *Proceedings* (1890).

IRWIN, Will.—"The United Press," *Harper's Weekly*, April 25, 1914.

JOHNSTON, Alexander.—*The United States* (1889).

JONES, Alexander.—*Historical Sketch of the Electric Telegraph* (1852).

Journal of Commerce (Centennial Edition), Sept. 29, 1927.

KENNEDY, J. H.—"Anson Stager," *Magazine of Western History* (Vol. IV, 1885).

KING, William L.—*The Newspaper Press of Charleston, South Carolina* (1872).

KING, J.—"The Press Association and its Objects," *Canadian Monthly*, June, 1876.

KIRK, John W.—"The First News Message by Telegraph," *Scribner's Magazine*, May, 1892.

LEE, James Melvin.—*History of American Journalism* (1923).

LIPPMANN, Walter.—*Public Opinion* (1922).

LIVESAY, J. F. B.—"The Canadian Press and Allied Organizations," (pamphlet, 1924).

LONG, Andrew.—"The Federated Press," *Survey*, October 23, 1920.

LOSSING, Benson J.—*History of New York City* (1884).

MACKEAN, Sidney H.—"How a Modern News Service Operates," *Publishers' Guide* (January, 1914).

MACLENNAN, Frank P.—*A Kansan in New York* (1918).

MCCULLOCH, Hugh.—*Men and Measures of Half a Century* (1888).

MCDERMOTT, E.—"Reporting by Telegraph," *Once a Week*, September, 1860.

McMaster, John Bach.—*A History of the People of the United States* (1910).

McRae, Milton A.—*Forty Years in Newspaperdom* (1924).

Mason, Gregory, and Kennan, George.—"The Associated Press," *Outlook*, May 30, 1914.

Maverick, Augustus.—*Henry J. Raymond and the New York Press for Thirty Years* (1870).

Medill, Joseph.—"Reminiscences," Associated Press *Report* (1897).

Memoirs of James Gordon Bennett, by a Journalist [said to be Isaac C. Pray] (1855).

Merriam, George S.—*Life and Times of Samuel Bowles* (1885).

Midgley, R. L.—*Boston Sights and Strangers' Guide* (1857).

Mitchell, E. P.—*Memoirs of an Editor* (1924).

Morse, Samuel F. B.—"Letter to the Secretary of the Treasury," Twenty-eighth Congress, 1st Session, House Document 270 (1884).

——— "Letter to the Secretary of the Treasury," Twenty-eighth Congress, 2nd Session, House Document 24 (1884).

——— *Letters and Journals*, 1914.

Nelson, William.—Notes toward a *History of American Newspapers* (1918).

New York State Associated Press.—Reports.

North, S. N. D.—"The Newspaper and Periodical Press in the United States," Tenth Census (Vol. VIII, 1881).

Northwestern Associated Press.—Reports.

Noyes, Frank B.—"Testimony," Sixty-second Congress, 1st Session, Senate Document 56 (Vol. II, 1911).

——— "The Associated Press," *North American Review*, May, 1913.

——— "The Battle for a Free Press," (pamphlet, 1927).

O'Brien, Frank M.—*The Story of The Sun* (1918).

"One of the Reasons for Telegraphic Reform: Power and Tyranny of the Associated Press" (pamphlet, 1873).

Owens, Dewey M.—"The Associated Press," *American Mercury*, April, 1927.

Parton, James.—"The New York *Herald*," *North American Review* (1866).

——— *Life of Horace Greeley* (1868).

——— *Captains of Industry* (1884).

Payne, George Henry.—*History of Journalism in the United States* (1920).

PHILIPS, Melville.—*The Making of a Newspaper* (1893).

PHILLIPS, Walter Polk.—*My Début in Journalism* (1882).

PERLEY POORE, Ben.—"Washington News," *Harper's Magazine*, January, 1874.

——— *Perley's Reminiscences* (1886).

PRAY, Isaac C.—*James Gordon Bennett and His Times* (1855).

PRESCOTT, George B.—*History, Theory and Practice of the Electric Telegraph* (1860).

Providence *Journal* (Semi-Centennial Edition), Jan. 3, 1870.

REGAN, John W.—"The Inception of the Associated Press," *Collections of the Nova Scotia Historical Society* (Vol. XIX, 1918).

REID, James D.—*The Telegraph in America* (1885).

REID, Whitelaw.—*Some Newspaper Tendencies* (1879).

——— "Introduction," *A Political History of Slavery*, by William Henry Smith (1903).

REYNAULD, H. W.—"The United Press," *Pacific Printer*, February, 1910.

RIPLEY, Philip.—"Newspapers in the United States," *American Cyclopedia* (1875).

RUSSELL, Robert W.—"Reply of the Executive Committee of the American Telegraph Company to the Pamphlet of D. H. Craig" (1860).

——— "The American Telegraph Company, Statement of Messrs. Abram S. Hewitt, Cyrus W. Field, Henry J. Raymond and others made at the Meeting of Stockholders on June 29th, 1860."

SANFORD, Edwards Sewall.—*In Memoriam* (1882).

SCHARF, J. Thomas.—*History of St. Louis* (1883).

SCHARF and WESTCOTT.—*History of Philadelphia* (1884).

SCHURZ, Carl.—"Intimate Letters," *Publications of the State Historical Society of Wisconsin* (edited by Joseph Schafer, 1922).

SCRIPPS, James E.—Circular letter, Sept. 1, 1893; also Leaflet (1894).

SEITZ, Don C.—*The James Gordon Bennetts* (1928).

SEWARD, William H.—Communication of William H. Seward, Secretary of State, upon the Subject of an Inter-Continental Telegraph (pamphlet, 1864).

SHANKS, W. F. S.—"How We Get Our News," *Harper's Magazine*, May, 1867.

SINCLAIR, Upton.—*The Brass Check* (1919).

SMITH, Francis Osmond Jonathan.—"An Exposition of the Differences Existing between Different Presses and Different Telegraph Lines Respecting the Transmission of Foreign News" (1850).

——— "Opening and Closing Arguments of Hon. Thomas M. Hayes and Hon. Francis O. J. Smith before the Superior Court of Suffolk County, Massachusetts, February 26, 1866, in the case of State vs. Smith" (1866).

SMITH, William Henry.—"The Press as a News Gatherer," *Century Magazine*, 1891.

Southern Associated Press.—*Confidential Reports and Documents* (1893).

STICKNEY, William.—*Autobiography of Amos Kendall* (1872).

STIMSON, A. L.—*History of the Express Business* (1881).

STONE, Melville Elijah.—"The Associated Press," *Century Magazine*, June, 1905.

——— *Memorabilia* (1908).

——— "Testimony," Sixty-second Congress, 1st Session, Senate Document 56 (Vol. II, 1911).

——— *"M. E. S.," Souvenir Volume* (1918).

——— *Fifty Years a Journalist* (1921).

TAYLOR, Charles H.—"Reminiscences," Associated Press *Report* (1901).

THOMPSON, Joseph P.—*Memoirs of David Hale* (1856).

THORPE, Merle.—*The Coming Newspaper* (1915).

TURNBULL, Laurence.—*Lectures on the Telegraph* (1852).

VILLARD, Oswald Garrison.—*Some Newspapers and Newspapermen* (1923).

WATSON, John Fanning.—*Annals of Philadelphia* (1830).

Annals of New York (1833).

WATTERSON, Henry.—*"Marse Henry," An Autobiography* (1919).

Western Associated Press.—Reports (1866 to 1892).

——— "Memorandum of Joint Executive Committee Contract" (leaflet, 1882).

——— "Confidential Circular," dated Cincinnati, April 15, 1867.

White's Cyclopedia of American Biography.

WILSON, James Grant.—*Memorial History of New York* (1893).

WILSON, James Harrison.—*The Life of Charles A. Dana* (1907).

WINGATE, Charles F.—*Views and Interviews on Journalism* (1875).

WINKLER, John K.—*Hearst* (1928).

WINSOR, Justin.—*Memorial History of Boston* (1881).

YOUNG, James P.—*Journalism in California* (1915).

INDEX

(1)